Listening To Go®

Dorothy A. Zelvis
Mary E. Schulz

Skill Areas:	Language
Ages:	4 through 9
Grades:	Preschool through 4

LinguiSystems, Inc.
3100 4th Avenue
East Moline, IL 61244-9700
1-800 PRO IDEA
1-800-776-4332

FAX: 1-800-577-4555
E-mail: service@linguisystems.com
Web: www.linguisystems.com
TDD: 1-800-933-8331
(for those with hearing impairments)

Printed in the U.S.A.

ISBN 0-7606-0479-7

About the Authors

Dorothy A. Zelvis, M.A., CCC-SLP, has enjoyed being a speech-language pathologist in Lakewood, Ohio for the past 23 years, working with preschool through high school students. Dorothy has a special interest in working with students with autism and multiple handicaps.

In 2001, the educational team at Dorothy's elementary school was awarded the Franklin B. Walter Award as outstanding educators in the state of Ohio.

Mary E. Schulz, M.A., CCC-SLP, works in the Lakewood City Schools in Lakewood, Ohio. She was a speech-language pathologist for fifteen years, and has been a library information specialist in two elementary schools for the last nine years. She enjoys teaching her students information-gathering skills and use of software applications.

Table of Contents

Introduction

Creating an environment that makes learning enjoyable is a challenge for all educators. Reinforcement like playing a game, getting an answer correct, receiving verbal praise, or getting a sticker on a worksheet all strengthen the learning process. Since listening skills provide the basis for language acquisition as well as the development of literacy skills, it is important to use materials which make learning through listening fun and enjoyable.

Listening To Go is a collection of motivating activities intended for use with children ages 4 through 9 in a one-on-one or small group setting and is designed to provide immediate reinforcement for attending to auditory information. The worksheets may be used by teachers and speech-language pathologists to meet specific educational goals and/or may be sent home with students as a follow-up to school intervention.

The activities in *Listening To Go* correlate with educational objectives and the acquisition of skills related to phonemic awareness, forming word associations, memory, making comparisons, and comprehending. These prerequisite skills are fundamental for developing literacy and the ability to reason using language.

The skills targeted in *Listening To Go* are divided into five sections:

- Listening for Sounds
- Listening for Associations
- Listening for Knowledge
- Listening for Recall
- Listening for Similarities

The skills covered in each section are not discrete, but complementary. The phonemic awareness skills in *Listening for Sounds* involve the process of perceiving and responding to differences between similar sounds, syllables, and words. *Listening for Associations* involves relating information to previous learning and storing new concepts for future learning. *Listening for Knowledge* requires the ability to attach meaning to words. *Listening for Recall* requires the ability to retain spoken information for a short time in order to repeat or process the content. And finally, students learn to organize their thoughts and words according to similarities in *Listening for Similarities*.

The worksheets in each section are organized as a hierarchy, progressing from easy to more difficult tasks whenever possible. This organization makes it easy to let children know how they have progressed. For example, "Now you're able to follow *three* directions in a row. Remember when you were learning to follow *two*!" The immediate feedback from verbal reinforcement is an intricate aspect of the effectiveness of these activities.

The organization of this book can also help you establish and evaluate goals. For example, if a student is having difficulty in early tasks (e.g., associating functions of objects or completing an analogy), she will have more difficulty with later tasks (e.g., comparing two objects).

We hope that *Listening To Go* will be an enjoyable and rewarding way for you to involve students in the enjoyment of listening for learning.

Dorothy and Mary

Don't let your ears fool you! Color a bead on the necklace each time you answer correctly. Listen to the sound at the beginning of each word. Tell if the words are the same or different.

1. weed · reed
2. wing · ring
3. ride · ride
4. west · rest
5. one · run
6. whale · whale
7. wink · rink
8. wag · rag
9. which · rich
10. wind · wind

Add a Bead

Name ______________________________

What a pretty necklace!

Don't leave the turkey featherless! Color a turkey feather each time you answer correctly. Listen to the sound at the beginning of each word. Tell if the words are the same or different.

1. thing · sing
2. song · song
3. thin · sin
4. thumb · sum
5. thought · thought
6. think · sink
7. thick · thick
8. that · sat
9. those · sews
10. sank · sank

Turkey Feathers! **Name** ____________________

That's one well-dressed turkey!

Good listening is just ducky! Color a duck or duckling each time you answer correctly. Listen carefully to the sounds at the beginning of each word. Tell whether the words are the same or different.

1. grip · drip
2. blue · glue
3. try · try
4. flea · free
5. steel · steel
6. skate · state
7. crack · clack
8. drag · brag
9. grape · grape
10. proud · plowed

Quack Quack!

Name ______________________

That's the way to listen!

Rockin' Words

Name ______________________

No horsing around! Trace the line from one dot to the next each time you answer correctly. Listen for the sound in the middle of each word. Tell whether the words are the same or different.

1. coat · cat
2. beat · bait
3. sit · sit
4. vale · veal
5. fan · fan
6. share · shore
7. pen · pen
8. tip · tip
9. ride · read
10. pool · pull

Hop on!

Draw the petals on a flower each time you answer correctly. Listen for the sound at the end of each word. Tell whether the words are the same or different.

1. cat · cap
2. tail · tail
3. teen · team
4. rack · rat
5. boot · boot
6. glass · glass
7. bath · bass
8. goat· goat
9. sun · some
10. safe · save

Flower Fun

Name ______________________________

You made such pretty flowers!

Listen carefully to the sound at the end of each word. Don't let your ears trick you! Put a smile on a face if the words are exactly the same. Put a frown on a face if they are different.

1. wrote · rope
2. knife · knife
3. can · can
4. shade · shape
5. look · look
6. bag · bad
7. hard · harp
8. dish · ditch
9. fat · fad
10. mule · mule

Smile or Frown?

Name ______________________

You're sure not easy to trick!

You'll have to be a very good listener! Color a bubble each time you answer correctly. Listen carefully. Tell if the words are the same or different.

1. frill · thrill
2. fin · thin
3. fat · fat
4. first · thirst
5. three · three
6. reef · wreath
7. roof · Ruth
8. rough · rough
9. oaf · oath
10. goof · goof

Blowing Bubbles

Name ______________________________

How many bubbles did the boy blow?

Take off with good listening! Draw a line on your way to the moon each time you answer correctly. Listen carefully. Tell if the words are the same or different.

1. ton · son
2. toe · sew
3. two · Sue
4. tie · tie
5. tick · sick
6. mitt · miss
7. pass · pass
8. late · lace
9. kiss · kiss
10. bat · bass

Words in Space

Name ____________________

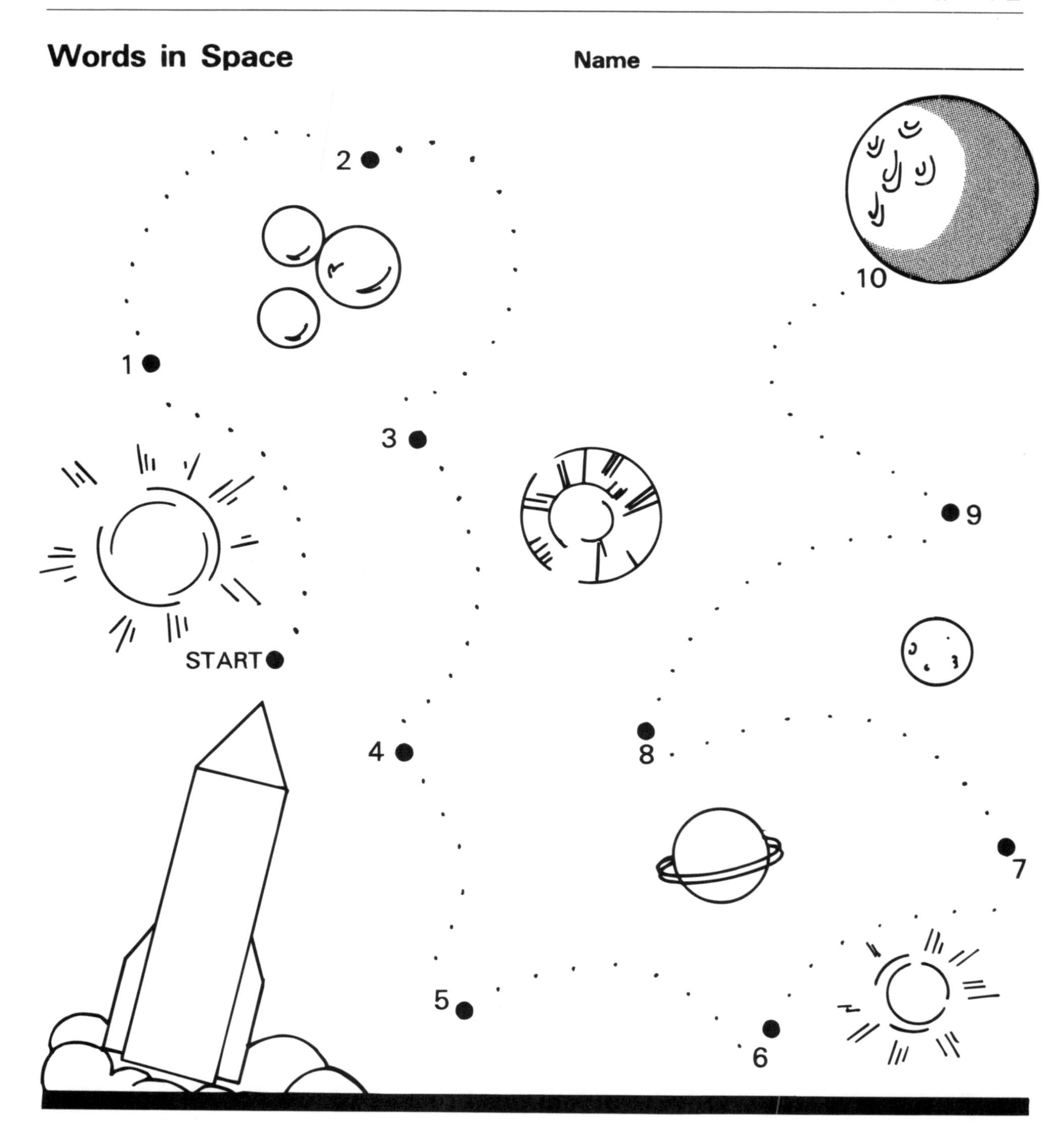

We're off to the moon!

Tell if the sounds are different at the beginning or at the end of the words. Color the front of a fish if the words are different at the beginning. Color the back of a fish if the words are different at the end.

1. shoot · suit
2. dish · ditch
3. beak · beep
4. life · knife
5. dig · pig
6. lit · lip
7. wire · fire
8. cat · pat
9. whip · wick
10. think · sink

Heads or Tails?

Name ______________________

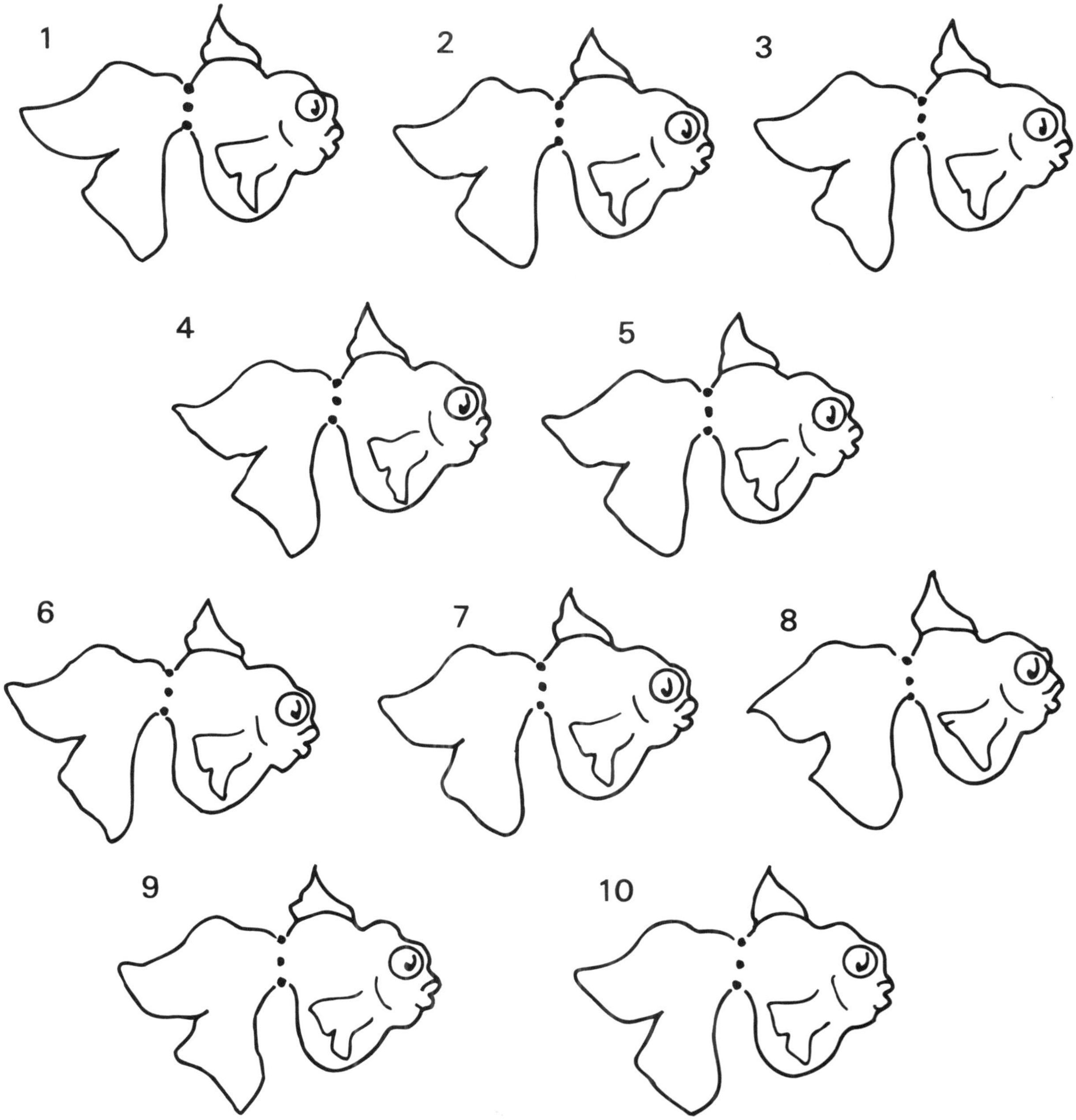

1 2 3

4 5

6 7 8

9 10

Good fishing!

This tiger is not happy. Cheer him up by tracing a stripe on him each time you tell which word does not rhyme with the other two.

1. slap · *lamp* · cap
2. stop · hop · *swan*
3. cape · grape · *train*
4. green · mean · *leap*
5. *kite* · time · rhyme
6. pill · bill · *rim*
7. mail · nail · *ache*
8. spoon · moon · *goose*
9. *rust* · bump · pump
10. then · *west* · when

Tearful Tiger

Name ______________________

The tiger says thank you!

Draw an X on a puff of smoke each time you answer correctly. Tell which word does not rhyme with the other two.

1. *cart* · farm · harm
2. night · *hike* · fight
3. suit · *boom* · loot
4. *cup* · run · bun
5. date · *made* · late
6. no · bow · *toad*
7. *keep* · peach · beach
8. sock · lock · *pond*
9. *perch* · twirl · girl
10. *tap* · man · can

Off We Go!

Name ____________________

1

2

3

4

5

6

7

8

9

10

Nice flying!

Climb On Up!

Name ______________________________

How high can you climb? Draw a rung through a number on the ladder each time you answer correctly. Tell which word doesn't rhyme with the other two.

1. band · land · *hat*
2. lake · *rate* · wake
3. bill · hill · *rim*
4. *load* · rope · hope
5. bull · full · *wood*
6. *food* · shoe · new
7. tie · lie · *find*
8. *itch* · match · patch
9. ten · hen · *pet*
10. ray · *make* · day

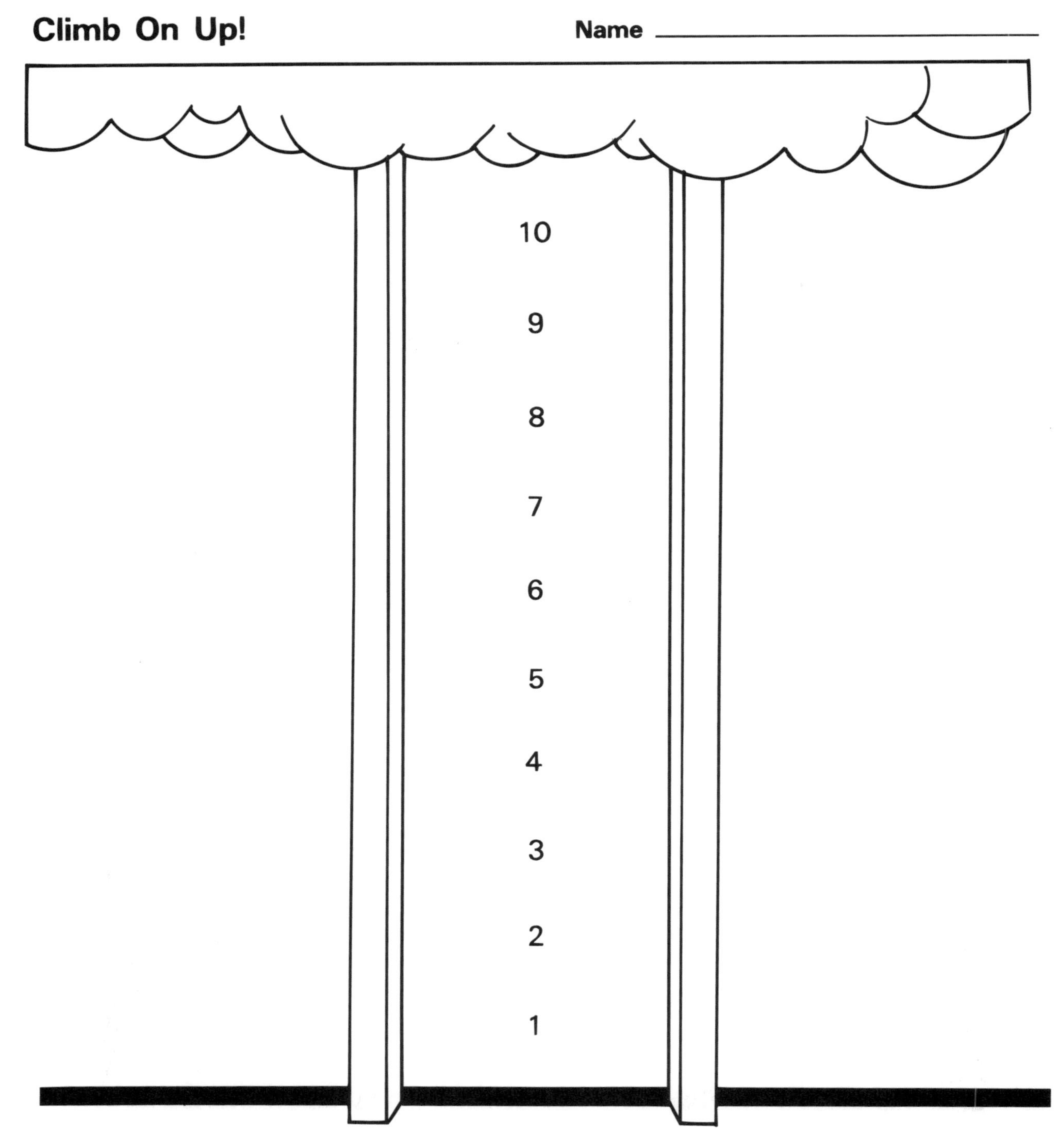

How's the air way up there?

Can you eat a ten-patty hamburger? Color a hamburger patty each time you answer correctly. Color the pickle if you get them all correct. Tell a rhyming word for:

1. dog
2. mouse
3. five
4. wing
5. fix
6. dish
7. truck
8. pear
9. ran
10. cut

Top It Off!

Name ______________________________

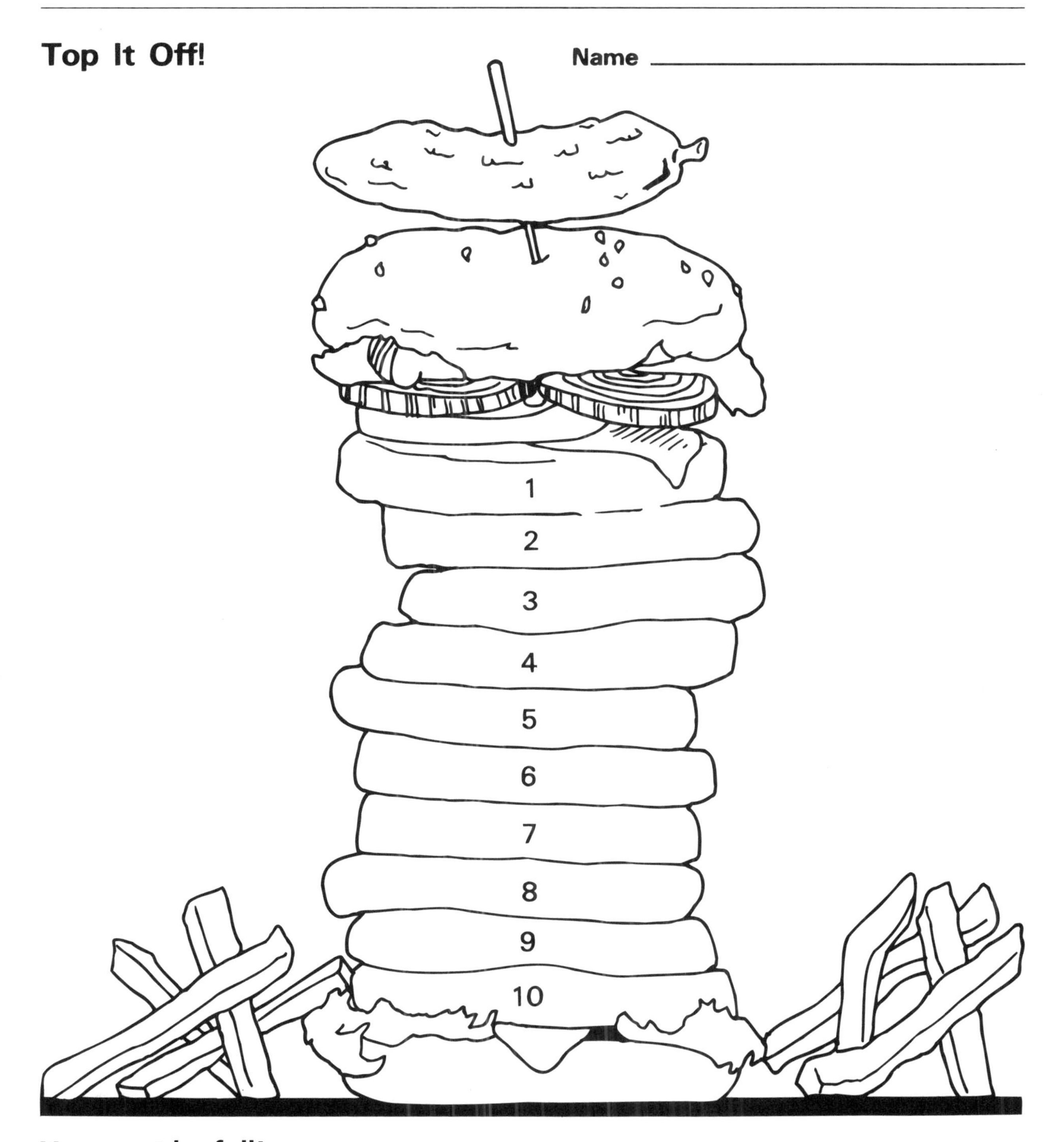

You must be full!

Color a different crayon each time you answer correctly. Tell a rhyming word for:

1. skip
2. run
3. star
4. cap
5. stick
6. heart
7. camp
8. nice
9. soap
10. coat
11. lock
12. train

Colorful Crayons

Name ______________________

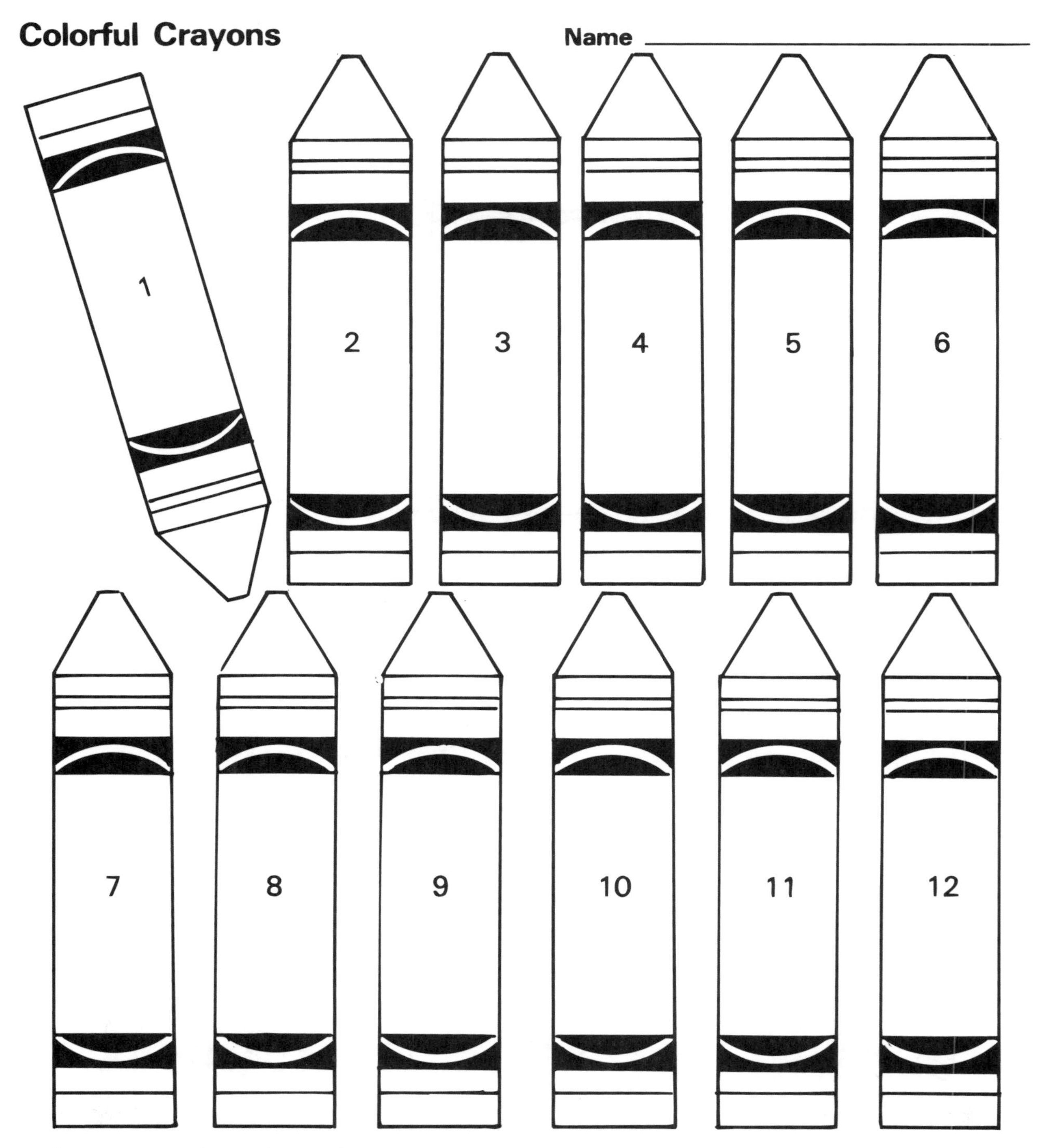

What's your favorite color?

Color a patch on Callie Cat if you answer correctly. Tell two rhyming words for:

1. door
2. cat
3. rag
4. rock
5. fox
6. tan
7. ball
8. like
9. hit
10. bee
11. dot
12. pipe
13. sun
14. rice
15. book

Calico Rhymes

Name ________________________

Isn't she pretty?

Watch your step! Color a toenail each time you answer correctly. Tell three rhyming words for:

1. book
2. big
3. loon
4. tall
5. bop
6. sat
7. hope
8. tar
9. bid
10. not

Follow the Footprints!

Name ______________________

Look at those colorful toenails!

Help Ryan mail a card to his girlfriend! Color a heart each time you answer correctly.

Does ____ start with the *t* sound?		Does ____ start with the *n* sound?		Does ____ start with the *d* sound?	
1. take	Y	7. mail	N	13. name	N
2. tall	Y	8. not	Y	14. dot	Y
3. dig	N	9. tell	N	15. did	Y
4. test	Y	10. nose	Y	16. toe	N
5. doll	N	11. knee	Y	17. date	Y
6. tick	Y	12. nut	Y	18. dust	Y

Hearts Away!

Name ______________________

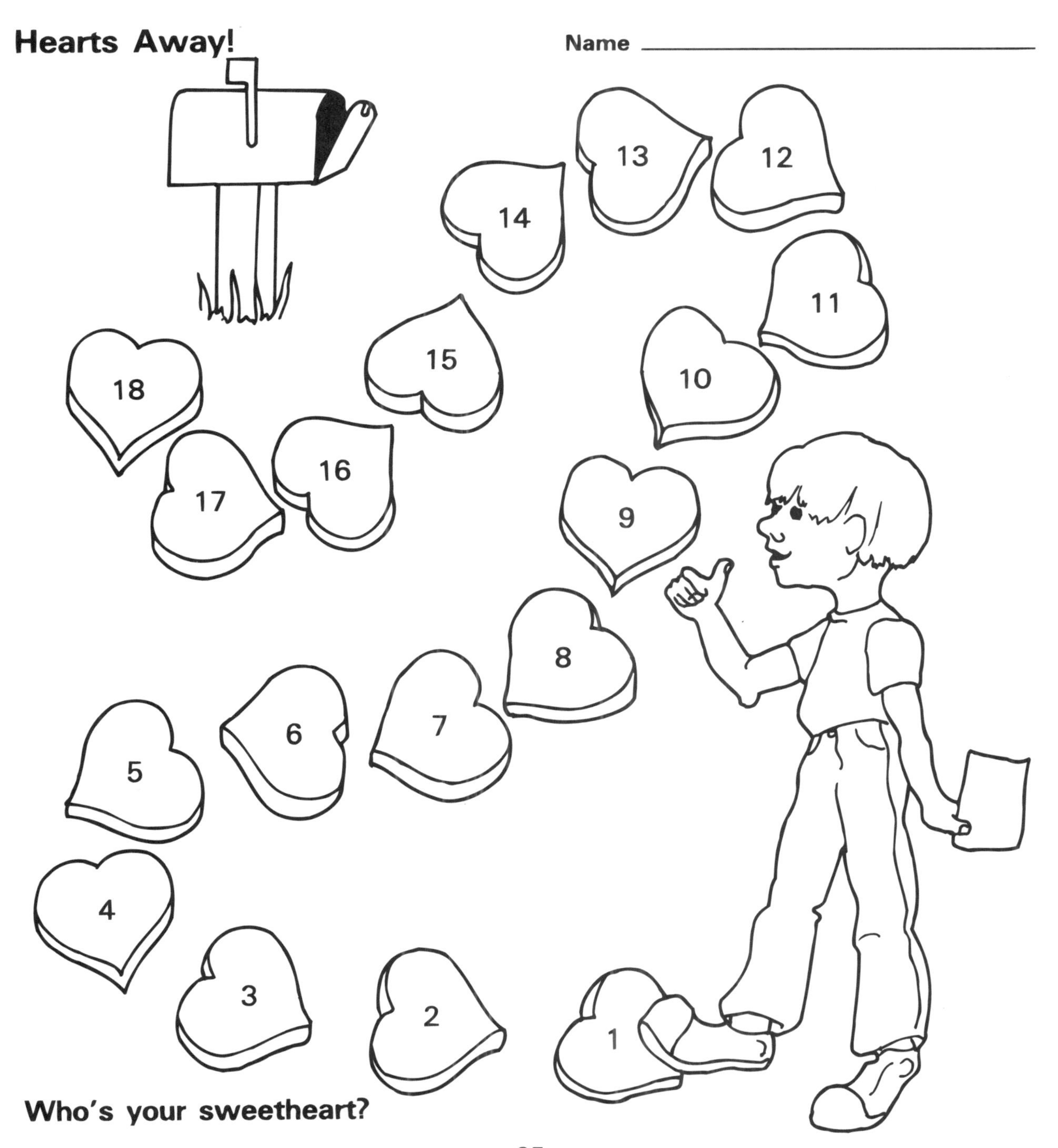

Who's your sweetheart?

How many butterflies can you catch? Color a butterfly each time you answer correctly.

Does ____ start with the *p* sound?

1. pop Y	2. pink Y	3. park Y	4. bike N
5. pie Y	6. boy N	7. mom N	8. pat Y

Does ____ start with the *m* sound?

9. mud Y	10. bug N	11. bed N	12. note N
13. make Y	14. my Y	15. man Y	16. knee N

Beautiful Butterflies **Name** ____________________

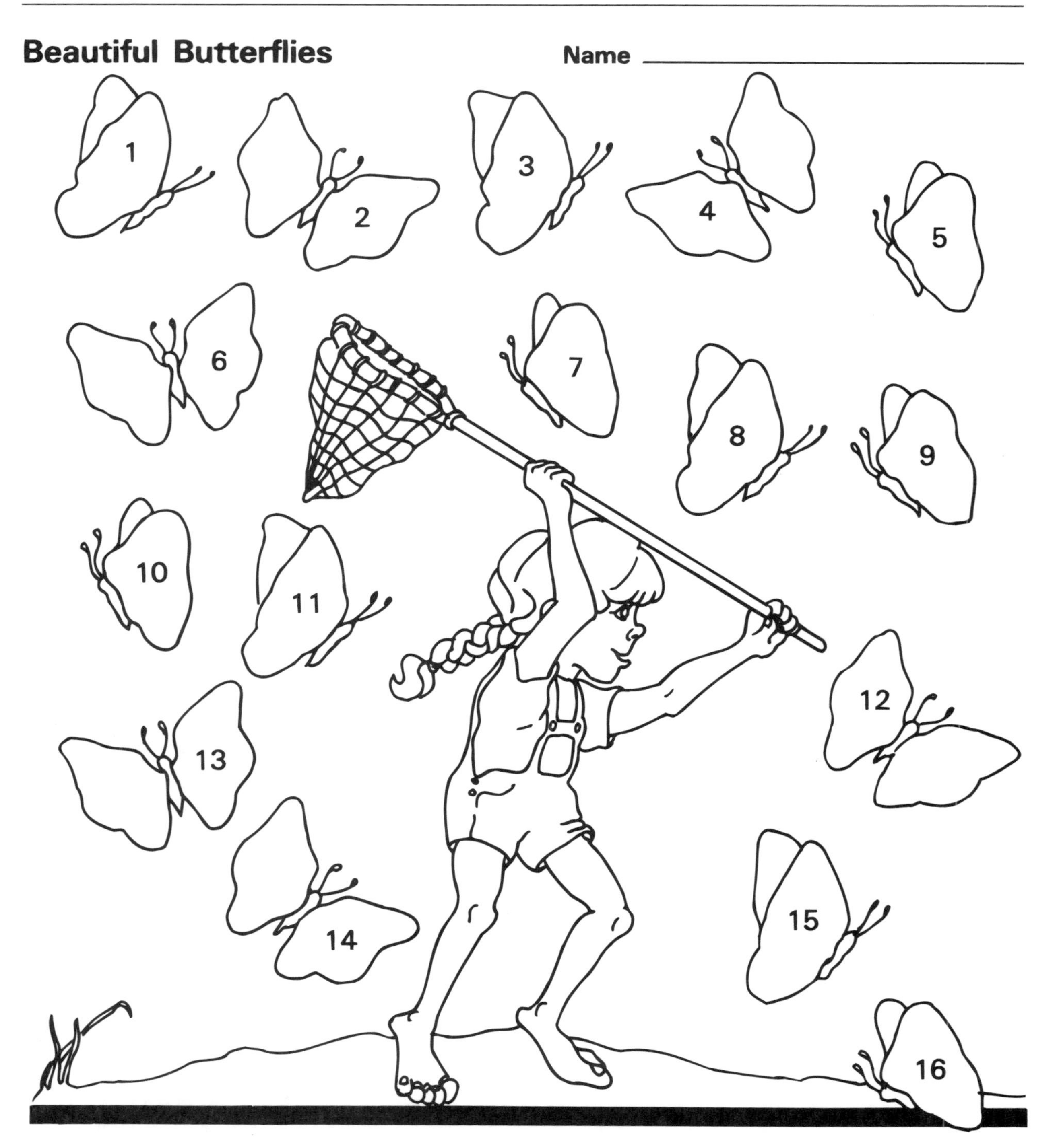

How many did you catch?

Dress up these penguins! Draw a bow tie on a penguin each time you answer correctly. Listen carefully to the sound at the beginning of each word. Do these words begin with the same sound?

1. yard • wake N
2. box • bag Y
3. tooth • ten Y
4. goat • dime N
5. come • coat Y
6. fish • vine N
7. wrong • right Y
8. lip • line Y
9. rug • win N
10. think • thin Y

Dress Up Time!

Name ______________________________

Good looking!

Can you "catch" the difference between two words by being a good listener? Trace a baseball each time you tell how the words are different. Name the sound that each word starts with.

1. coat • goat
2. lake • rake
3. ban • pan
4. hat • fat
5. rest • west
6. gate • date
7. call • tall
8. fire • wire
9. vest • west
10. pool • tool

Word Pair Baseball

Name ______________________________

Good catch!

Draw an X on a chick each time you answer correctly.

Does ____ end with the *k* sound?

1. pick Y
2. take Y
3. rug N
4. back Y
5. twig N

Does ____ end with the *g* sound?

6. pig Y
7. ring N
8. rag Y
9. mug Y
10. bake N

Does ____ end with the *ng* sound?

11. song Y
12. talk N
13. bag N
14. thing Y
15. rang Y

Chicks A Poppin!

Name ____________________

Peep, peep!

Make a big splash! Trace a splash of water each time you answer correctly.

Does ___ end with the *s* sound?		Does ___ end with the *z* sound?		Does ___ end with the *sh* sound?	
1. bush	*N*	6. buzz	*Y*	11. fish	*Y*
2. guess	*Y*	7. kiss	*N*	12. maze	*N*
3. rose	*N*	8. nose	*Y*	13. mash	*Y*
4. fuss	*Y*	9. raise	*Y*	14. cash	*Y*
5. face	*Y*	10. wash	*N*	15. bus	*N*

High Diving

Name ______________________

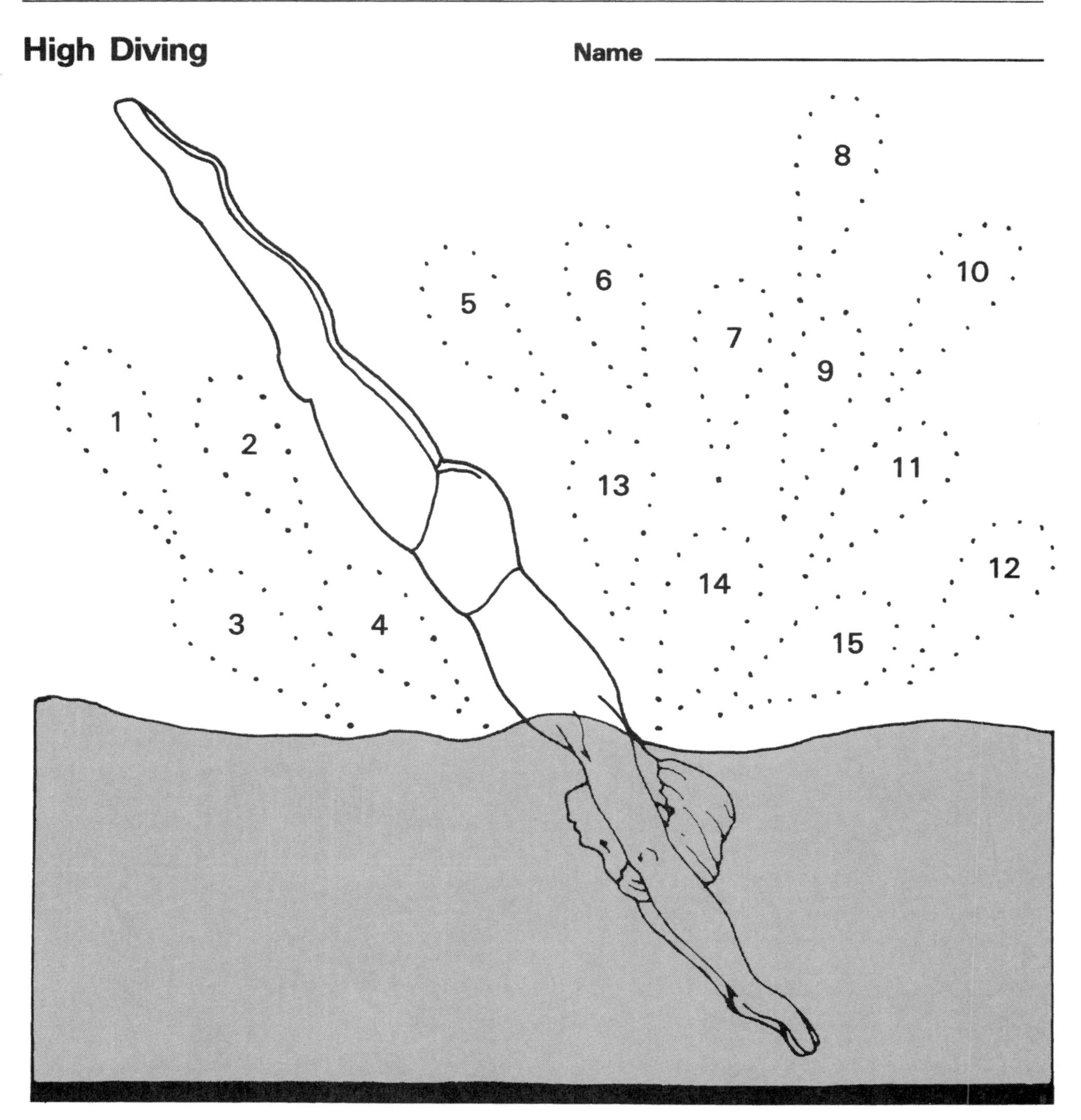

Nice dive!

Draw a box around a number each time you answer correctly. Listen carefully to the sounds at the end of each word. Tell whether the words end with the same sound.

1. pot · what Y
2. bit · bid N
3. calm · cream Y
4. wall · sail Y
5. is · eyes Y
6. knife · love N
7. beg · rug Y
8. wash · brush Y
9. take · bite N
10. pine · trim N

Phone Fun

Name ______________________

Way to go!

I am going to say two words. Listen carefully to the sound at the end of each word. Color the smiling pumpkin if the words end with the same sound. Color the frowning pumpkin if the words end with different sounds.

1. hop · Bob *D*
2. bug · egg *S*
3. ice · is *D*
4. jail · wall *S*
5. corn · bin *S*
6. brush · catch *D*
7. act · rack *D*
8. Mom · farm *S*
9. mug · mud *D*
10. did · trip *D*

Pumpkin Patch

Name ______________________

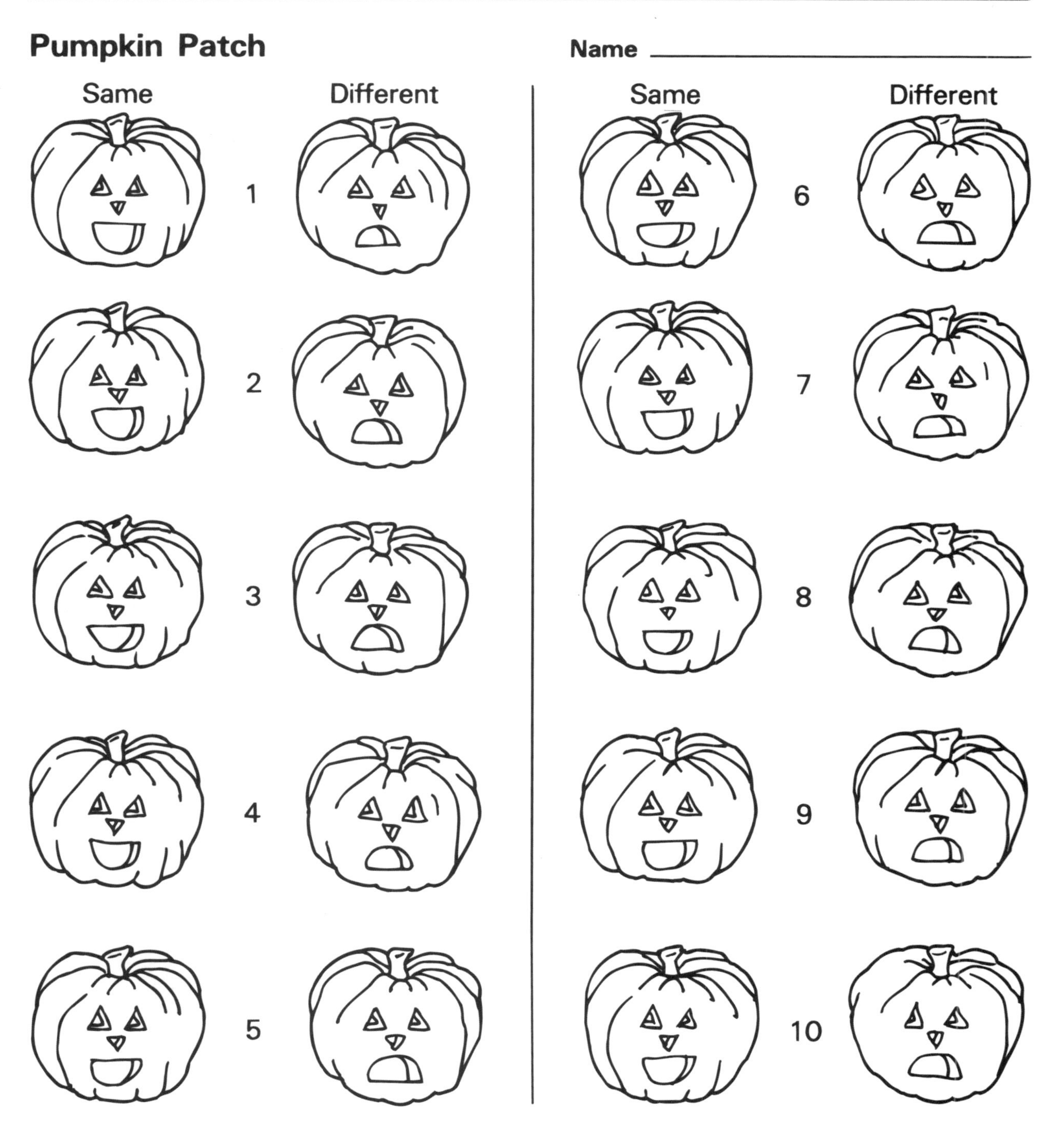

How many smiling pumpkins did you color?

Draw a face on a Wutsit each time you tell how the words are different. Listen carefully to the sound at the end of each word. Tell what sound each of these words ends with.

1. cup · cut
2. bug · bud
3. kiss · kit
4. mad · mat
5. leaf · math
6. bat · back
7. tall · tan
8. gum · sun
9. cap · cab
10. buff · bus

Listen Up!

Name ______________________________

Good listening!

Color one of the clown's balloons each time you tell a word that starts with the _____ sound.

1. *p*
2. *m*
3. *n*
4. *r*
5. *w*
6. *s*
7. *j*
8. *ch*
9. *sh*
10. *k*

Clown Around

Name ______________________________

No clowning around here!

Color a lucky clover each time you tell two words that start with the _____ sound.

1. *b*
2. *t*
3. *d*
4. *f*
5. *v*
6. *z*
7. *y*
8. *j*
9. *h*
10. *l*

Luck O' the Irish!

Name ____________________________

Have you ever found a four-leaf clover?

Check out your listening skills! Put a check in a box if your answer is *yes*.

(Note: Have the child say the word after you to improve his listening ability. For example, tell the child, "*Say the word* cow." Wait for his response and then ask, "*Do you hear the word* cow *in* farmer?" Continue with the exercise in this manner.)

Say the word __________. Do you hear the word __________ in __________?

1. cow . . . farmer? *N*
2. cowboy? *Y*

3. ball . . . bowling? *N*
4. baseball? *Y*

5. see . . . seesaw? *Y*
6. saddle? *N*

7. car . . . card? *Y*
8. drive? *N*

9. all . . . ball? *Y*
10. hallway? *Y*

11. ant . . . candy? *N*
12. anthill? *Y*

13. ray . . . rain? *Y*
14. radio? *Y*

15. knee . . . needle? *Y*
16. beetle? *N*

17. pay . . . daytime? *N*
18. paper? *Y*

19. can . . . candy? *Y*
20. candle? *Y*

Can You Hear It?

Name ____________________

1	2	3	4	5
6	7	8	9	10
11	12	13	14	15
16	17	18	19	20

You heard it well!

Color a *Y* or *N* to answer each question.

(Note: Have the child say the word after you to improve his listening ability. For example, tell the child, *"Say the word* cake." Wait for his response and then ask, *"Do you hear the word* cake *in* cupcake?" Continue with the exercise in this manner.)

1. cake ... cupcake? *Y*
2. Dale ... birthday? *N*
3. tooth ... toothbrush? *Y*
4. cloth ... tablecloth? *Y*
5. bell ... baseball? *N*
6. slide ... outside? *N*
7. corn ... popcorn? *Y*
8. note ... notebook? *Y*
9. pick ... pocketbook? *N*
10. snow ... snowman? *Y*

YES or NO?

Name ____________________

1 Y N

2 Y N

3 Y N

4 Y N

5 Y N

6 Y N

7 Y N

8 Y N

9 Y N

10 Y N

Such fine listening!

Help Dino reach his dinner! Be a good listener and put an X on a dinosaur track each time you answer the question correctly.

(Note: Have the child say the word after you to improve his listening ability. For example, tell the child, *"Say the word cat."* Wait for his response and then ask, *"Do you hear the word* cat *in* caterpillar?*"* Continue with the exercise in this manner.)

1. cat ... caterpillar? *Y*
2. fat ... father? *N*
3. pain ... paint? *Y*
4. leaf ... laughter? *N*
5. shell ... shelter? *Y*
6. class ... closet? *N*
7. bath ... batter? *N*
8. car ... carpenter? *Y*
9. print ... footprint? *Y*
10. time ... daytime? *Y*

Dinosaur Tracks

Name ______________________________

Dino says thanks!

Be a good listener. Color a shell each time you tell how many syllables are in each word.

1. lunch *1*
2. hundred *2*
3. signature *3*
4. between *2*
5. people *2*
6. answer *2*
7. dictionary *4*
8. furniture *3*
9. squirrel *2*
10. elevator *4*

Seashells

Name ______________________________

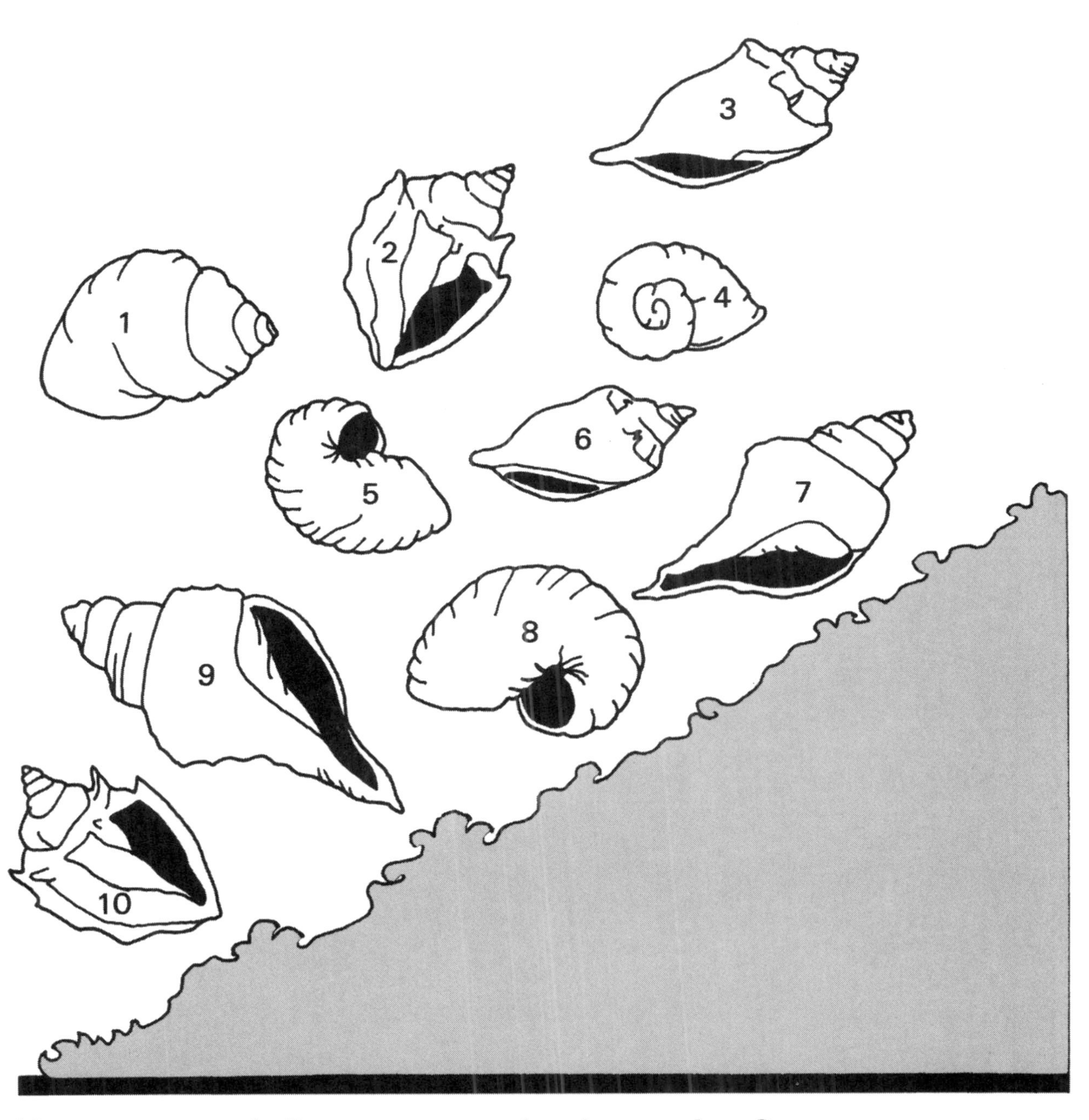

How many seashells can you see by the seashore?

Shoot for a basket! Trace a basketball each time you tell how many syllables are in each word.

1. picnic 2
2. watermelon 4
3. yesterday 3
4. arithmetic 4
5. basketball 3
6. dinosaur 3
7. television 4
8. radio 3
9. notebook 2
10. supper 2

Two Points

Name ______________________

It's overtime! Try these for extra credit.

Help Freddy Frog reach the lily pad by tracing a line each time you tell how many syllables are in each word.

1. preposition 4
2. paragraph 3
3. headache 2
4. subtraction 3
5. magnify 3
6. intelligent 4
7. amazement 3
8. bracelet 2
9. poetry 3
10. finger 2

Leapin' Lily Pads!

Name ______________________

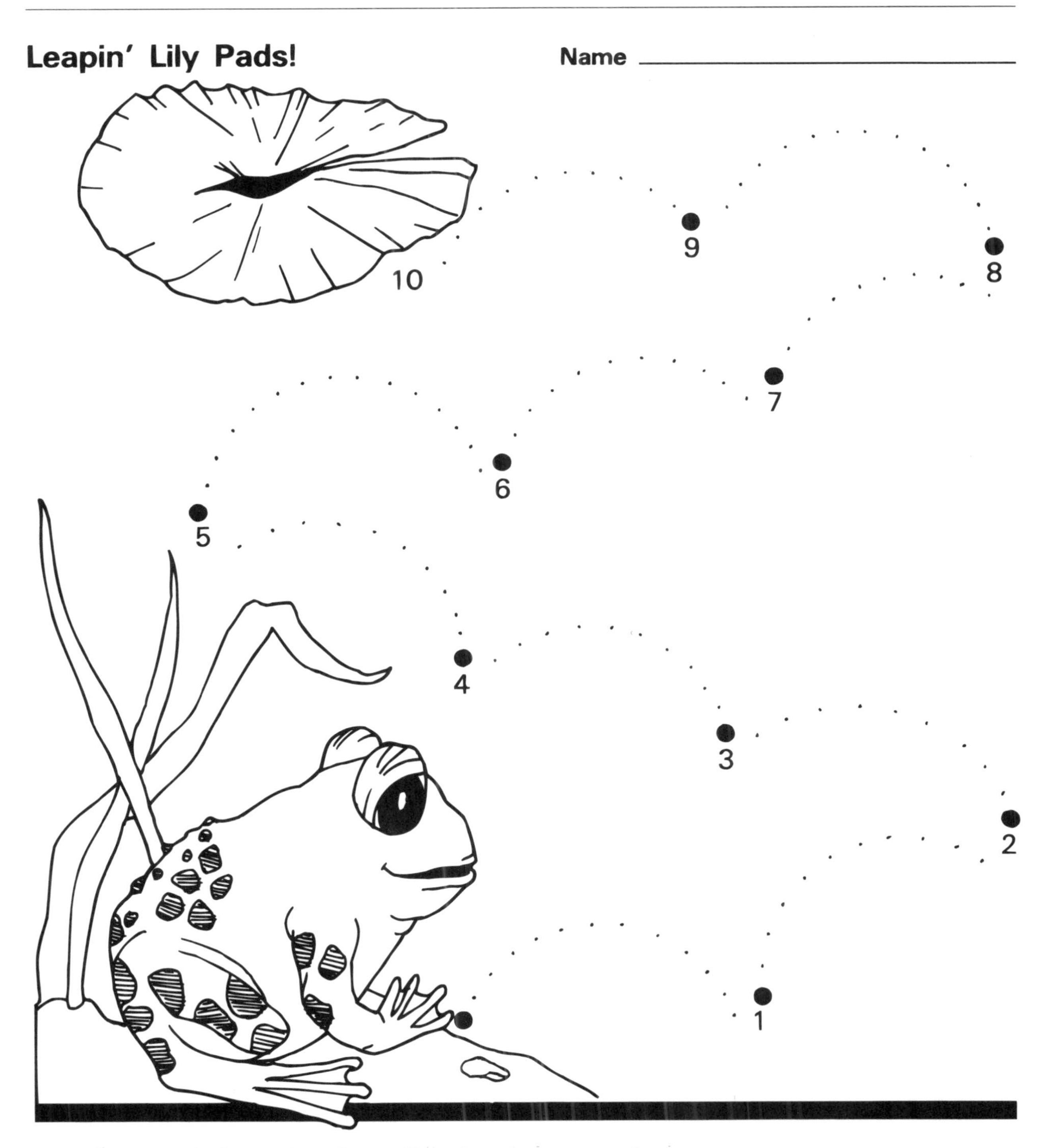

Freddy Frog is hopping happily, thanks to you!

Salty Words

Name ____________________

This pretzel is tasteless. Draw a piece of salt around a number on the pretzel each time you answer correctly. Tell which word in the sentence is incorrect. Then, change it to the correct word.

1. *Zip* your milk slowly.
2. The *sank* is filling up with water.
3. He needs a drink of water because he is *thirty*.
4. Wear a *cymbal* on your finger when you sew.
5. Clean off your dirty lunch *gray*.
6. The quarterback *true* the football.
7. My mother and *fodder* are waiting for me.
8. It's raining cats and *bogs*.
9. That flower is a *wheel* one, not a plastic one.
10. *Sank* you very much for the gift.

8 9 2 1 3 10 7 4 5 6

That looks much better!

Mouse Munch

Name ______________________________

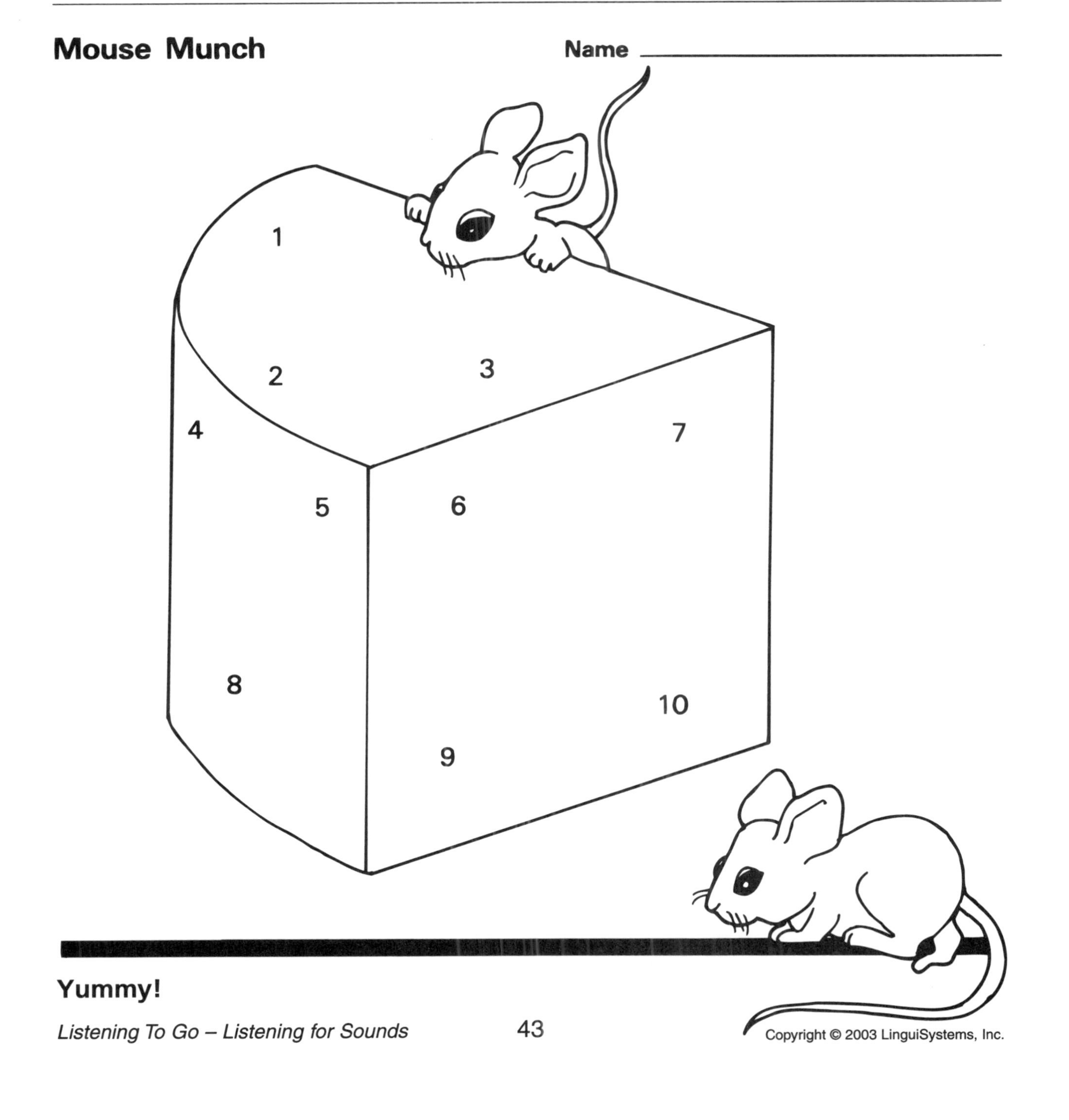

Yummy!

Draw a circle around a number in the Swiss cheese block each time you answer correctly. Tell which word in the sentence is incorrect. Then, change it to the correct word.

1. I don't *mow* the answer to that question.
2. *Wish* way did the boy go?
3. Give your pencil to *hair*.
4. The building is *berry* tall.
5. "Oink" said the *big*.
6. Don't *Dutch* the hot stove.
7. The *coat* is eating the grass.
8. I was sick, but now I'm *vine*.
9. The man with the fancy car is very *hitch*.
10. I cut my *whip* on my tooth.

Listening for Associations

Auditory association is how we attach meaning to the words we hear. For example, when we are asked, "Do bricks float?" we must understand the meaning of the noun and the verb in the question and make an association in order to answer correctly. Even children with verbal expression difficulties can benefit from these auditory association activities because only one-word responses are required.

Since a child learns most when learning is enjoyable, the listening activities in this section encourage the growth of auditory association skills in a fun way. These activities also help to improve the child's understanding of language.

These listening worksheets may be used with individuals or small groups in a therapy setting, within a classroom environment, or for homework assignments. The speech-language clinician, classroom teacher, or parent reads the statements and question, and the child answers aloud. For each correct answer, the child colors, traces, or draws a simple picture numbered to correspond with the question. To ensure that the activities are auditory tasks, the questions have been printed upside-down on each worksheet.

Color a fruit or vegetable for the basket each time you answer YES or NO correctly.

1. Are you a boy?
2. Are you a girl?
3. Are you cold?
4. Are you a child?
5. Are you short?
6. Are you tall?
7. Are you a mother?
8. Are you a plant?
9. Are you a pet?
10. Are you a person?

All About You! **Name** ______________________

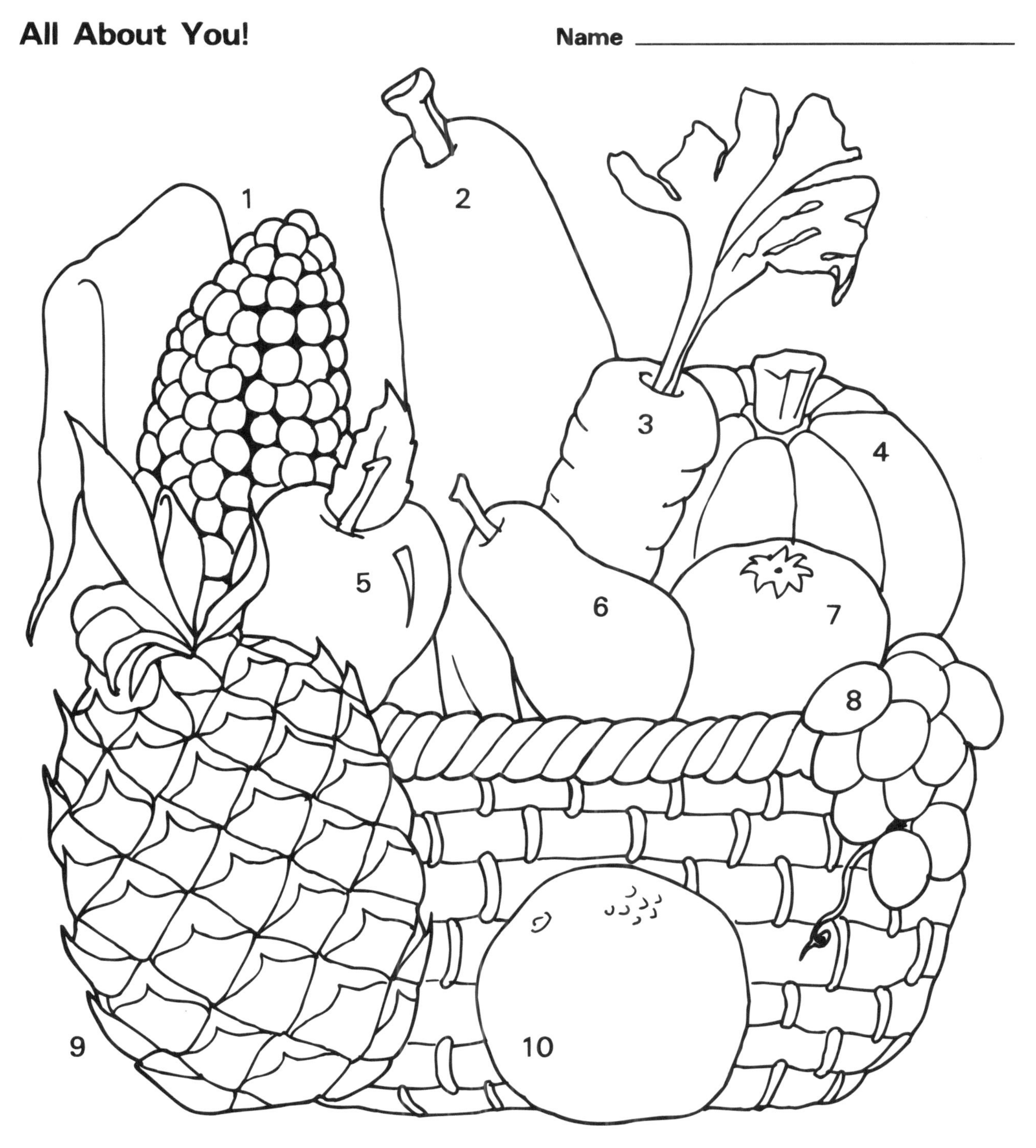

You're super!

Trace the legs on a spider each time you answer a question correctly.

1. Is a goat an animal? Y
2. Is a plant a tool? N
3. Is a parent a person? Y
4. Is a bee honey? N
5. Is a ghost scary? Y
6. Is a tack sharp? Y
7. Is an elephant tiny? N
8. Is a penny money? Y
9. Is a raindrop wet? Y
10. Is a rock soft? N

Listen Carefully

Name ______________________________

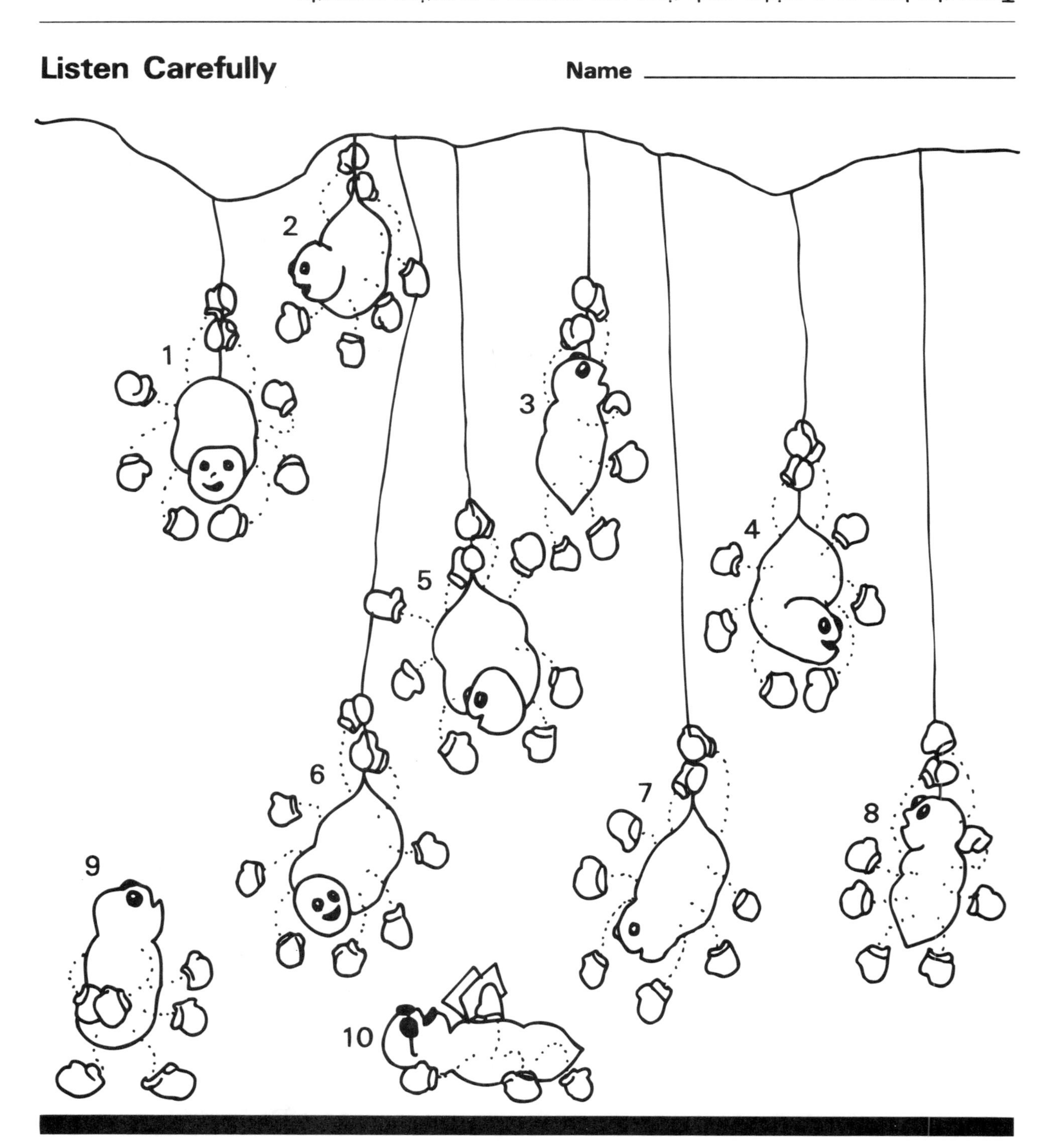

Good thinking!

Color the zigzags on a balloon each time you answer correctly.

1. Is a girl a person? Y
2. Is a cup a container? Y
3. Is a banana a vegetable? N
4. Is an automobile a vehicle? Y
5. Is a desk a piece of furniture? Y
6. Is a lemon sour? Y
7. Is a princess a male? N
8. Is an ant large? N
9. Is a doll alive? N
10. Is a violin an instrument? Y

Zigzags

Name ______________________

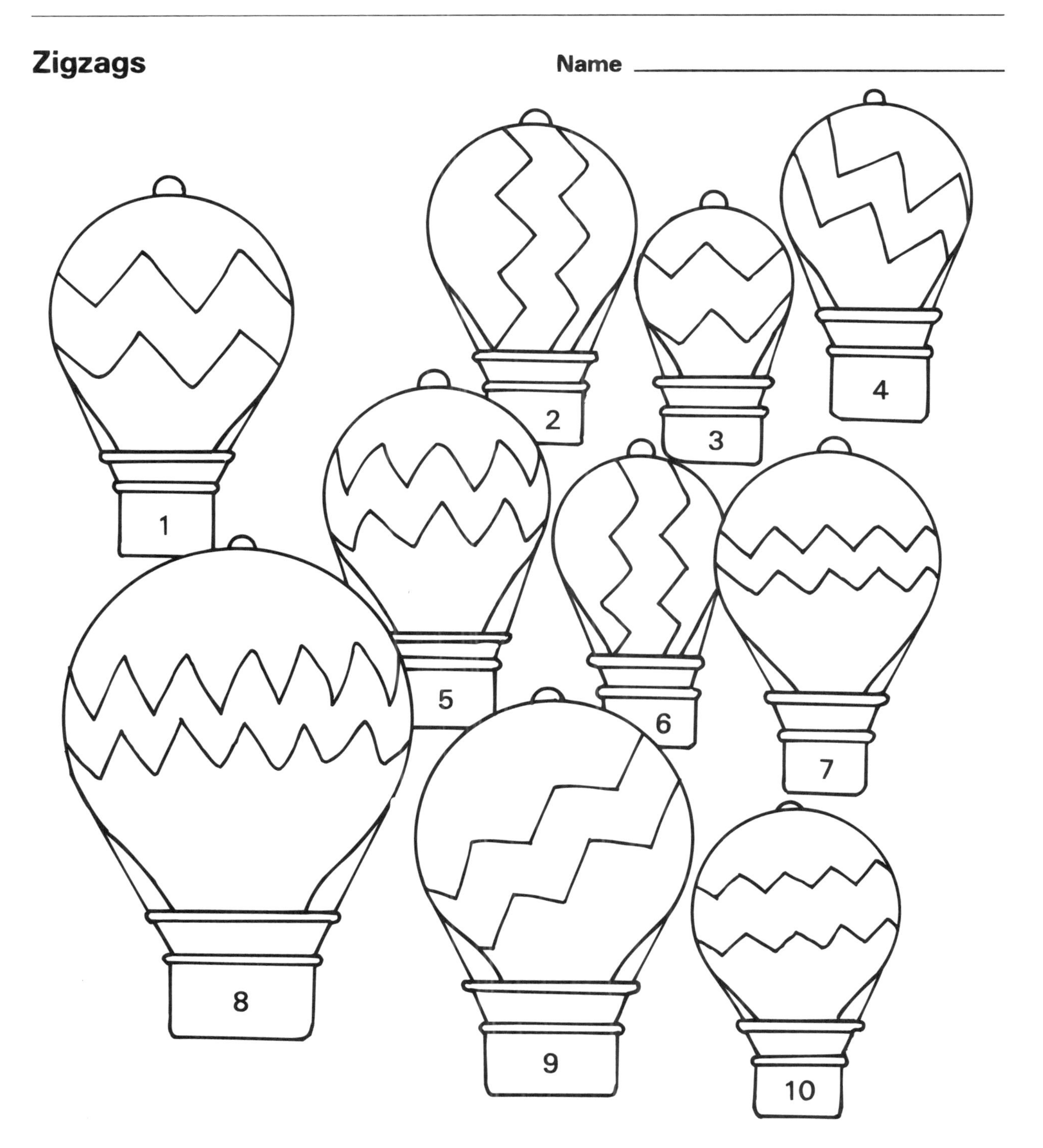

How many zigzags did you color?

Color a section of Samantha Snake each time you answer a question correctly.

1. Is fire hot? *Y*
2. Is night late? *Y*
3. Are pillows hard? *N*
4. Is a marshmallow red? *N*
5. Is the sun bright? *Y*
6. Are cars heavy? *Y*
7. Is water dry? *N*
8. Is popcorn a snack? *Y*
9. Are buildings places? *Y*
10. Is a joke sad? *N*

Yes-s-s-s? **Name** ______________________

Good answers!

Listen carefully to the questions. Color a mitten with a check if the answer is YES. Color a mitten with an X if the answer is NO.

1. Are dogs four-legged animals? *Y*
2. Are squares round shapes? *N*
3. Is a lemon a sweet fruit? *N*
4. Is a drum a loud instrument? *Y*
5. Are lions farm animals? *N*
6. Is a coat warm clothing? *Y*
7. Are saws sharp tools? *Y*
8. Is pop a bubbly liquid? *Y*
9. Is yellow a dark color? *N*
10. Is one hundred a small number? *N*

Pairs of Mittens

Name ____________________

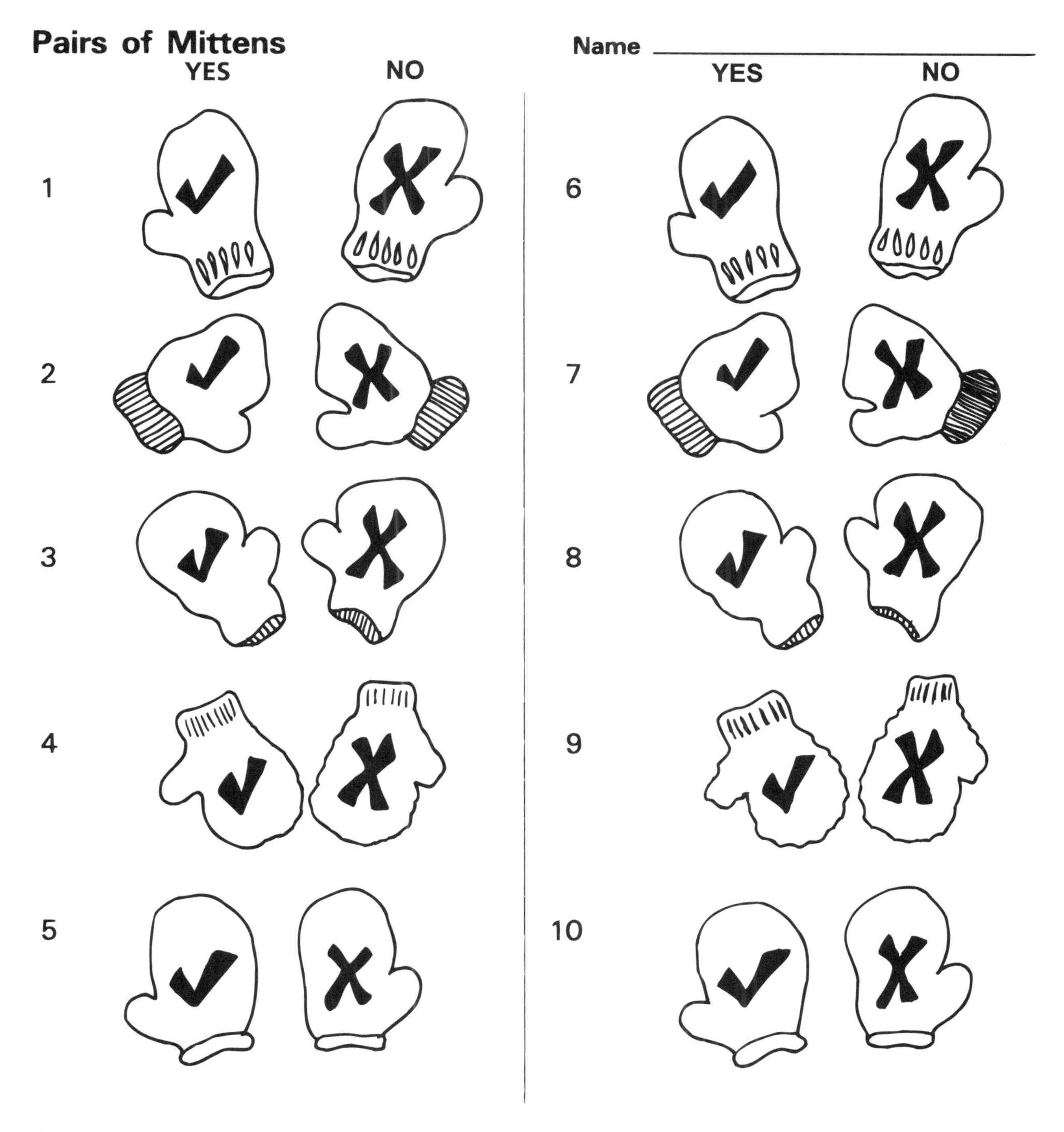

That's the way to pair 'em up!

Get revved up for good listening! Color a section of the race car each time you answer correctly.

1. Are skyscrapers short buildings? *N*
2. Is a crocodile a long reptile? *Y*
3. Are astronauts imaginary creatures? *N*
4. Is steel a hard metal? *Y*
5. Is a mountain a flat surface? *N*
6. Are alleys wide roads? *N*
7. Are airplanes speedy transportation? *Y*
8. Is a diamond an expensive gem? *Y*
9. Is an astronaut a factory worker? *N*
10. Is a cub a baby bear? *Y*

Rev 'Em Up!

Name ______________________

Look at that fancy car!

Color a section of the jack-in-the-box each time you answer a question correctly.

1. Can a chair cough? N
2. Can a candle break? Y
3. Can a pencil bend? N
4. Can a purse open? Y
5. Can a grape melt? N
6. Can a lamp hop? N
7. Can a sweater rip? Y
8. Can a door lock? Y
9. Can a plate crack? Y
10. Can a clock tick? Y

Surprise!

Name ____________________

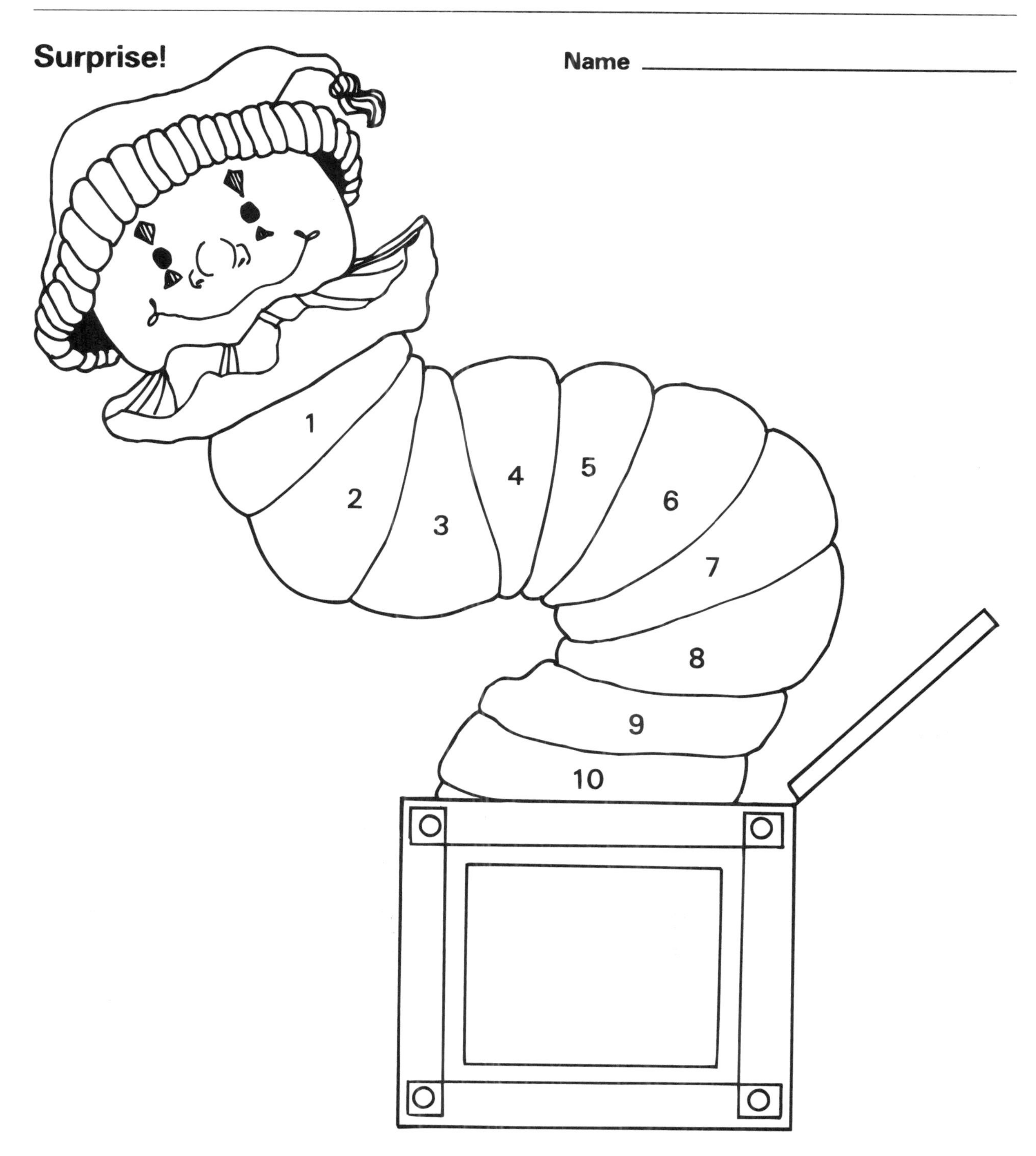

It's no surprise that you work hard!

Help Clyde the Clown juggle the balls! Color a ball each time you answer a question correctly.

1. Can a book read? N
2. Can a man paint? Y
3. Can a tree climb? N
4. Can water drink? N
5. Can a rubber band stretch? Y
6. Can a boat sail? Y
7. Can a door creak? Y
8. Can a chair sit? N
9. Can a bell ring? Y
10. Can a car fly? N

Juggling Act

Name ______________________

Clyde couldn't do it without you!

Help Mrs. Mouse get to the cheese. Put an X on a line each time you answer correctly.

1. Can you ride a horse? Y
2. Can you climb a ladder? Y
3. Can you roll a box? N
4. Can you turn off a lamp? Y
5. Can you drink a hamburger? N
6. Can you catch a ball? Y
7. Can you draw a picture? Y
8. Can you cook a toy? N
9. Can you eat a fish? Y
10. Can you fly a train? N

Cheese Trail

Name ______________________________

1 2 3 4 5 6 7 8 9 10

Mrs. Mouse loves cheese!

Help the baby birds hatch. Trace a crack in an egg each time you answer a question correctly.

1. Can you bounce a table? N
2. Can you catch a cloud? N
3. Can you dust a dresser? Y
4. Can you erase a mistake? Y
5. Can you find a penny? Y
6. Can you grow a vegetable? Y
7. Can you hang a desk? N
8. Can you keep a present? Y
9. Can you lose a hat? Y
10. Can you wear a lion? N

Hatching Time!

Name ______________________

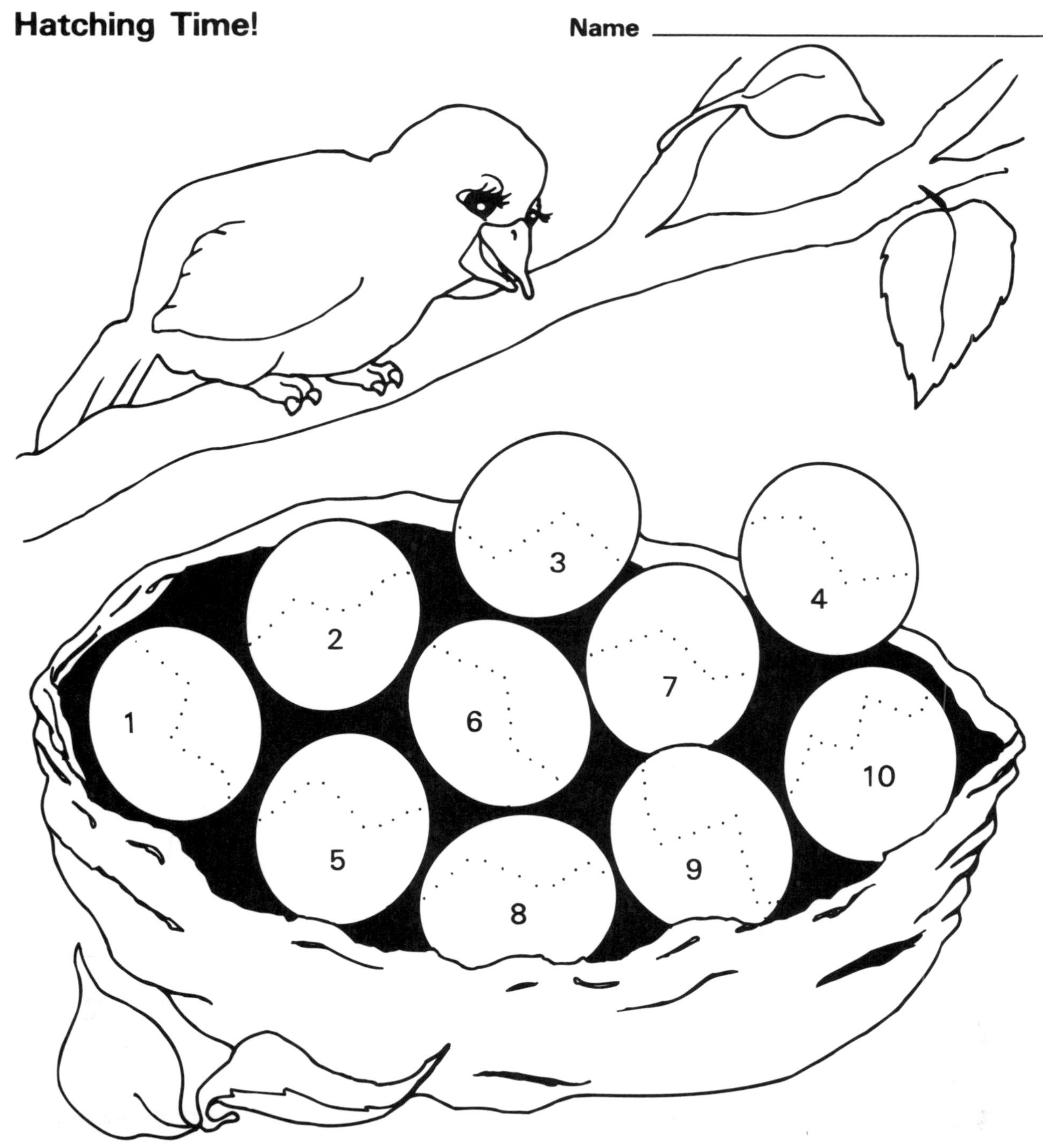

How many birds are ready to hatch?

Make a safe landing for the parachutist. Trace a parachute string each time you answer a question correctly.

1. Can you water a plant with a straw? *N*
2. Can you dust a table with aluminum foil? *N*
3. Can you write a letter with a pencil? *Y*
4. Can you watch TV with the electricity off? *N*
5. Can you cook food in a sink? *N*
6. Can you light a candle with a toothpick? *N*
7. Can you eat soup with a spoon? *Y*
8. Can you read a magazine in the dark? *N*
9. Can you touch your ear with your nose? *N*
10. Can you look at something with binoculars? *Y*

Look Out Below!

Name ______________________________

Congratulations on a safe landing!

Color an apple each time you answer correctly.

1. Does a bear growl? Y
2. Does a bird chirp? Y
3. Does a cat bark? N
4. Does a horse fly? N
5. Does a fish run? N
6. Does a bug crawl? Y
7. Does a cow moo? Y
8. Does a monkey quack? N
9. Does a bee buzz? Y
10. Does a sheep roar? N

Pick the Apples!

Name ______________________

Yummy apples!

Color a section of the fan each time you answer correctly.

1. Does a baby cry? Y
2. Does a teacher talk? Y
3. Does a rock grow? N
4. Does a table cry? N
5. Does a fire heat? Y
6. Does a clock tick? Y
7. Does a tree cut? N
8. Does a flower write? N
9. Does a lamp light? Y
10. Does a phone ring? Y

Cool! **Name** ____________________

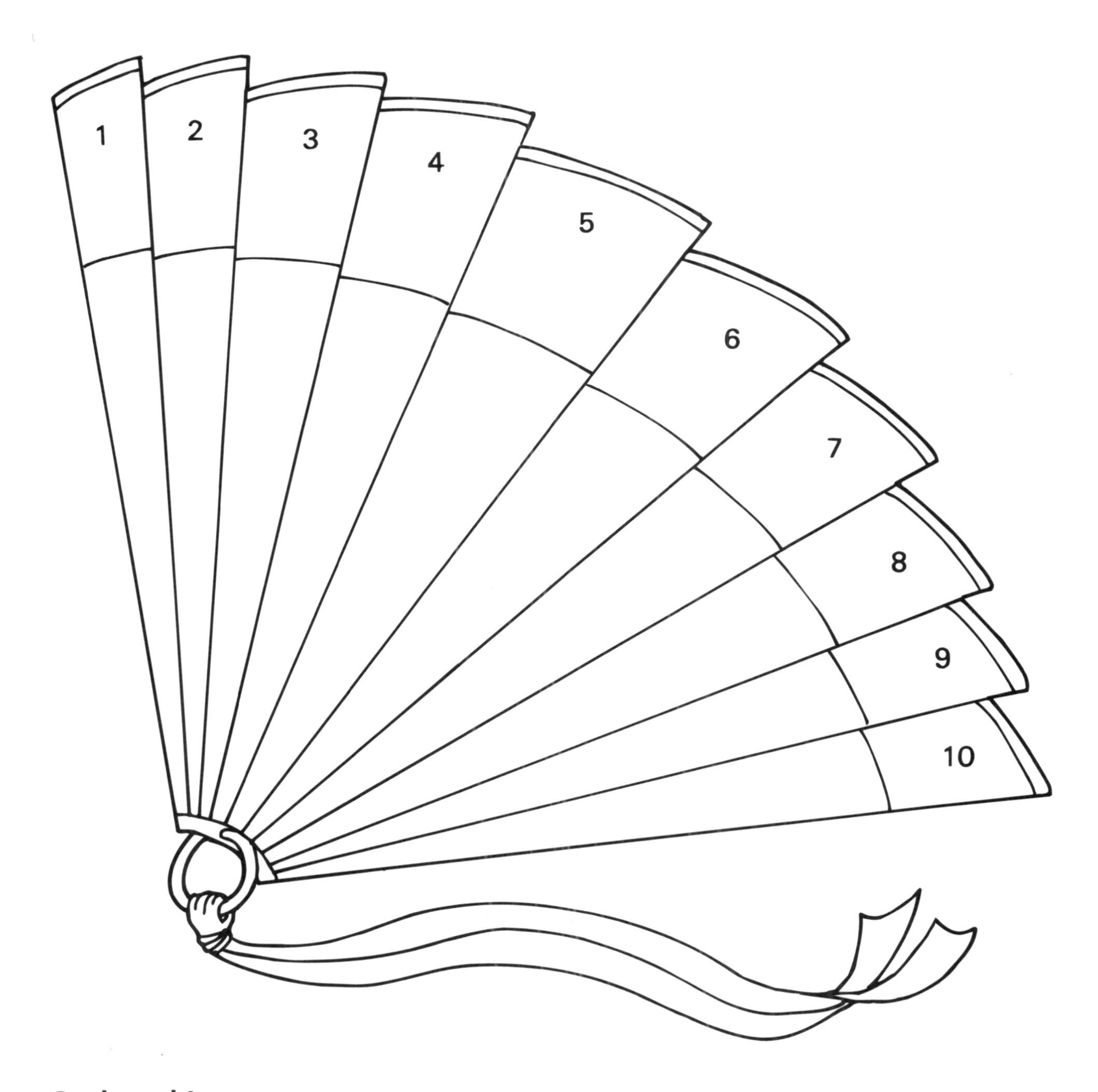

Cool work!

Add a wheel to a sports car each time you answer a question correctly.

1. Do shoulders sit? N
2. Do bats fly? Y
3. Do thorns prick? Y
4. Do blocks cry? N
5. Do parents help? Y
6. Do potatoes blink? N
7. Do secretaries type? Y
8. Do buildings freeze? N
9. Do drawers close? Y
10. Do eggs melt? N

Sporty Cars

Name ______________________

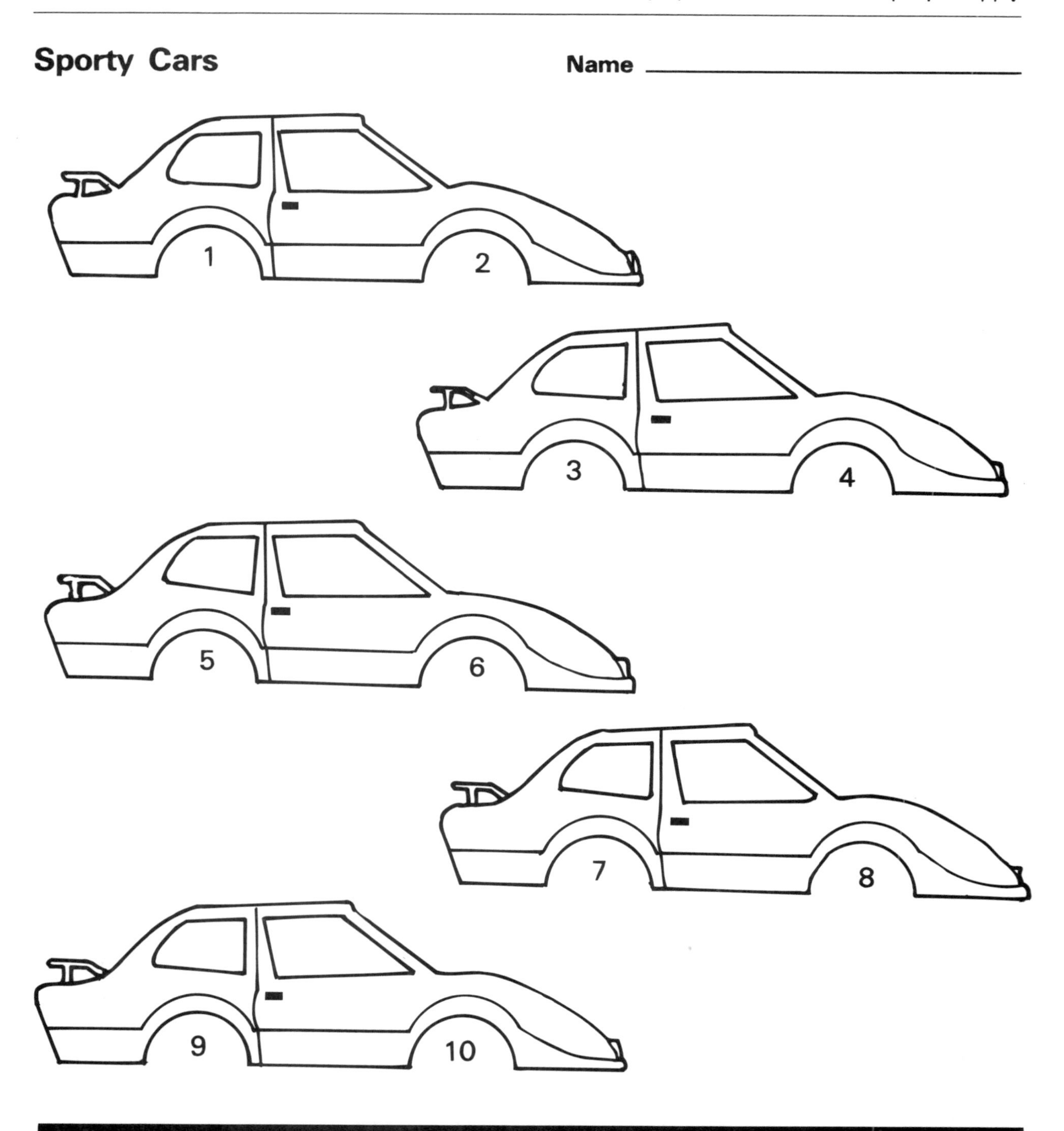

Now, color your favorite car!

Don't let these ladybugs fly away. Catch each one by coloring a dot on a wing each time you answer a question correctly.

1. Does spaghetti shrink? N
2. Does milk pour? Y
3. Does honey hope? N
4. Does sugar sweeten? Y
5. Does water drip? Y
6. Does makeup cover? Y
7. Does paper rip? Y
8. Does ink scream? N
9. Does water flow? Y
10. Does sand freeze? N

Lucky You! **Name** ______________________

How many ladybugs did you catch?

Listen carefully to the questions. Color a stone for a ring each time you answer correctly.

1. Does an artist paint pictures? Y
2. Does a plumber fix lights? N
3. Does a dentist fix teeth? Y
4. Does a baker sew clothes? N
5. Does a teacher use chalk? Y
6. Does a carpenter hammer nails? Y
7. Does a farmer grow rocks? N
8. Does a grocer sell furniture? N
9. Does a baseball player hit balls? Y
10. Does a clown wear makeup? Y

Sparkling Stones

Name ______________________________

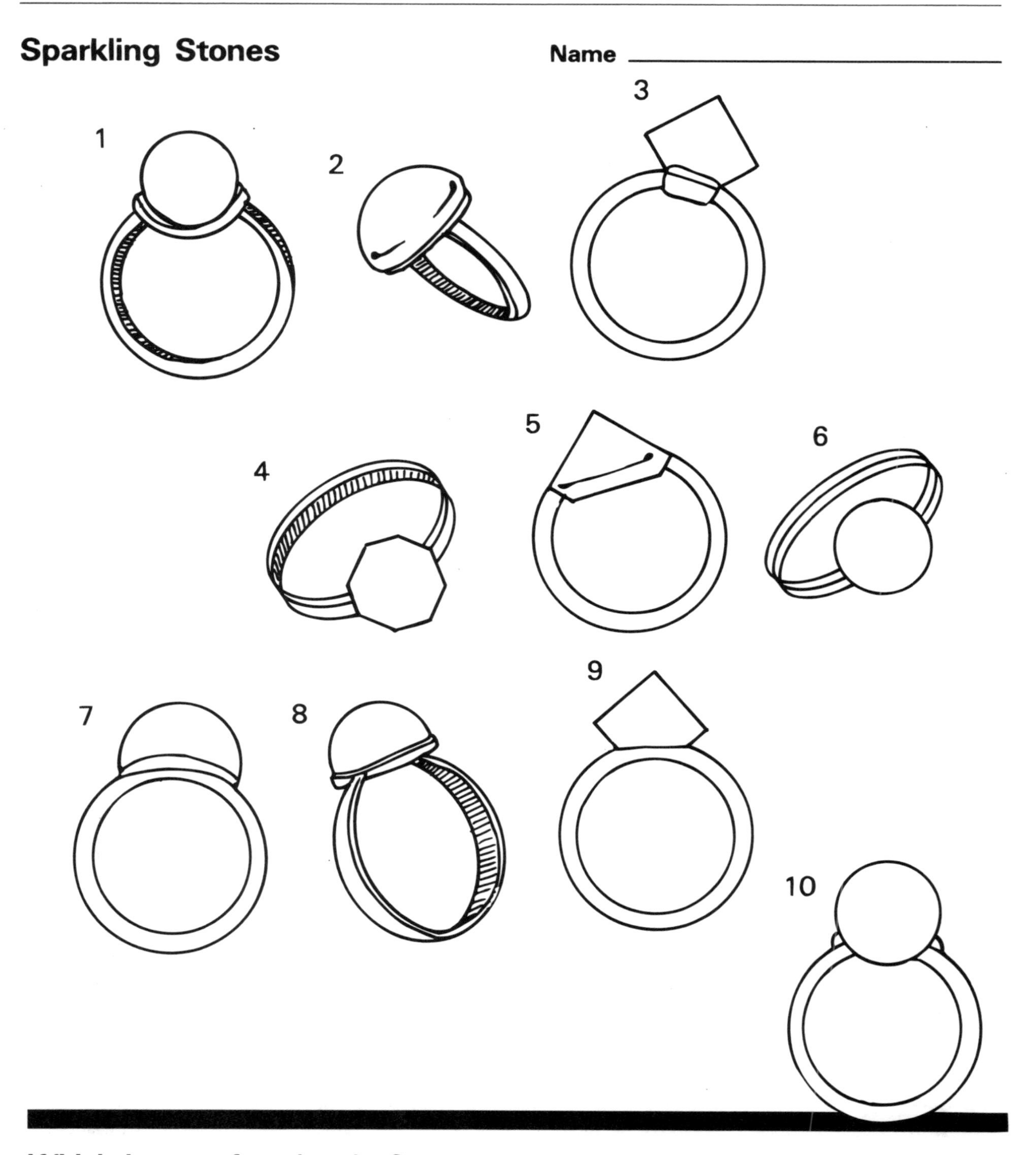

Which is your favorite ring?

Help the seals do their tricks. Color a ball each time you answer a question correctly.

1. Does an aquarium hold cats? N
2. Does a watermelon have juice? Y
3. Does a teacher give you information? Y
4. Does an airplane have wheels? Y
5. Does a nurse take your temperature? Y
6. Does a necktie have a button? N
7. Does a calculator subtract? Y
8. Does a neighbor live on your street? Y
9. Does an earthquake shake clouds? N
10. Does a post office sell magazines? N

Balancing Balls

Name ____________________

Tricky!

Color a piece of chocolate candy each time you answer a question correctly.

1. Do fireplaces light candles? *N*
2. Do irons wrinkle your clothes? *N*
3. Do trees grow taller? *Y*
4. Do clocks have hands? *Y*
5. Do combs make your hair neat? *Y*
6. Do people skate in the kitchen? *N*
7. Do kangaroos live in bushes? *N*
8. Do fire fighters direct traffic? *N*
9. Do pictures belong in a museum? *Y*
10. Do windows let sunshine through? *Y*

Sweets for the Sweet!

Name ______________________

What is your favorite kind of candy?

Help feed Polly Parrot. Put an X on a cracker each time you answer a question correctly.

1. If you were a bee, could you sting? Y
2. If you were a shark, could you fly? N
3. If you were a horse, could you race? Y
4. If you were a goat, could you talk? N
5. If you were a kangaroo, could you hop? Y
6. If you were a lion, could you roar? Y
7. If you were a pig, could you moo? N
8. If you were a snake, could you walk? N
9. If you were a frog, could you jump? Y
10. If you were a mouse, could you squeak? Y

Polly Want a Cracker?

Name ______________________

Polly says thanks for all the crackers!

These pigs are unhappy because their tails are missing. Trace a curly tail on a pig each time you answer a question correctly.

1. If you wanted dessert, could you go to a bakery? *Y*
2. If the electricity went out, could you turn on a lamp? *N*
3. If there are no leaves on the trees, is it summer? *N*
4. If you need a taxi, would you wait at the bus stop? *N*
5. If you were a lifeguard, would you be at the ice rink? *N*
6. If you went to the circus, would you see a lion? *Y*
7. If you were using a racquet, would you be playing baseball? *N*
8. If you were eating a candy cane, would it be Halloween? *N*
9. If you were wearing mittens and boots, would it be winter? *Y*
10. If a screen had holes in it, could bugs get in? *Y*

Oink! Oink! **Name** ____________________

My, what happy pigs!

Give each elf pointed shoes before he runs away! Trace a shoe for an elf each time you answer a question correctly.

1. If a pool is shallow, should you dive into it? *N*
2. If something weighs 300 pounds, can you lift it? *N*
3. If you are a teacher, do you work at school? *Y*
4. If you are sick, do you go to the doctor? *Y*
5. If it is Saturday, are you in school? *N*
6. If you are poor, do you have much money? *N*
7. If a ladder is missing rungs, can you climb it? *N*
8. If two things are separated, are they touching each other? *N*
9. If something is frozen, is it cold? *Y*
10. If you are asleep, can you dream? *Y*

Sharp Shoes

Name ______________________________

How many elves did you catch?

Color a car on the train each time you answer correctly.

1. If you are hot, do you turn up the heat? *N*
2. If you are lost, do you ask a police officer for directions? *Y*
3. If you break your leg, do you go to the hospital? *Y*
4. If you move to a new home, do you have a new bedroom? *Y*
5. If you need to know a phone number, do you look in the dictionary? *N*
6. If you get married, do you change your first name? *N*
7. If you draw a triangle, are you drawing three sides? *Y*
8. If you have a birthday, are you younger? *N*
9. If you take a shower, do you get wet? *Y*
10. If you have a sister, are you an only child? *N*

I Think You Can!

Name ______________________________

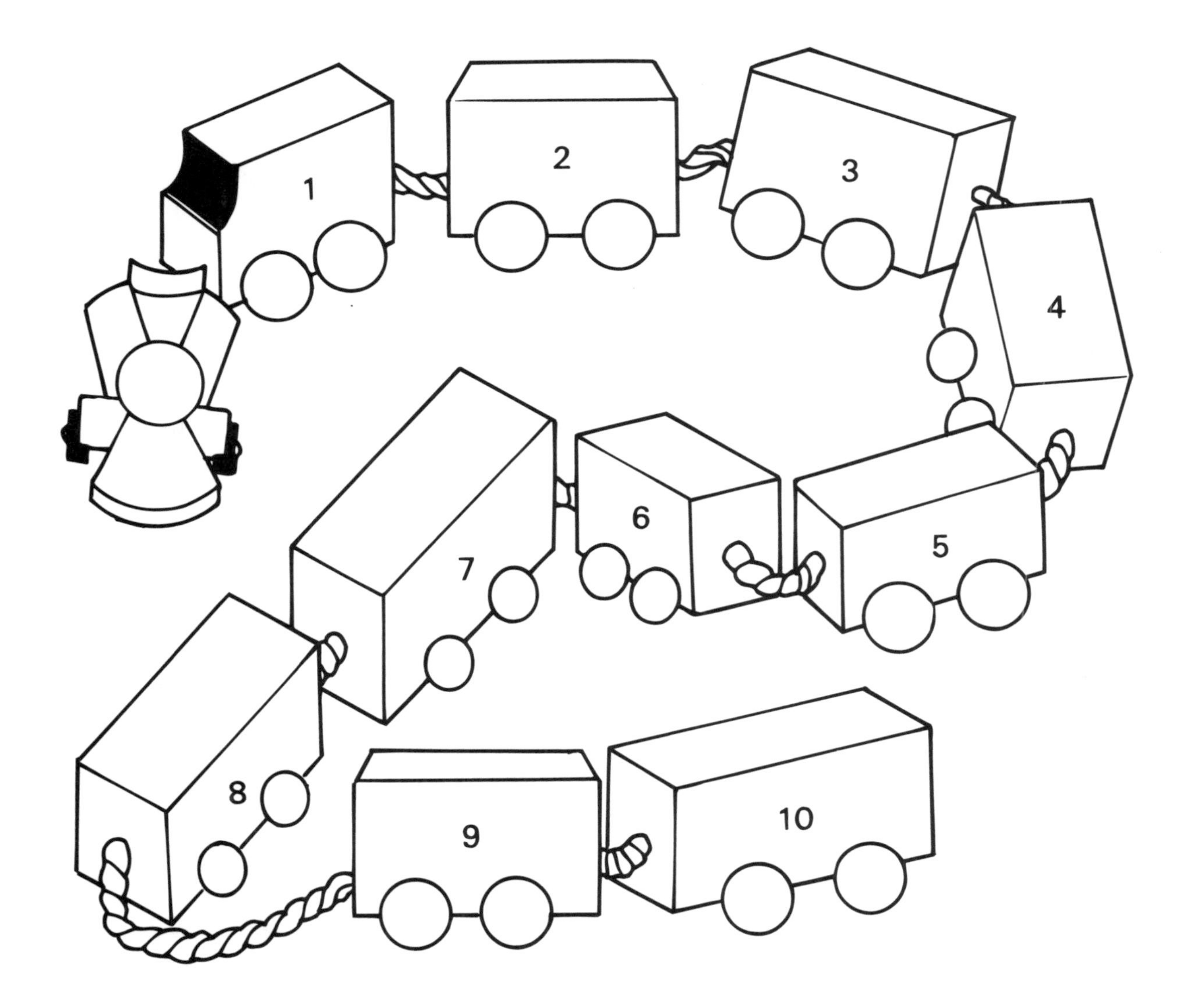

Did you reach the caboose?

Make a shape by connecting the dots between the numbers each time you answer a question correctly.

1. Is a house smaller than a garage? *N*
2. Is your leg longer than your arm? *Y*
3. Is a needle fatter than a pencil? *N*
4. Is eight more than ten? *N*
5. Is having a friend better than having an enemy? *Y*
6. Is the sun brighter than the moon? *Y*
7. Is a shovel bigger than a spoon? *Y*
8. Is a lemon more sour than sugar? *Y*
9. Is a princess uglier than a monster? *N*
10. Is a whisper quieter than a yell? *Y*

Let It Shine!

Name ______________________

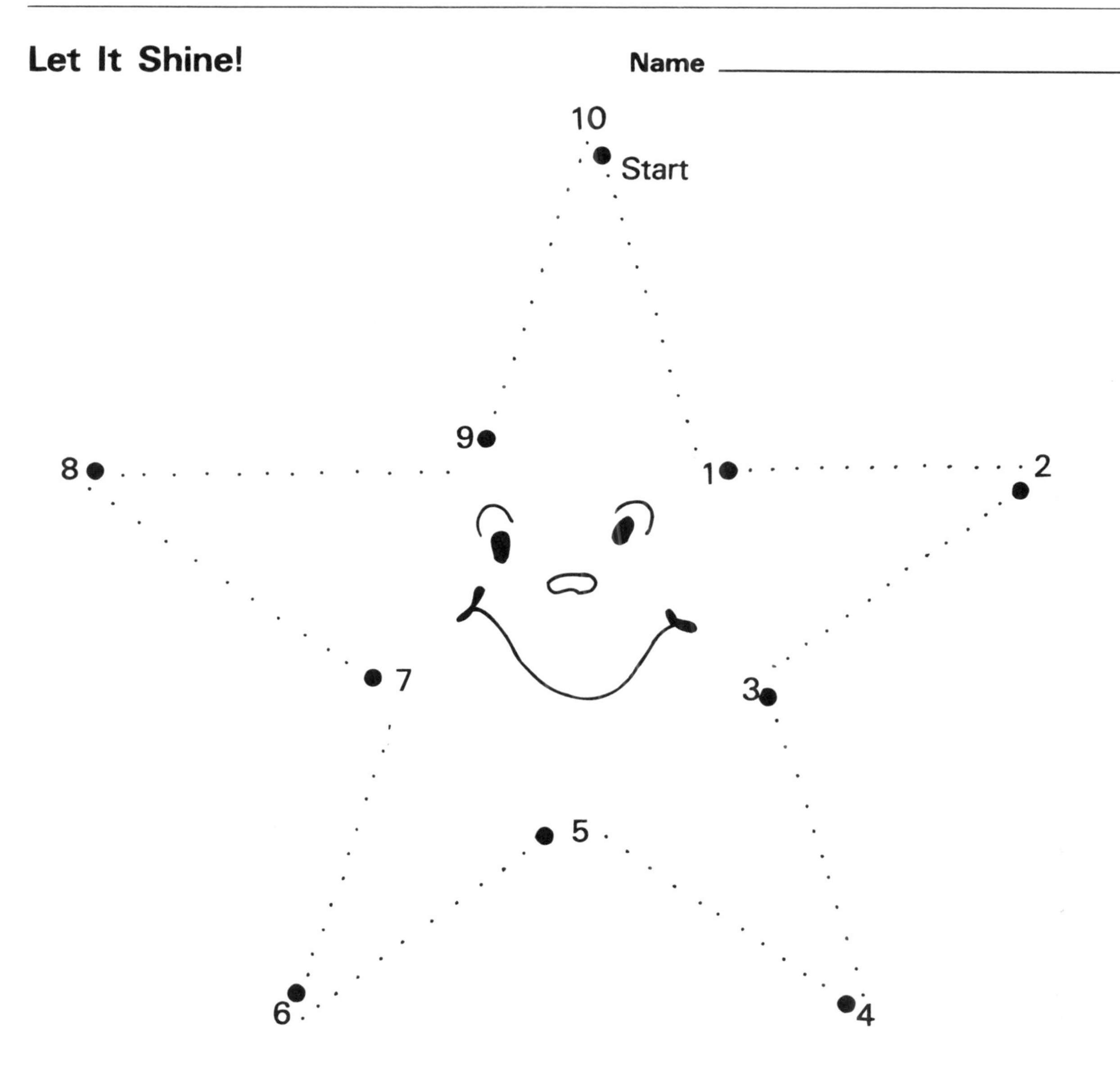

What did you draw?

Snuggle under the quilt you decorate! Color a section of the quilt each time you answer a question correctly.

1. Does a chair have more than four legs? N
2. Are there more than thirty seconds in a minute? Y
3. Are quarters worth less than dimes? N
4. Does a skyscraper have more than three floors? Y
5. Is a carton of eggs more than ten eggs? Y
6. Is cinnamon sweeter than sugar? N
7. Does brushing your teeth take longer than taking a bath? N
8. Does jewelry cost more than candy? Y
9. Is ice colder than milk? Y
10. Is a towel bigger than a washcloth? Y

Snuggle Time

Name ____________________

1 2 3

4 5 6 7

8 9 10

What a cozy-looking quilt!

Take Off!

Name ______________________________

Fly high with good thinking! Trace the wings on an airplane each time you answer a question correctly.

1. Is a car worth more than a bike? Y
2. Are feathers lighter than books? Y
3. Are grapefruits sweeter than oranges? N
4. Is a month longer than a year? N
5. Are cars heavier than buses? N
6. Are parents older than their children? Y
7. Is a pair more than three of something? N
8. Is a whole more than half? Y
9. Is four more than two? Y
10. Is a rock shinier than a diamond? N

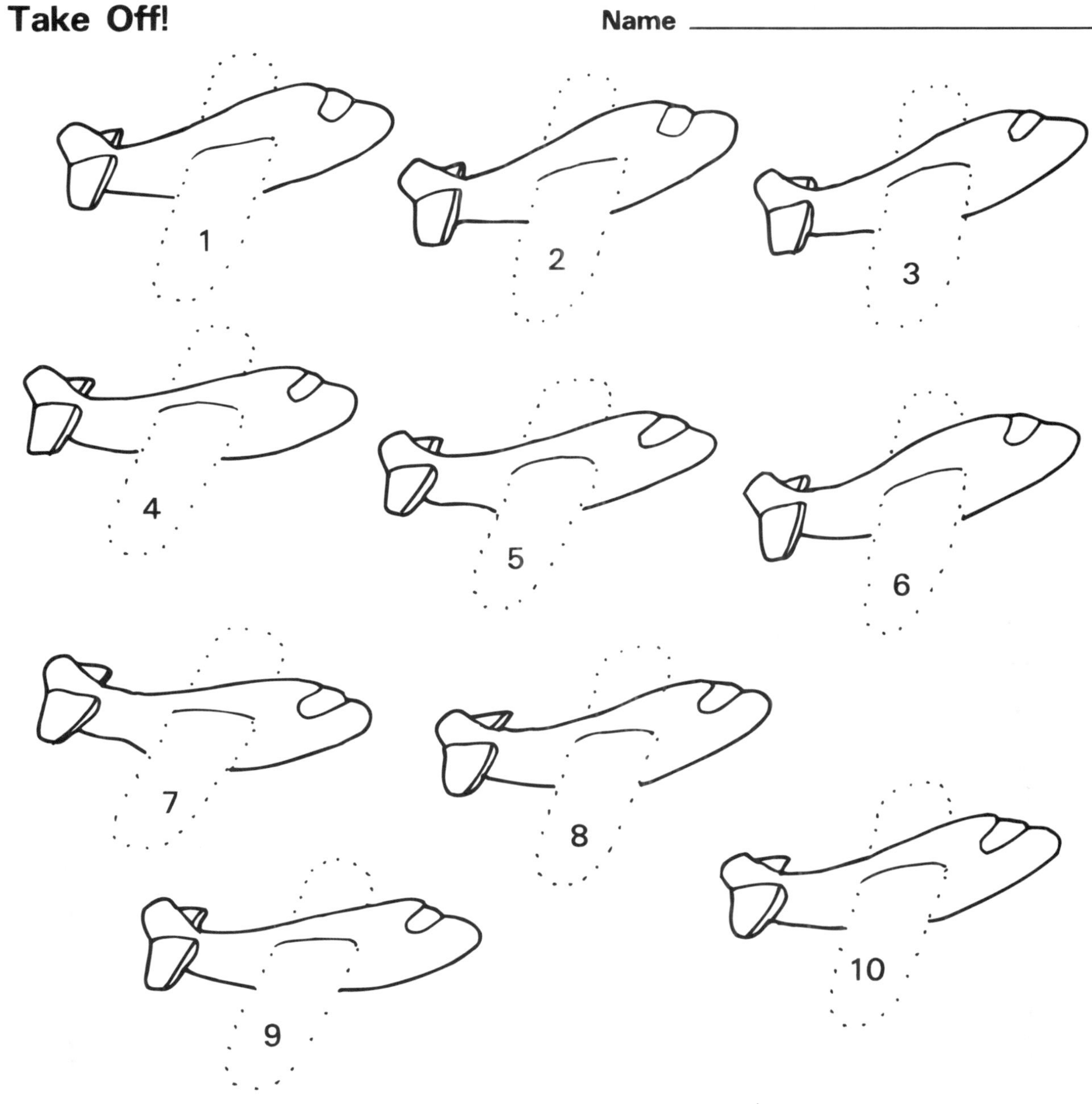

Nice flying!

Color a bell each time you answer a question correctly.

1. Is a cup more than a gallon? *N*
2. Does a refrigerator weigh more than a TV? *Y*
3. Are twins more than two people? *N*
4. Does *several* mean more than *one*? *Y*
5. Is an inch smaller than a foot? *Y*
6. Does a year have fewer than twelve months? *N*
7. Are your hips lower than your waist? *Y*
8. Is a dollar more than four quarters? *N*
9. Is a bus faster than a train? *N*
10. Is the United States bigger than California? *Y*

Ding Dong!

Name ______________________________

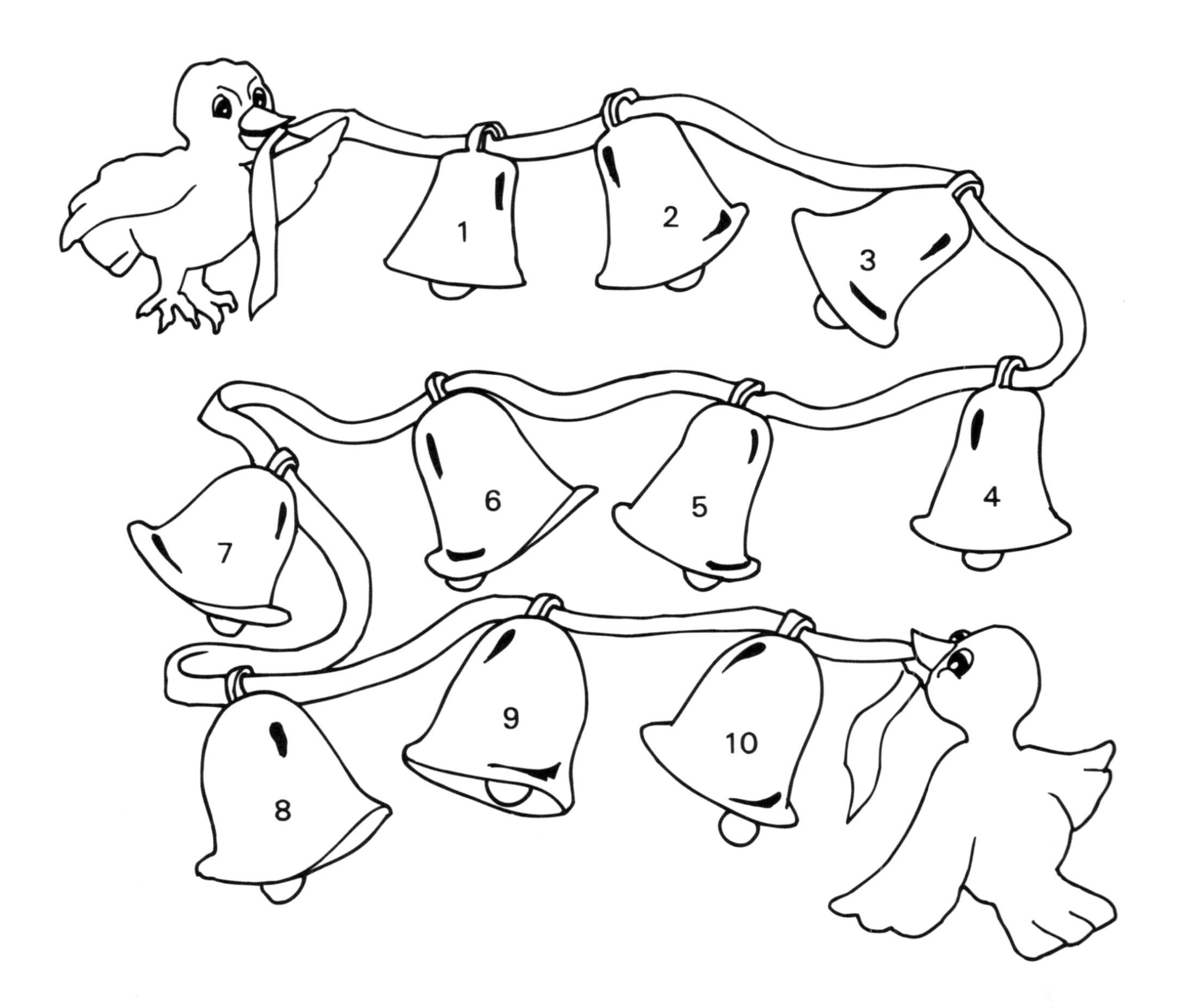

What colorful bells!

Color a car on the Ferris wheel each time you correctly tell whether a sentence is true or false.

1. We sit on a chair. *T*
2. We eat trees. *F*
3. We climb stairs. *T*
4. We see with our ears. *F*
5. We button our shirts. *T*
6. We write with a pencil. *T*
7. We fly a bike. *F*
8. We hate our friends. *F*
9. We chew milk. *F*
10. We chew bubblegum. *T*

Ferris Wheel Fun

Name ______________________________

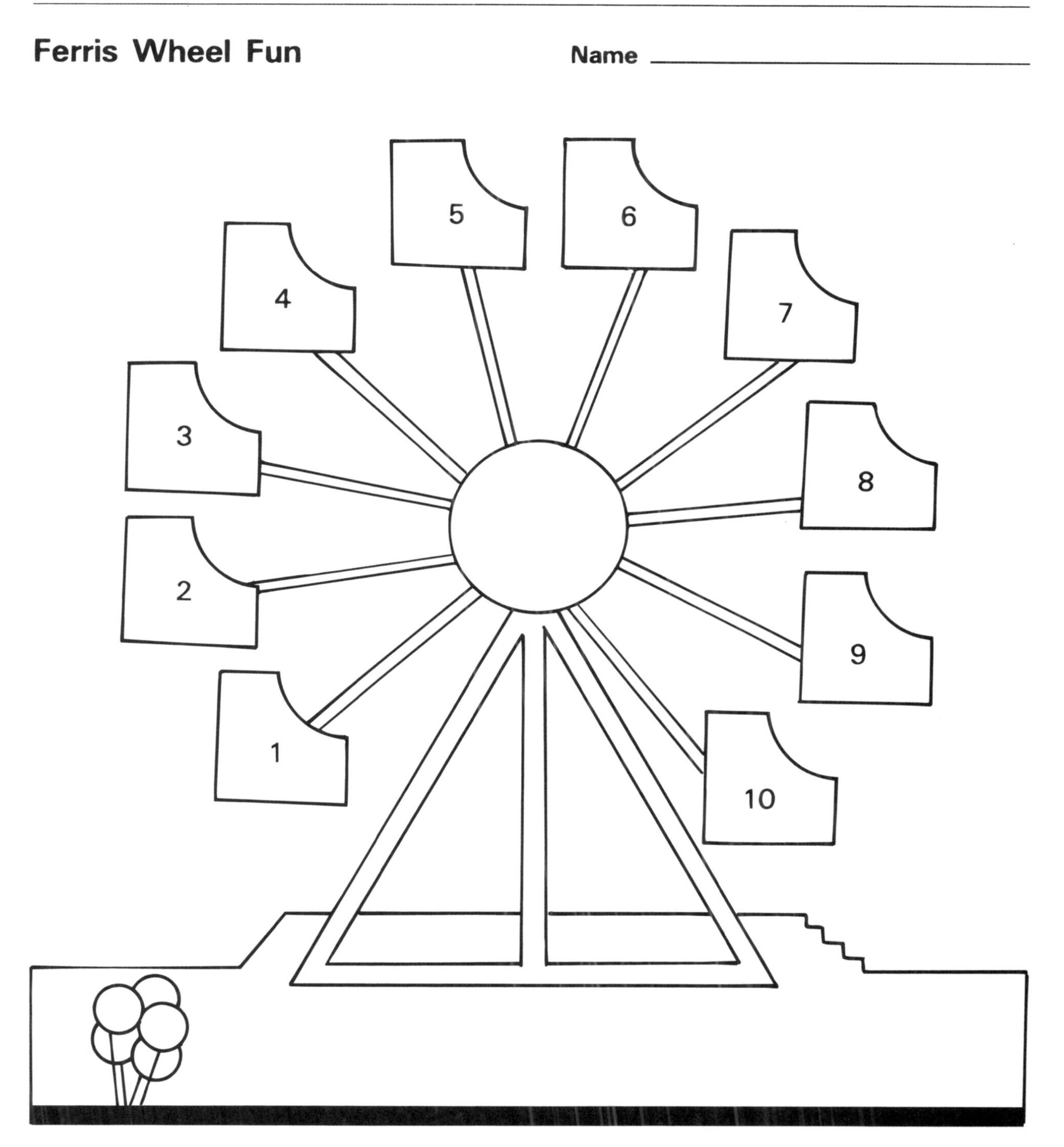

What's your favorite ride?

Are you a match for these true and false questions? Draw a line to match the shapes each time you correctly tell whether a sentence is true or false.

1. The sun shines during the night. *F*
2. People often go swimming in lakes. *T*
3. A horse can carry a man on its back. *T*
4. A giraffe lives on a farm. *F*
5. A pencil writes in ink. *F*
6. Gas makes a car go. *T*
7. A pilot builds houses. *F*
8. Summer is a hot season. *T*
9. A bicycle has four wheels. *F*
10. Some people eat cereal for breakfast. *T*

Matching Shapes

Name ______________________

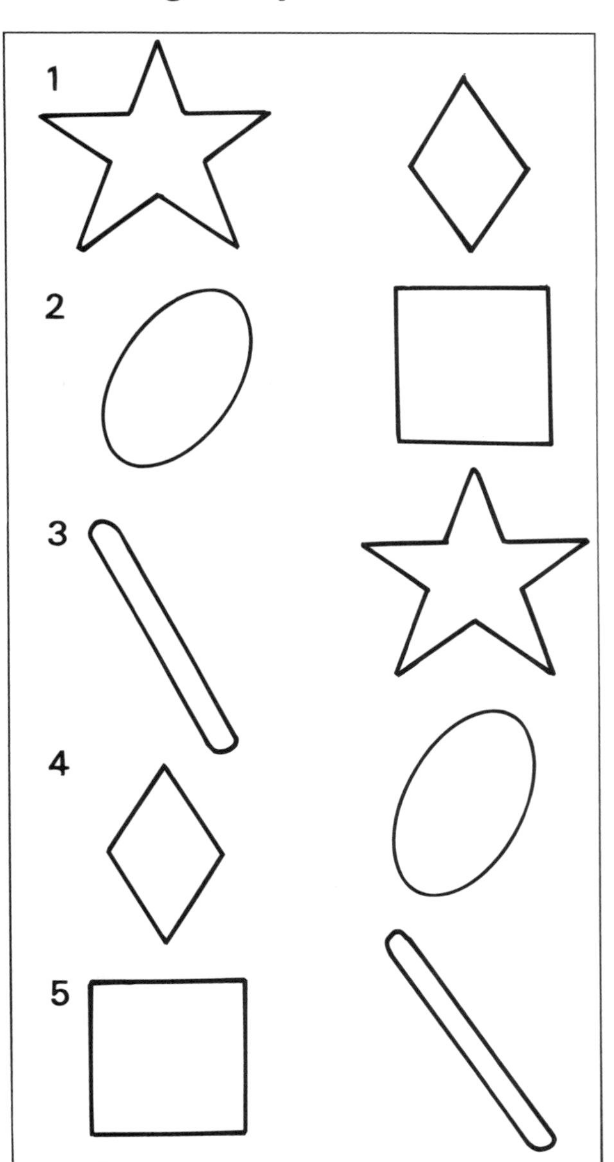

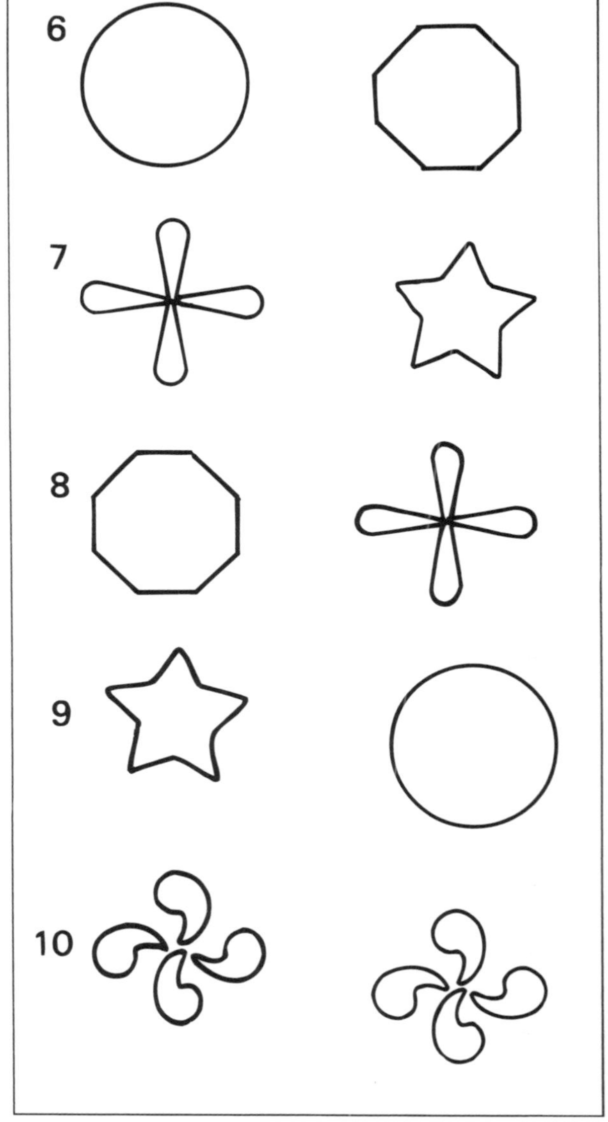

Great matching!

Color a section of the monkey each time you correctly tell whether a sentence is true or false.

1. Ice will melt at room temperature. *T*
2. Ten comes before eight. *F*
3. A minute is longer than an hour. *F*
4. A caboose is the last car on a train. *T*
5. Winter is a cold month. *F*
6. Florida is a warmer place than Alaska. *T*
7. The sun is larger than the moon. *T*
8. Cake is sweeter than popcorn. *T*
9. A bird flies higher than a jet. *F*
10. We get vitamins from eating vegetables. *T*

Hanging Around **Name** ______________________________

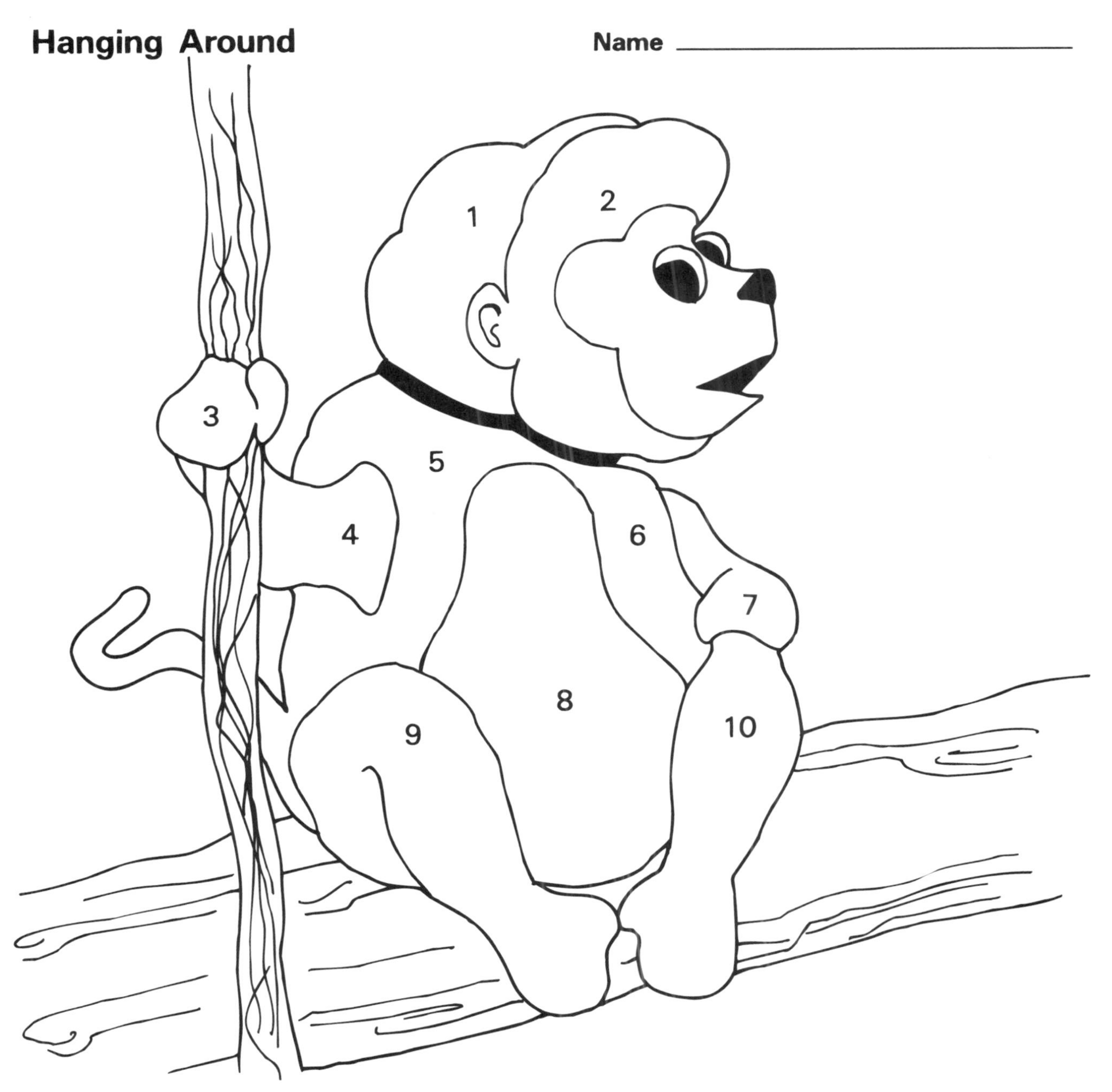

You don't monkey around, do you?

Color a kite each time you answer a question correctly.

1. Can some or all kangaroos hop? *all*
2. Can some or all bugs fly? *some*
3. Can some or all people swim? *some*
4. Can some or all birds talk? *some*
5. Can some or all paper rip? *all*
6. Can some or all shoes be worn on the feet? *all*
7. Can some or all liquids be poured? *all*
8. Can some or all watches tell the time? *all*
9. Can some or all bells ring? *all*
10. Can some or all doors have windows? *some*

Flying High! **Name** ____________________

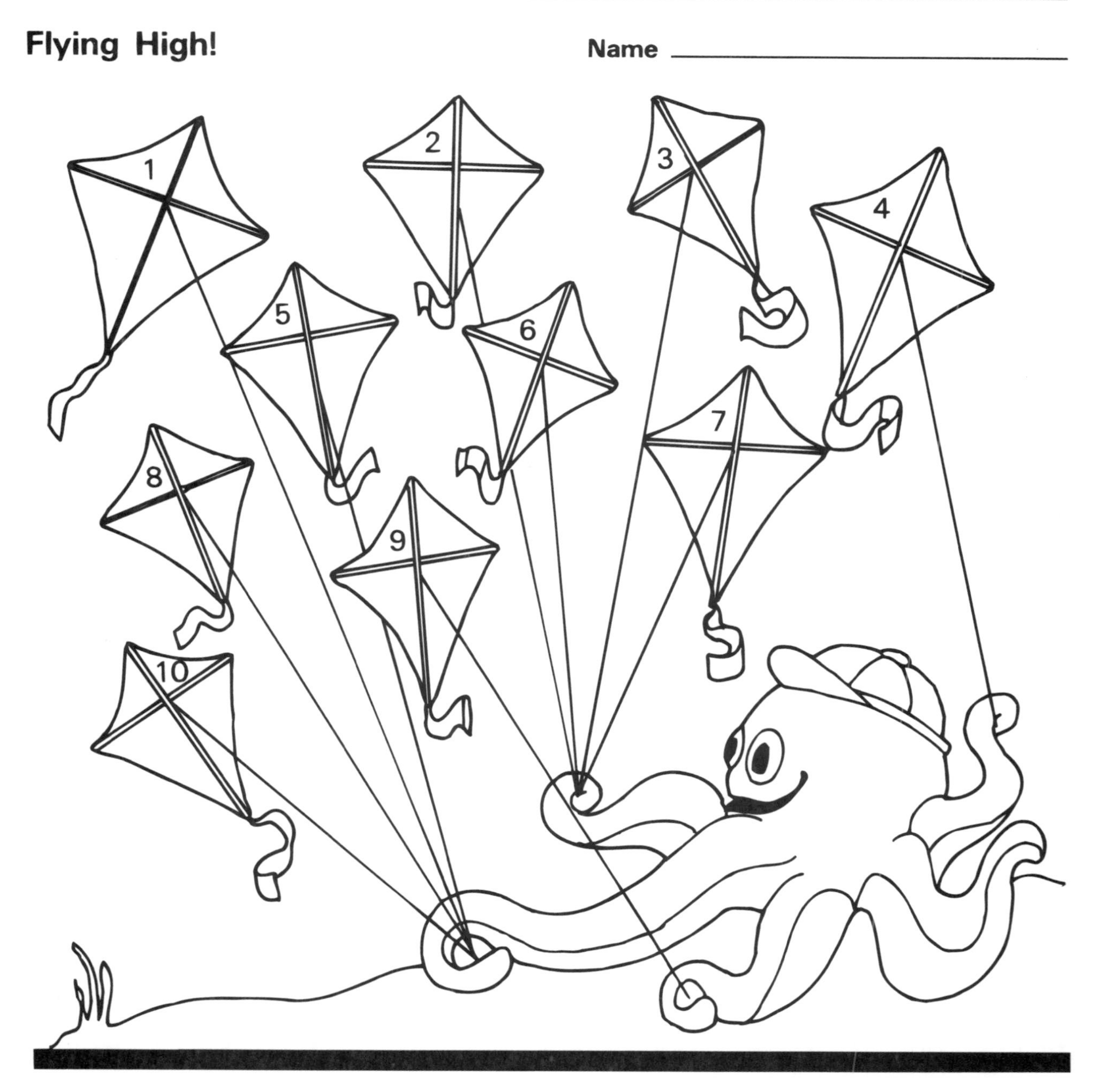

Way to fly!

Color a link of the chain each time you answer a question correctly.

1. Do some or all cars have wheels? *all*
2. Do some or all pants have two legs? *all*
3. Do some or all zebras have stripes? *all*
4. Do some or all garages hold two cars? *some*
5. Do some or all coats have a zipper? *some*
6. Do some or all rings have a diamond? *some*
7. Do some or all sinks hold water? *all*
8. Do some or all games have dice? *some*
9. Do some or all bikes have handlebars? *all*
10. Do some or all houses have a basement? *some*

Link Up

Name ______________________________

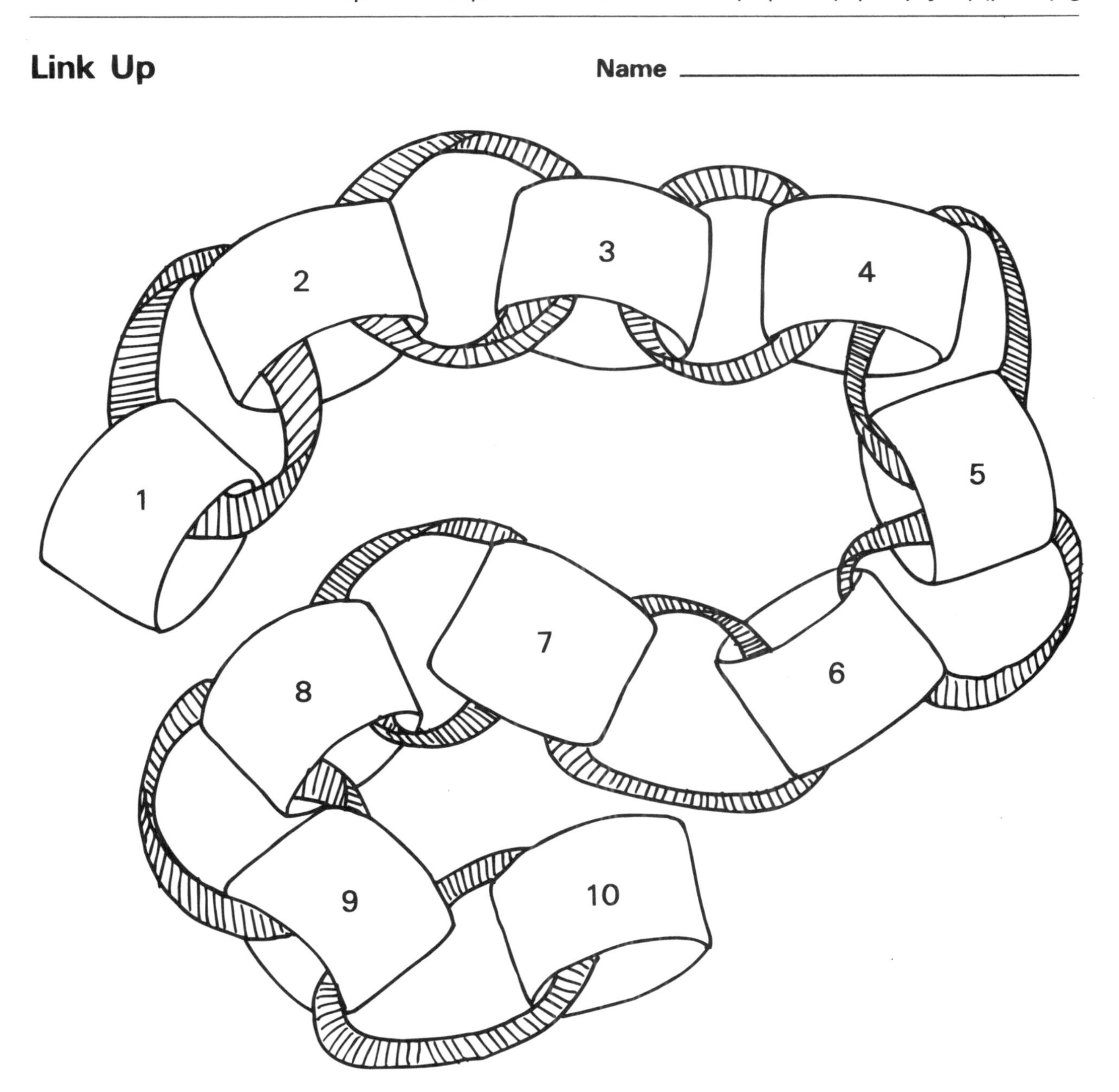

Did you complete the chain?

Help Andy Ant reach his home. Trace an arrow each time you answer a question correctly.

1. Do some or all people have eyes? *all*
2. Do some or all fish live in the water? *all*
3. Do some or all houses have walls? *all*
4. Do some or all animals live on a farm? *some*
5. Do some or all children have brothers? *some*
6. Do some or all people eat food? *all*
7. Do some or all animals fly? *some*
8. Do some or all cats have black fur? *some*
9. Do some or all schools have teachers? *all*
10. Do some or all shirts have pockets? *some*

Lost Ant

Name ______________________

Did the ant make it home?

Color part of the pinwheel each time you answer a question correctly.

1. Are some or all tables made of wood? *some*
2. Are some or all pillows soft? *all*
3. Are some or all children babies? *some*
4. Are some or all vegetables food? *all*
5. Are some or all nights dark? *all*
6. Are some or all ants small? *all*
7. Are some or all teachers women? *some*
8. Are some or all birds pets? *some*
9. Are some or all movies happy? *some*
10. Are some or all tornados windy? *all*

Spinning 'Round

Name ______________________________

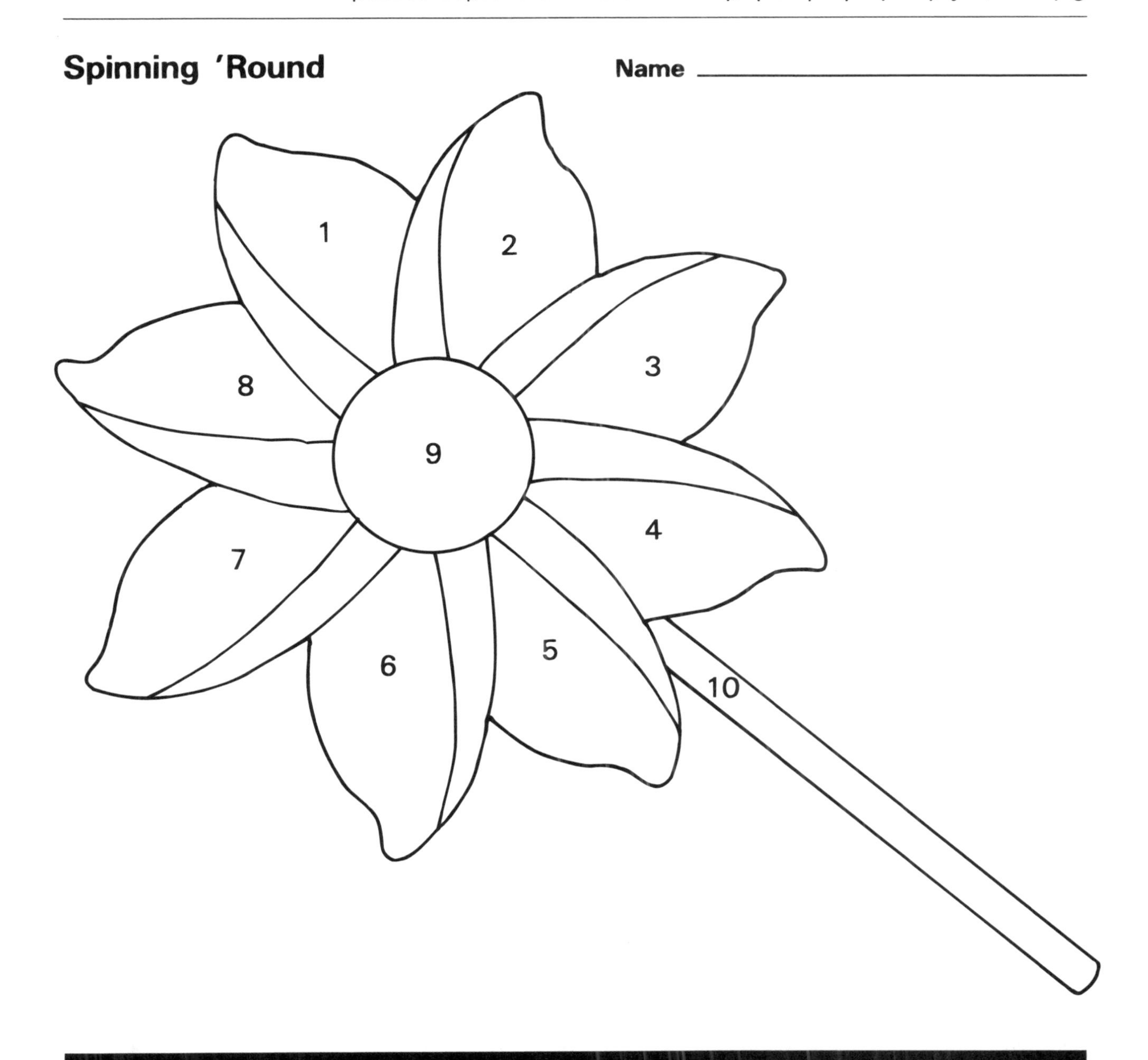

What a pretty pinwheel!

Tell if each statement is true *always*, *sometimes*, or *never*. Trace a raindrop each time you answer correctly.

1. A clock has batteries. *sometimes*
2. A phone book has numbers. *always*
3. A man has fur. *never*
4. A pen has ink. *always*
5. A shoe has sleeves. *never*
6. A car has a motor. *always*
7. A coat has buttons. *sometimes*
8. A house has a roof. *always*
9. A telephone has pages. *never*
10. A woman has children. *sometimes*

Falling Raindrops

Name ______________________________

What do you like best about rainy days?

Color a section of the flower if you answer correctly. Tell if each statement is true *always*, *sometimes*, or *never*.

1. People are tall. *sometimes*
2. Carrots are vegetables. *always*
3. Cold is hot. *never*
4. Milk is a liquid. *always*
5. The library is open. *sometimes*
6. Wives are women. *always*
7. Letters are numbers. *never*
8. Apples are red. *sometimes*
9. A tire is flat. *sometimes*
10. A circle is round. *always*

Finish the Flower

Name ____________________

Look at that colorful flower!

Color a sailboat each time you answer correctly. Tell if each statement is true *always*, *sometimes*, or *never*.

1. Doctors are concerned with good health. *always*
2. Five is larger than four. *always*
3. Birds fly south in winter. *sometimes*
4. Junk food contains many vitamins. *never*
5. A duck is a reptile. *never*
6. Sunday is on the weekend. *always*
7. Adults are younger than children. *never*
8. Tables are made of plastic. *sometimes*
9. A president is a leader. *always*
10. The sky is blue. *sometimes*

Win First Place

Name ____________________

You won!

Listening for Knowledge

Listening for knowledge involves listening to information presented and recalling specific bits of information. Recognition and recall are important aspects of this basic skill. By developing a knowledge base, we are able to associate new information and are able to attach meaning to something that we hear.

Since a child learns most when learning is enjoyable, the listening activities in this section encourage the growth of language skills in a fun way. The activities contribute to the acquisition of skills related to phonemic awareness by creating a knowledge base of word associations and by developing word memory. These parameters might be compared to descriptors in Bloom's Taxonomy. They are prerequisite skills which are fundamental for developing literacy and the ability to reason using language.

These listening worksheets may be used with individuals or small groups in a therapy setting, within a classroom environment, or for homework assignments. The speech-language clinician, classroom teacher, or parent reads the statements and question, and the child answers aloud. For each correct answer, the child colors, traces, or draws a simple picture numbered to correspond with the question.

Whenever it is advisable to maintain a purely auditory task, have the child just listen to each item as you read it. After the child responds correctly, present the worksheet for the child to complete the appropriate reinforcing picture.

Kitchen or Bathroom?

Name ______________________

Color a lollipop for each correct answer. Tell whether each thing belongs in the kitchen or the bathroom.

1. toothbrush
2. mixer
3. shampoo
4. stove
5. eggbeater

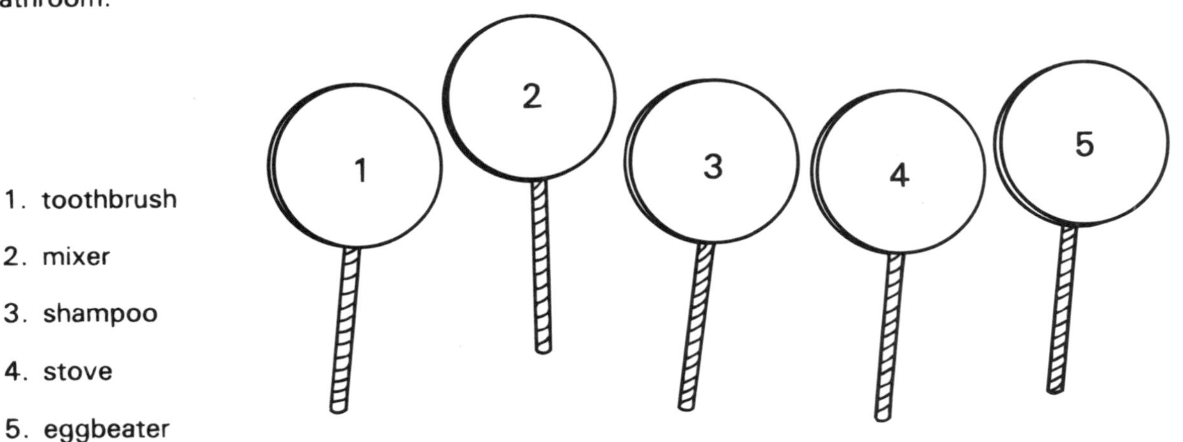

6. spoons
7. blender
8. bathrobe
9. bandages
10. cake

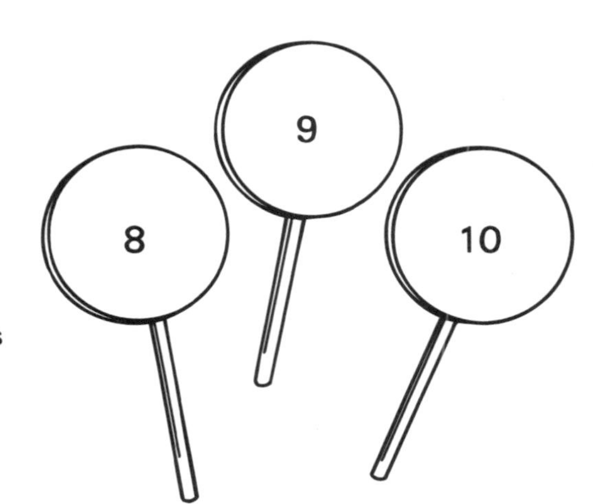

11. razor
12. dishes
13. toilet paper
14. toothpaste
15. dishwasher

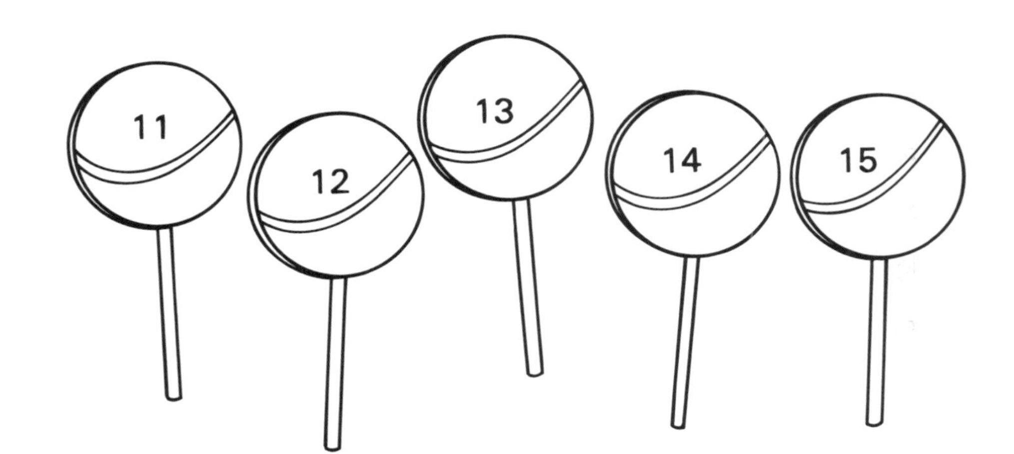

How many lollipops did you color?

Farm or Tree?

Name ______________________________

Trace an X each time you answer correctly. Tell whether each animal lives on a farm or in a tree.

1 2 3 4 5

1. squirrel
2. cow
3. monkey
4. eagle
5. duck

10 7 8 9 6

6. sheep
7. turkey
8. blue jay
9. pony
10. chicken

13 11 15 12 14

11. chipmunk
12. horse
13. robin
14. pig
15. goat

X-CELLENT!

Up, Up and Away!

Name ______________________________

Draw a string on a balloon each time you answer correctly. Tell something that goes with each word.

1. broom
2. needle
3. bee
4. candle
5. hammer
6. key
7. belt
8. fork
9. sock

Try these for extra credit!

______ egg ______ picture ______ kite ______ teacher

Target Practice

Name ______________________________

Color the point of the arrow each time you answer correctly. Tell something that goes with each word.

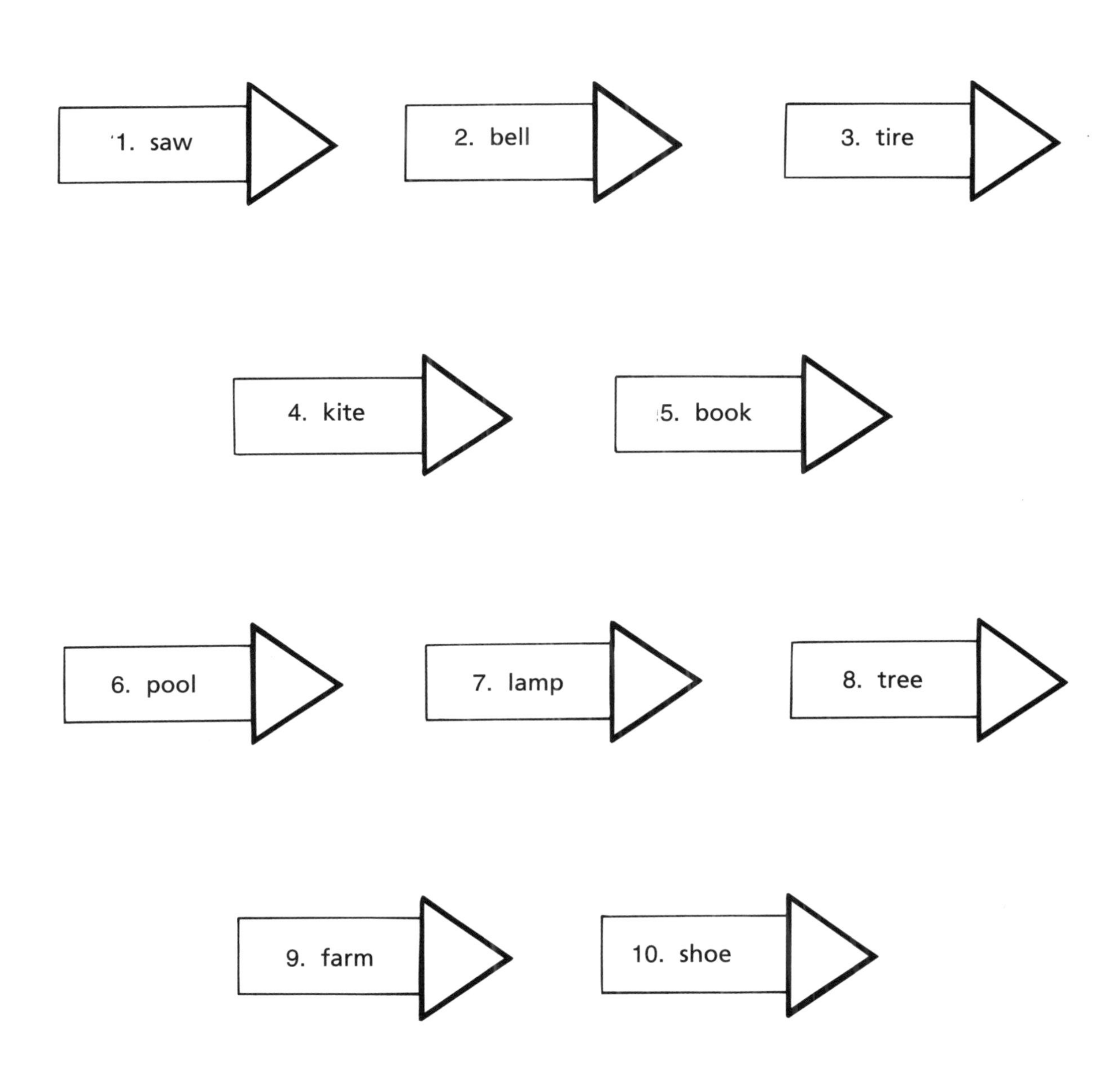

Try these for extra credit!

_____ engine _____ eraser _____ clock _____ soldier

Make a Face

Name ______________________

Make a face for a mask each time you finish a sentence correctly.

1. A faucet is part of a ___________.
2. A beak is part of a ___________.
3. A paw is part of a ___________.
4. A mattress is part of a ___________.
5. A collar is part of a ___________.
6. A lid is part of a ___________.
7. A steering wheel is part of a ___________.
8. A frame is part of a ___________.
9. An eraser is part of a ___________.
10. A seat is part of a ___________.

1

2

3

4

5

6

7

8

9

10

How many scary masks did you draw?

Caterpillar Color Fun

Name ______________________________

Color a part of Katie Caterpillar each time you finish a sentence correctly.

1. A thumb is part of a ____________.
2. A stem is part of a ____________.
3. A floor is part of a ____________.
4. A shade is part of a ____________.
5. A wheel is part of a ____________.
6. Pages are part of a ____________.
7. Drawers are part of a ____________.
8. Teeth are part of a ____________.
9. Leaves are part of a ____________.
10. Feathers are part of a ____________.

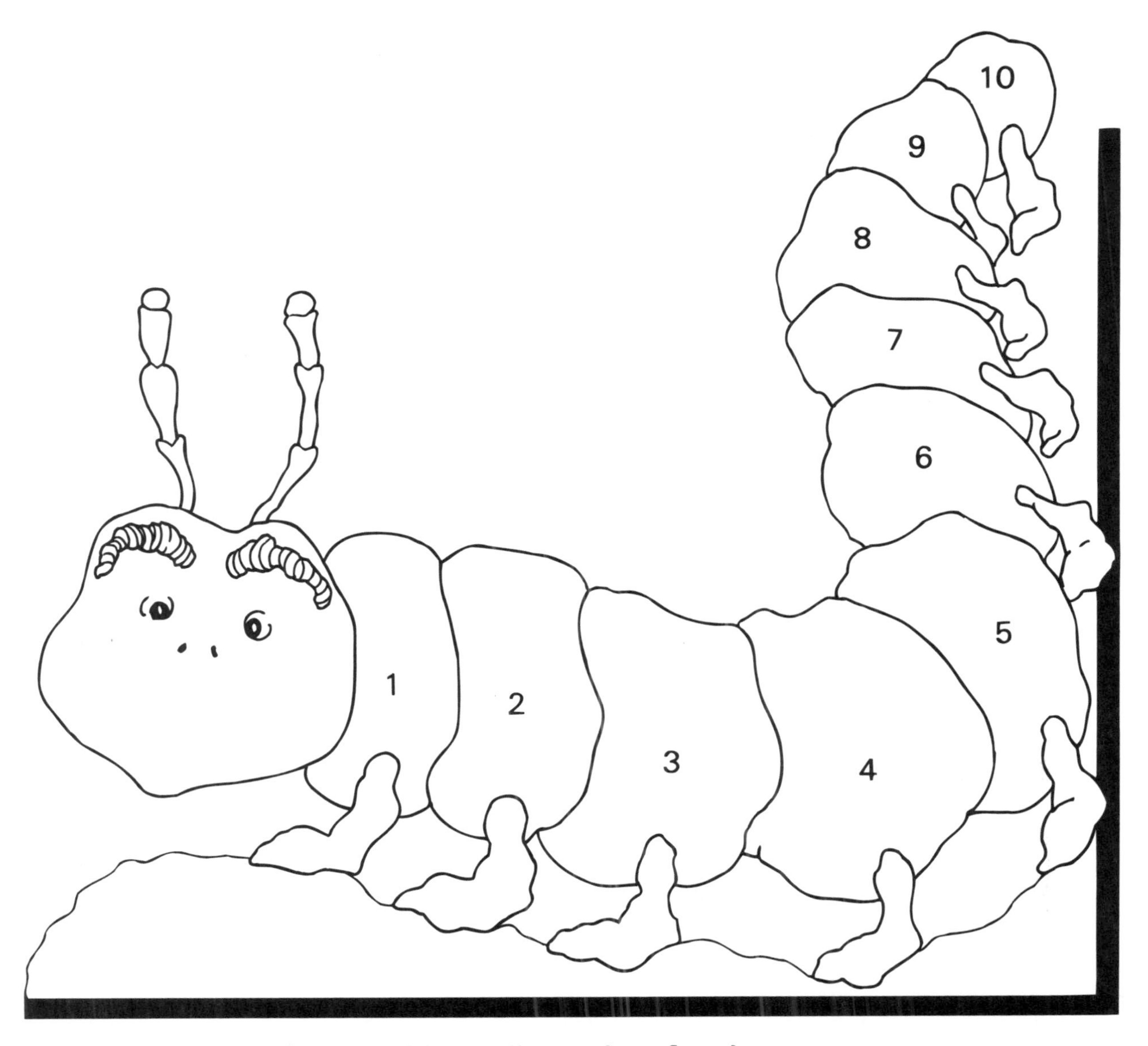

Katie is happy. Draw a big smile on her face!

Toot! Toot!

Name ______________________________

How are these things different? Color a puff of smoke coming from the train each time you answer correctly.

Think of a sheep and a pig.

1. Which one is woolly?
2. Which one has a curly tail?
3. Which one eats grass?

Think of a table and a couch.

4. Which one do we sit on?
5. Which one is softer?
6. Which one do we put our legs under?

Think of fingers and toes.

7. Which ones hold things?
8. Which ones do you use for kicking?
9. Which ones do we wear rings on?

Think of a watermelon and a lemon.

10. Which one is sweet?
11. Which one is bigger?
12. Which one do we eat with a fork?

Blow your whistle for a job well done!

Chewy Choices

Name ______________________________

Answer YES or NO to each question. Color a cookie each time you answer correctly. Don't burn your fingers.

1. Are bees smaller than grasshoppers?
2. Is a house taller than a tent?
3. Is the moon brighter than the sun?
4. Is a stick heavier than a log?
5. Is a pumpkin bigger than an apple?
6. Are turtles faster than rabbits?
7. Is hot chocolate hotter than pop?
8. Is a baby younger than its parents?
9. Is mud harder than cement?
10. Are boats larger than ships?

Yummy, don't those cookies look delicious?

Blow Your Horn!

Name ___________________________

Circle a note each time you answer correctly.

Which is lighter?

1. a bed or a chair
2. a car or a bus

Which is hotter?

3. the sun or a piece of toast
4. fall or summer

Which is louder?

5. a tuba or a flute
6. a sheep or a lion

Which is sharper?

7. a butter knife or a saw
8. a pencil or a needle

Which is taller?

9. a tree or a skyscraper
10. a giraffe or a camel

What beautiful music you made!

Fly Away!

Name ______________________________

Color a leaf each time you answer correctly. Help the caterpillar become a butterfly!

Which is the biggest?

1. a house, a horse, or an elephant
2. a man, a truck, or a car
3. a lemon, a seed, or a grapefruit

Which is the prettiest?

4. a duck, a princess, or a snowman
5. a flower, an ant, or an apple
6. a giant, a leaf, or a rainbow

Which is the coldest?

7. pop, milk, or ice
8. snow, rain, or water
9. winter, spring, or fall

Which is the shortest?

10. a dog, a man, or a hamster
11. a baby, a cat, or a frog
12. a chair, a door, or a wall

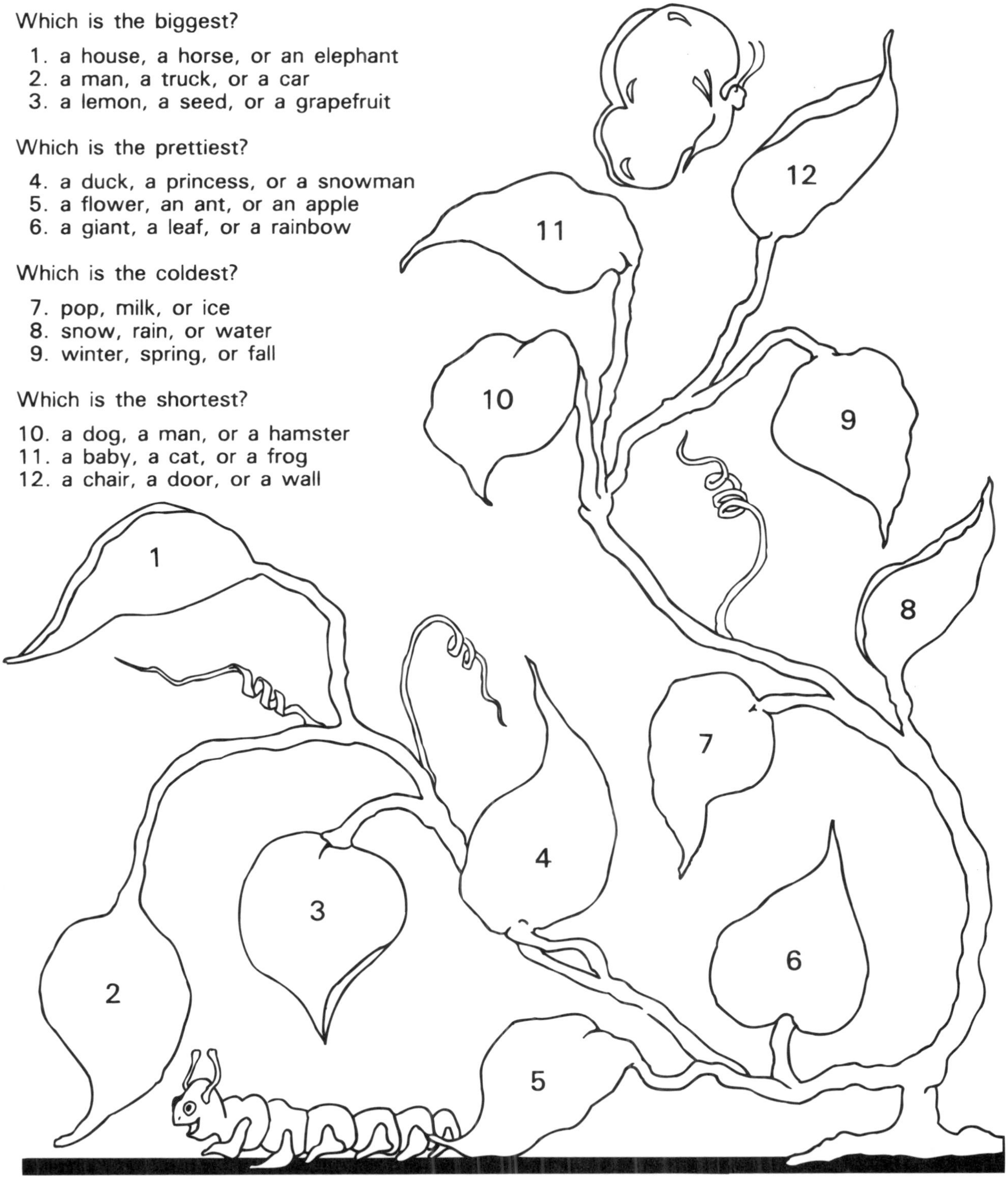

1 2 3 4 5 6 7 8 9 10 11 12

Spread your wings and fly, butterfly!

Cr-r-runch!

Name ______________________________

Trace a bunny hop for a bunny each time you answer correctly.

1. What animal barks?
2. What animal meows?
3. What buzzes?
4. What oinks?
5. What neighs?
6. What quacks?
7. What chirps?
8. What moos?
9. What roars?
10. What growls?
11. What clucks?
12. What baas?

Do you like carrots?

Flower Fun

Name ______________________

Trace a flower in a vase each time you answer correctly.

1. What rolls?
2. What rips?
3. What cracks?
4. What breaks?
5. What freezes?
6. What walks?
7. What opens?
8. What cuts?
9. What pops?
10. What hangs?
11. What folds?
12. What stretches?

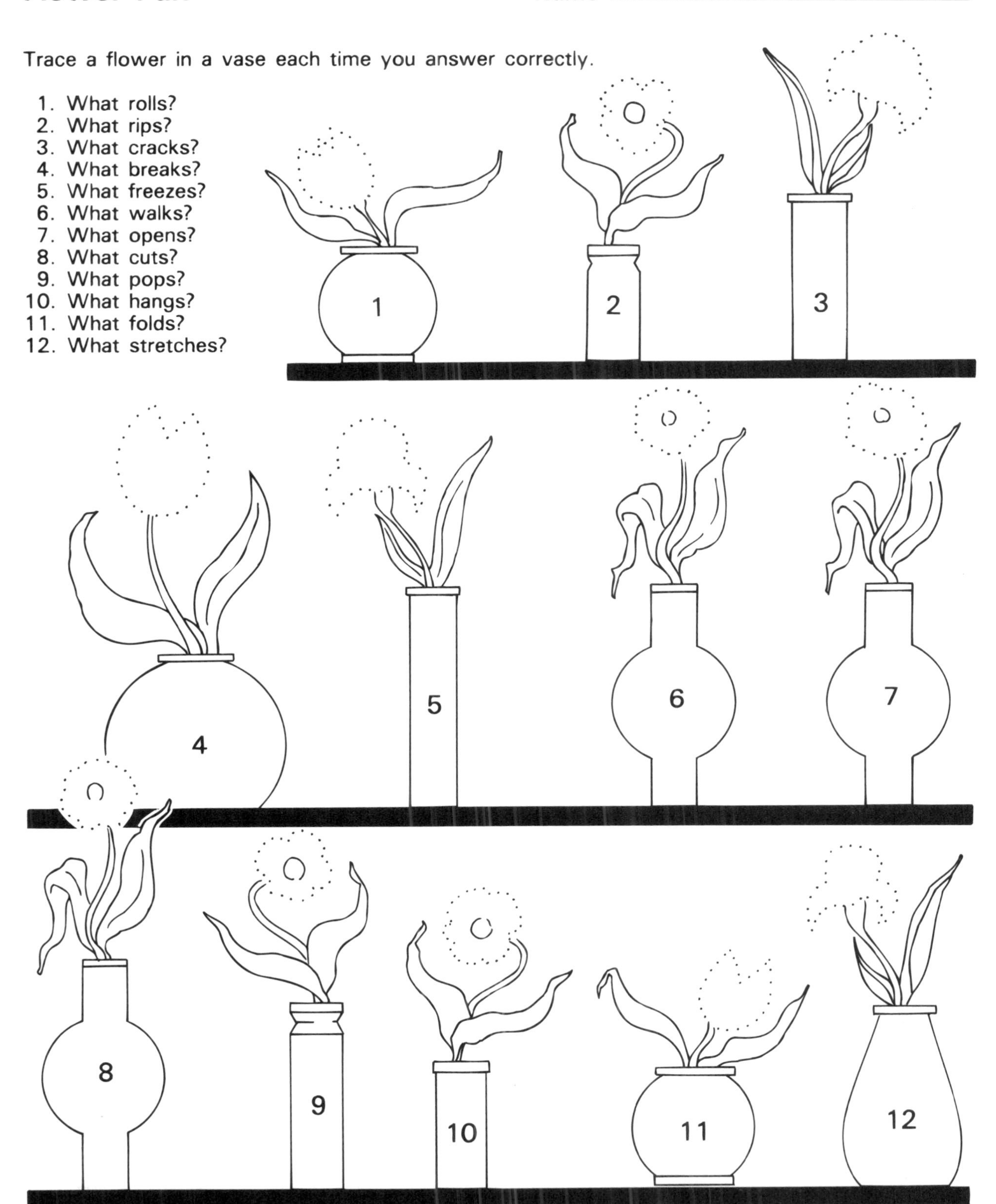

How many flowers did you trace?

An Apple a Day

Name ______________________________

Trace a worm coming out of an apple each time you answer correctly. What does __________ do?

1. a kangaroo
2. a cow
3. a bird
4. a bee
5. a lion
6. a fish
7. a bunny
8. a hen
9. a dog
10. a rooster

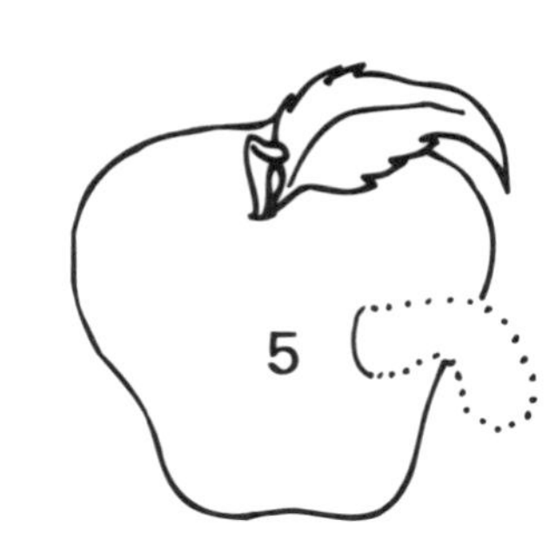

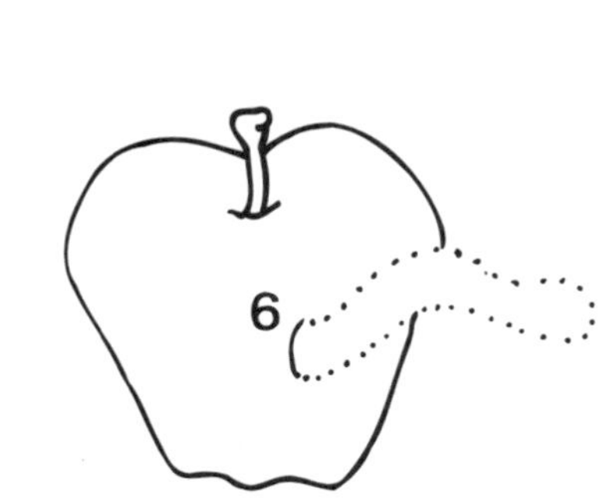

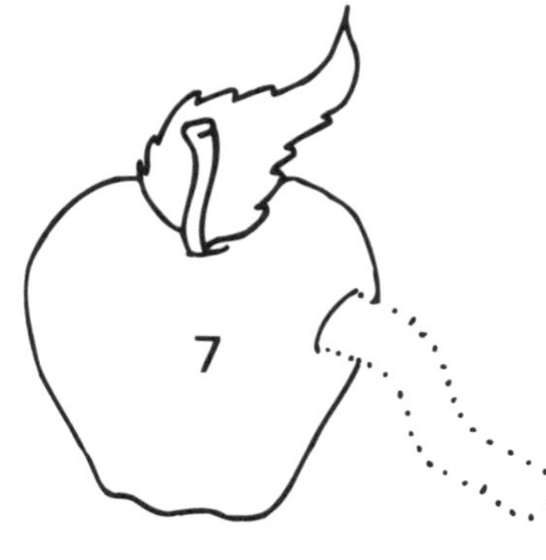

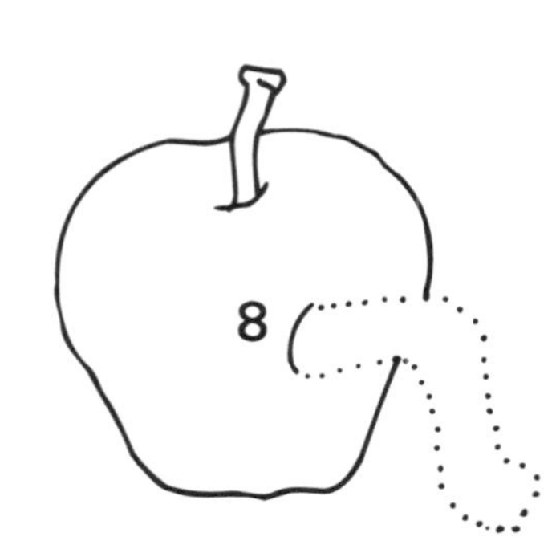

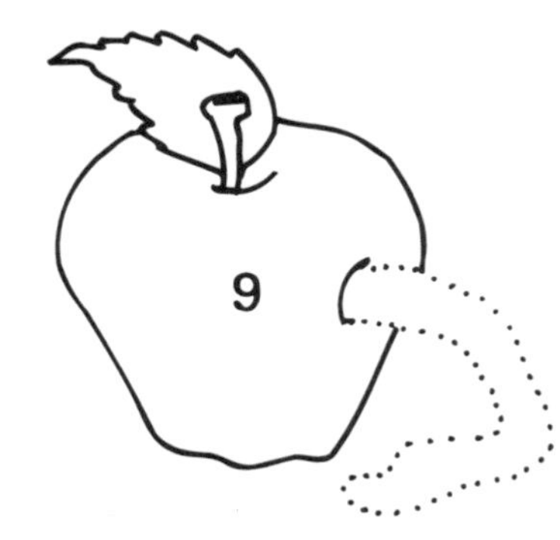

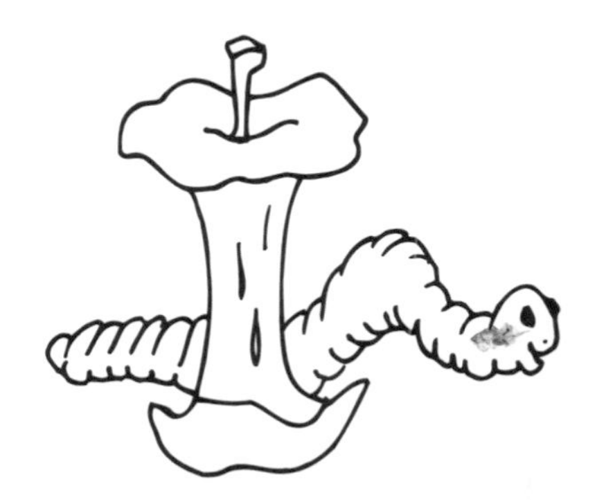

What kind of apples do you like?

Get Rich Quick!

Name ____________________

Color a piece of gold each time you answer correctly. What does __________ do?

1. a baby
2. a barber
3. an artist
4. a ballerina
5. a repair person
6. a pilot
7. a farmer
8. a police officer
9. a dentist
10. an actor

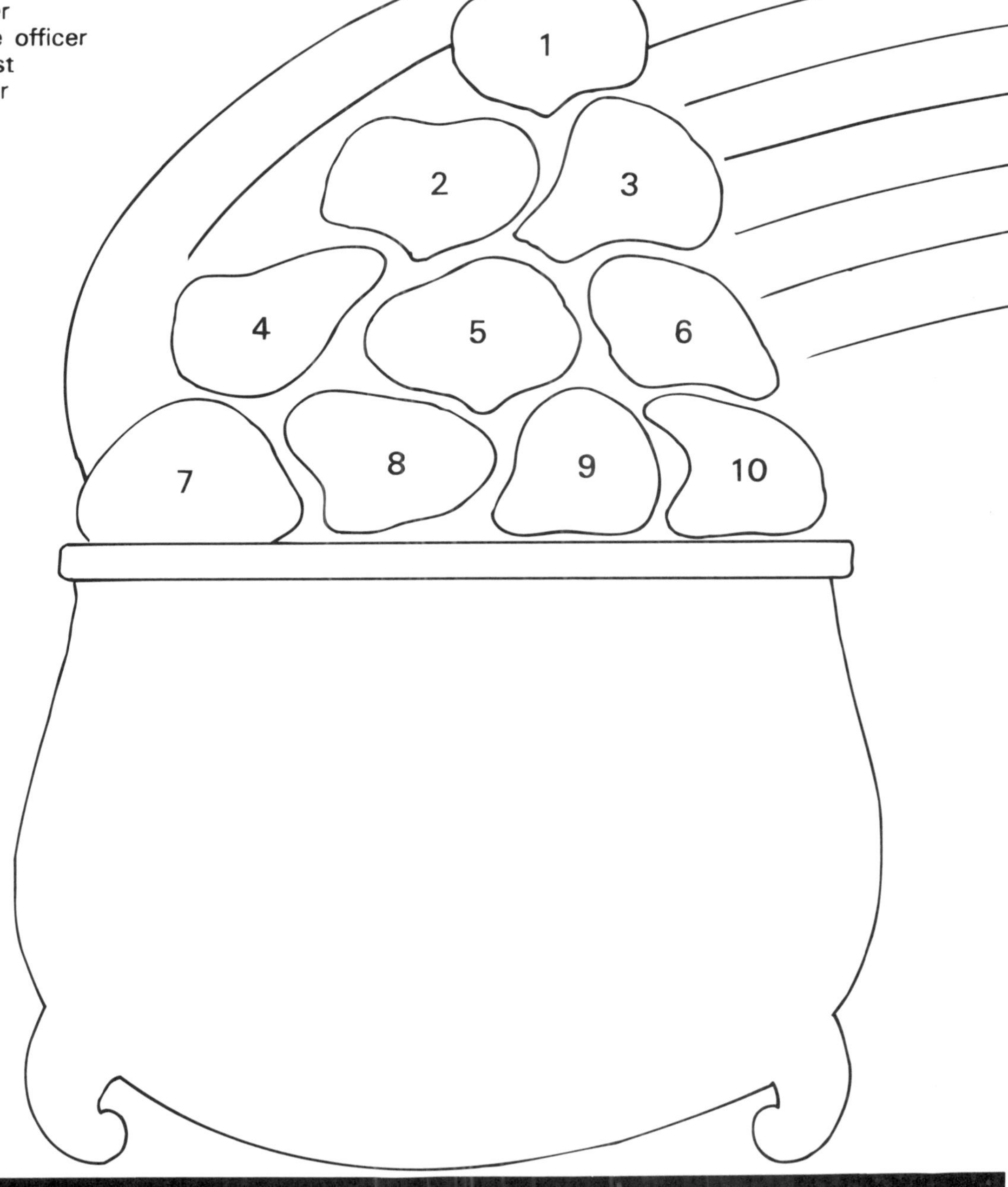

If you won a million dollars, what would you do?

Sunny Days!

Name ______________________________

Draw a big smile on a sun each time you answer correctly. What does __________ do?

1. a hammer
2. chalk
3. a kite
4. a pair of scissors
5. a wheel
6. a stove
7. a flashlight
8. a spoon
9. a jet
10. a clock

Good work! Smile to show you're proud!

Check It Out!

Name ______________________________

Check off each number on the chalkboard each time you answer correctly. What does ____________ do?

1. a siren
2. a scale
3. a toaster
4. a yardstick
5. soap
6. a thermometer
7. wind
8. a furnace
9. a camera
10. an alarm

Right on!

Glub, Glub!

Name ______________________

Color an air bubble for the fish each time you answer correctly.

1. Who cries?
2. Who marches?
3. Who paints?
4. Who cooks?

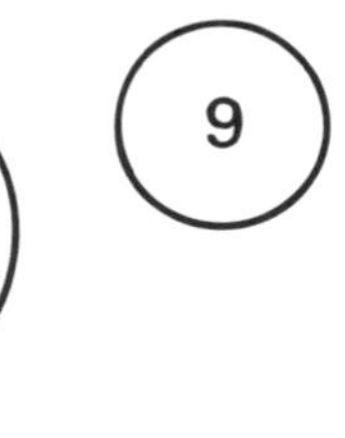

5. Who fixes things?
6. Who heals?
7. Who types?
8. Who dances?

9. Who fights?
10. Who cuts hair?
11. Who grows food?
12. Who acts?

Bubble bubble, no trouble!

Crack Up

Name ______________________

Color an egg each time you answer correctly. Don't crack any!

This is something noisy and heavy.

1. Is it an airplane?
2. Is it a grasshopper?

This is something big and fast.

3. Is it a mouse?
4. Is it a train?

This is something round and light.

5. Is it a baseball?
6. Is it a balloon?

This is something that rolls and bounces.

7. Is it a cat?
8. Is it a beachball?

This is something that closes and locks.

9. Is it a mouth?
10. Is it a window?

This is something that floats and swims.

11. Is it a person?
12. Is it a boat?

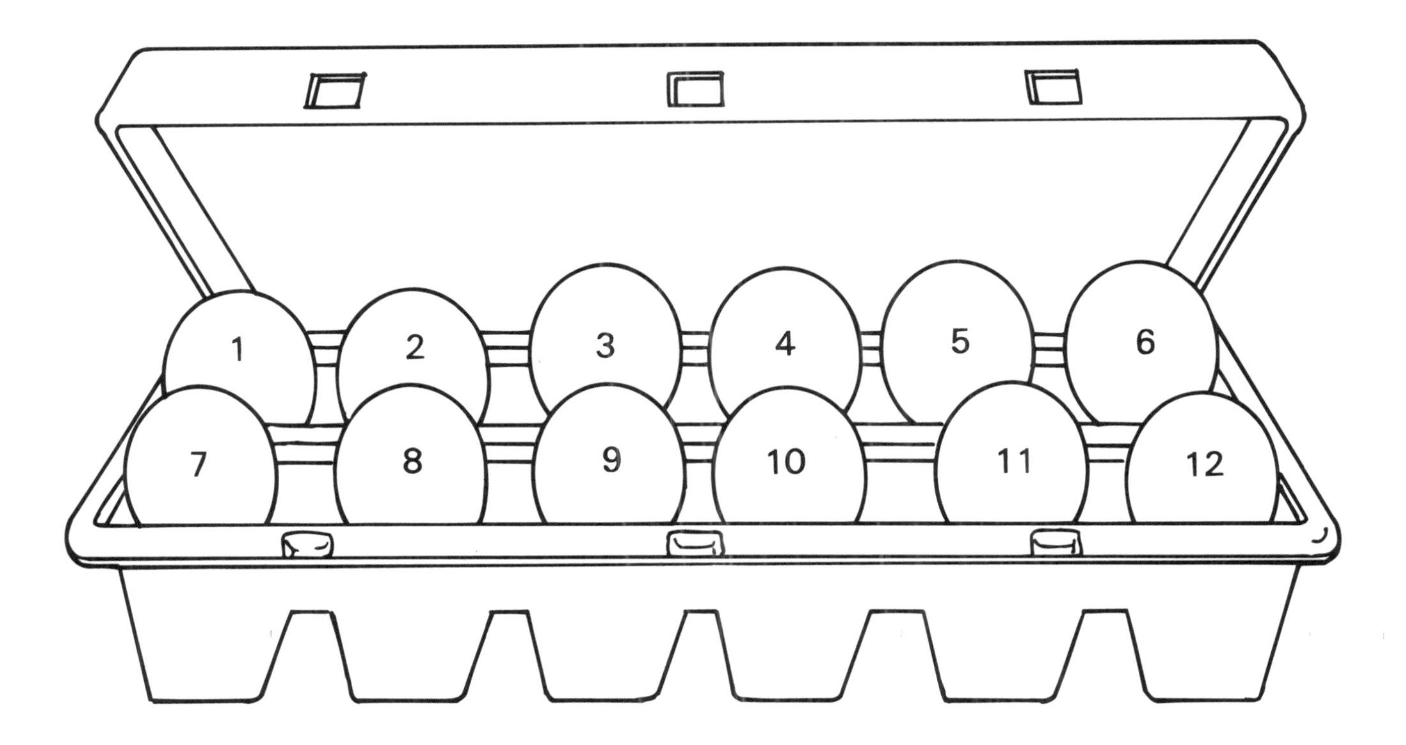

You're a good egg!

Cool Scoops

Name ____________________

Color a scoop of ice cream on the cone each time you answer correctly. Add your favorite flavors!

1. What is fast and little?
2. What smells good and tastes good?
3. What can we hear and see?
4. What shines and is hot?
5. What is big and light?
6. What flies and walks?
7. What is round and light?
8. What closes and locks?
9. What is noisy and little?
10. What floats and is heavy?

M-m-m, good!

Up-Down Fun

Name ____________________________

Draw a string on a yo-yo each time you answer a question correctly. Where do you find ____________?

1. a chalkboard
2. a wallet
3. a ring
4. ice cream
5. mail
6. money
7. a nest
8. medicine
9. a monkey
10. a carpet

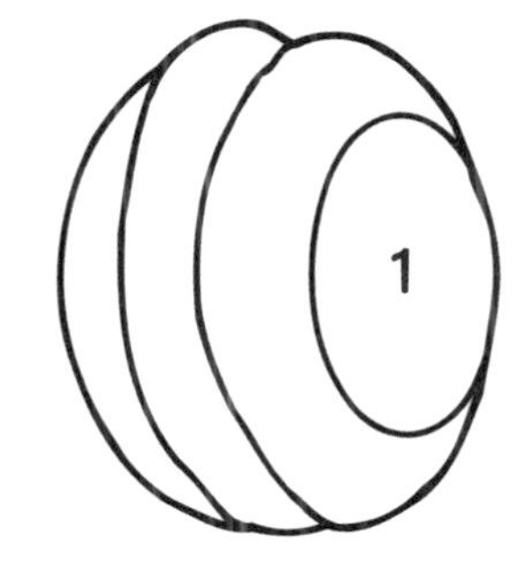

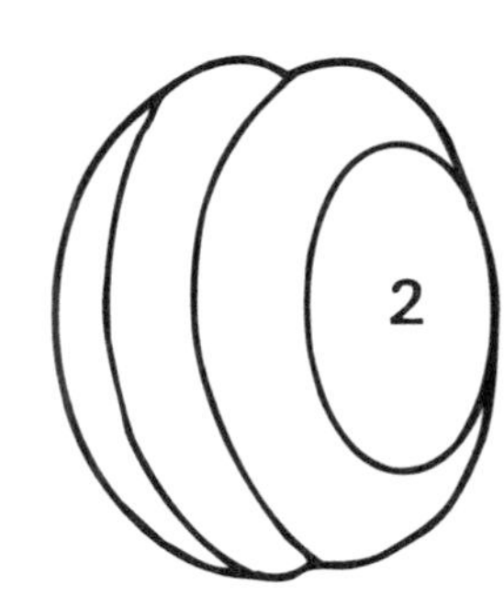

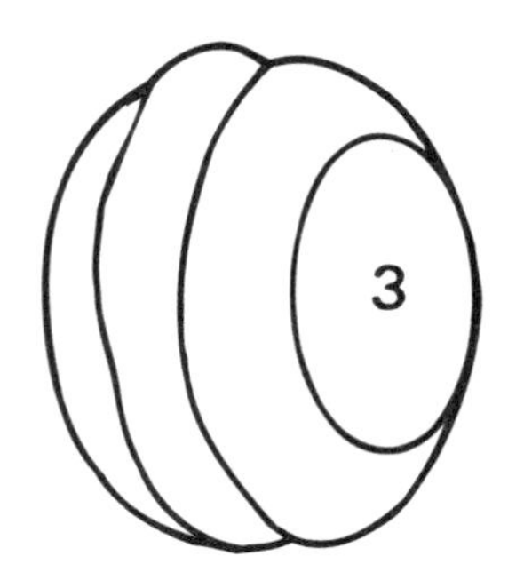

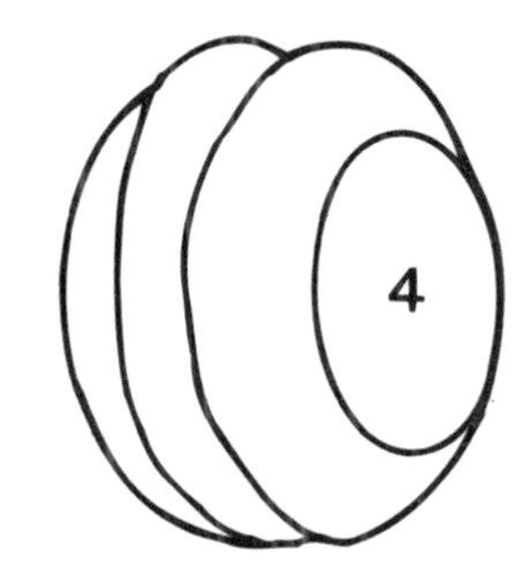

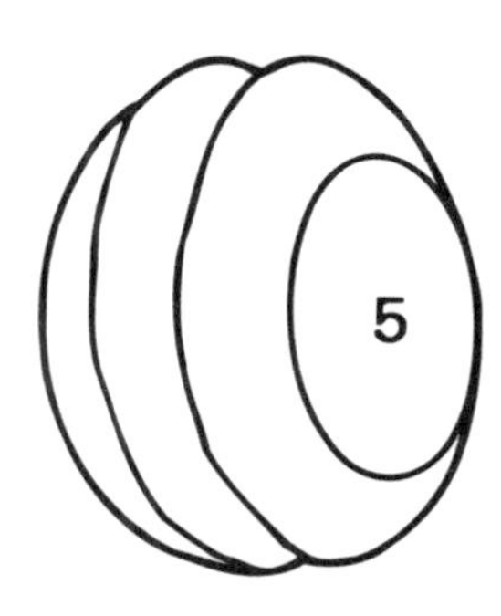

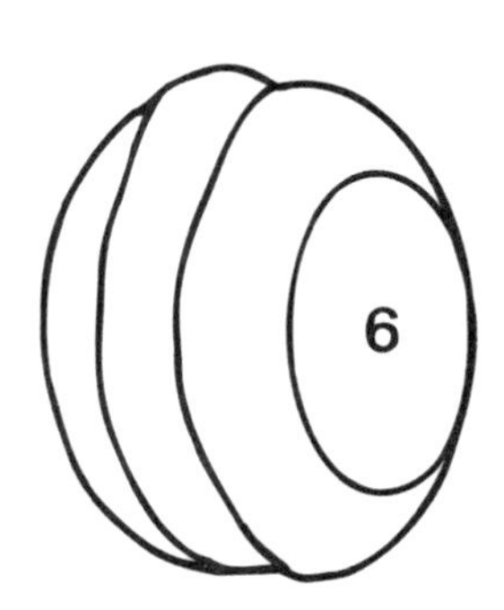

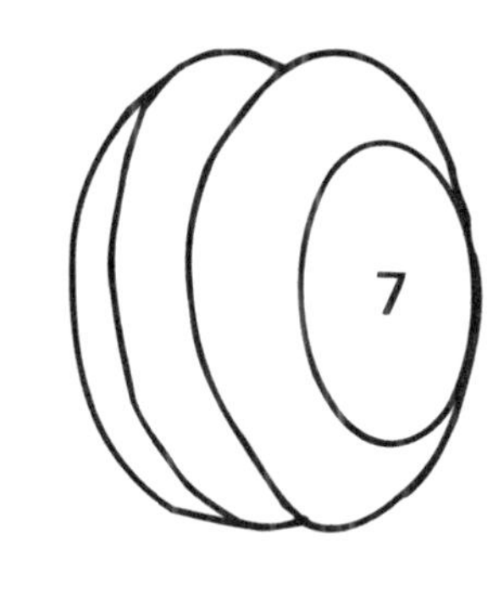

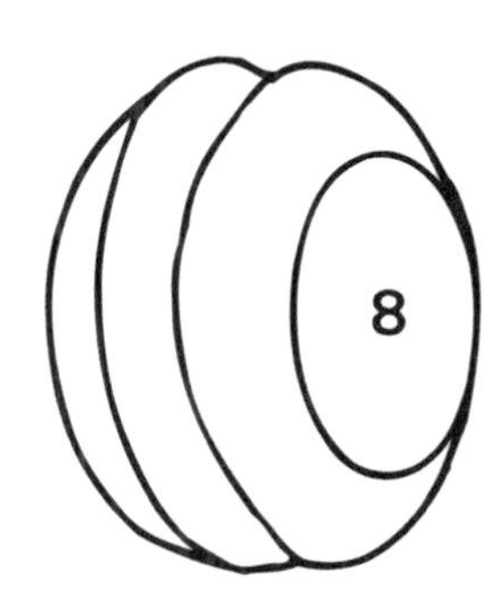

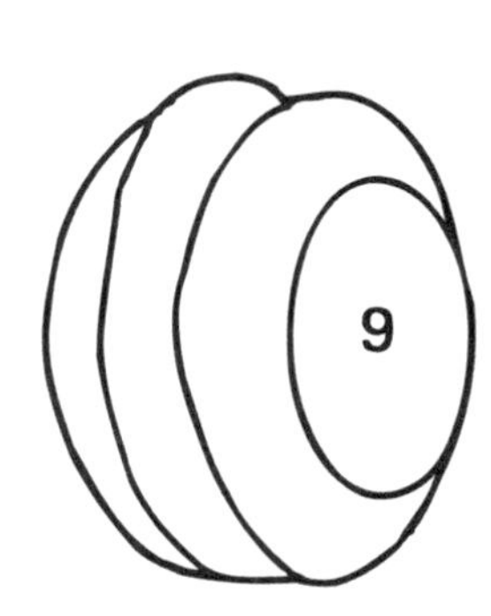

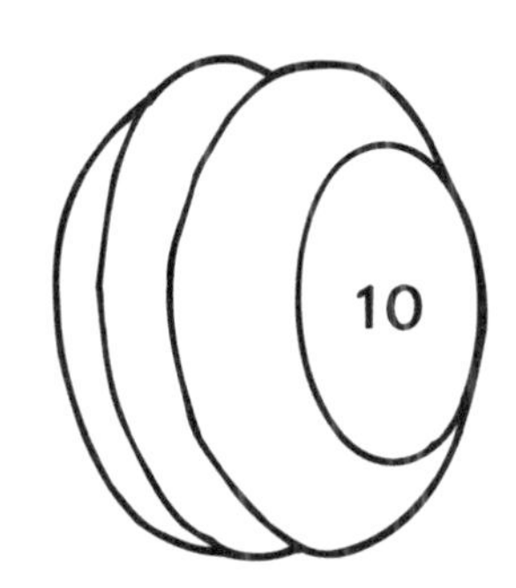

Way to go!

Stack 'Em Up!

Name ______________________________

Trace a number on a block each time you answer a question correctly. Where does _______ work?

1. a teacher
2. a food server
3. a clown
4. a nurse
5. a cook
6. a sailor
7. a doctor
8. a pilot
9. a mechanic
10. a mail carrier

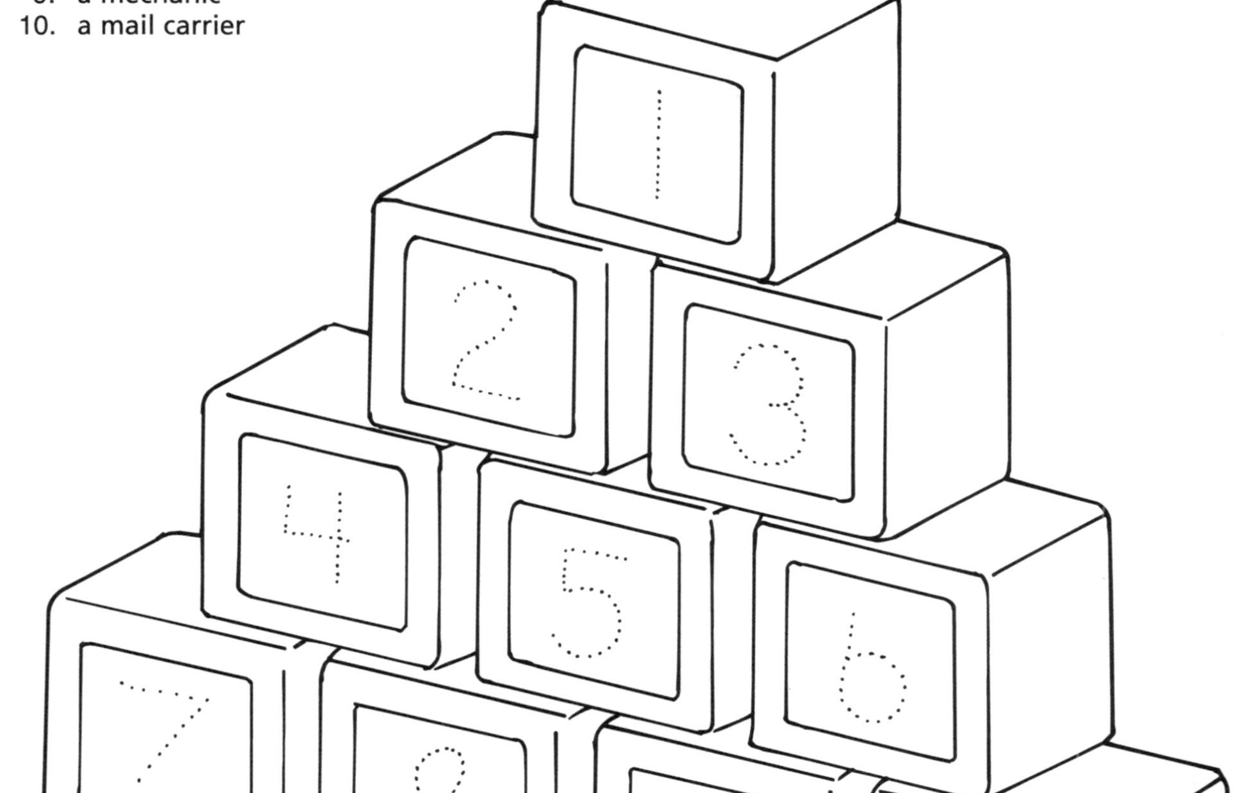

How many did you get right?

S-T-R-I-K-E

Name ______________________

Draw an X on a bowling pin each time you answer a question correctly. Get a strike! Where does ______ work?

1. a firefighter
2. a miner
3. a diver
4. a secretary
5. a lawyer
6. a reporter
7. a chef
8. a mechanic
9. a detective
10. an astronaut

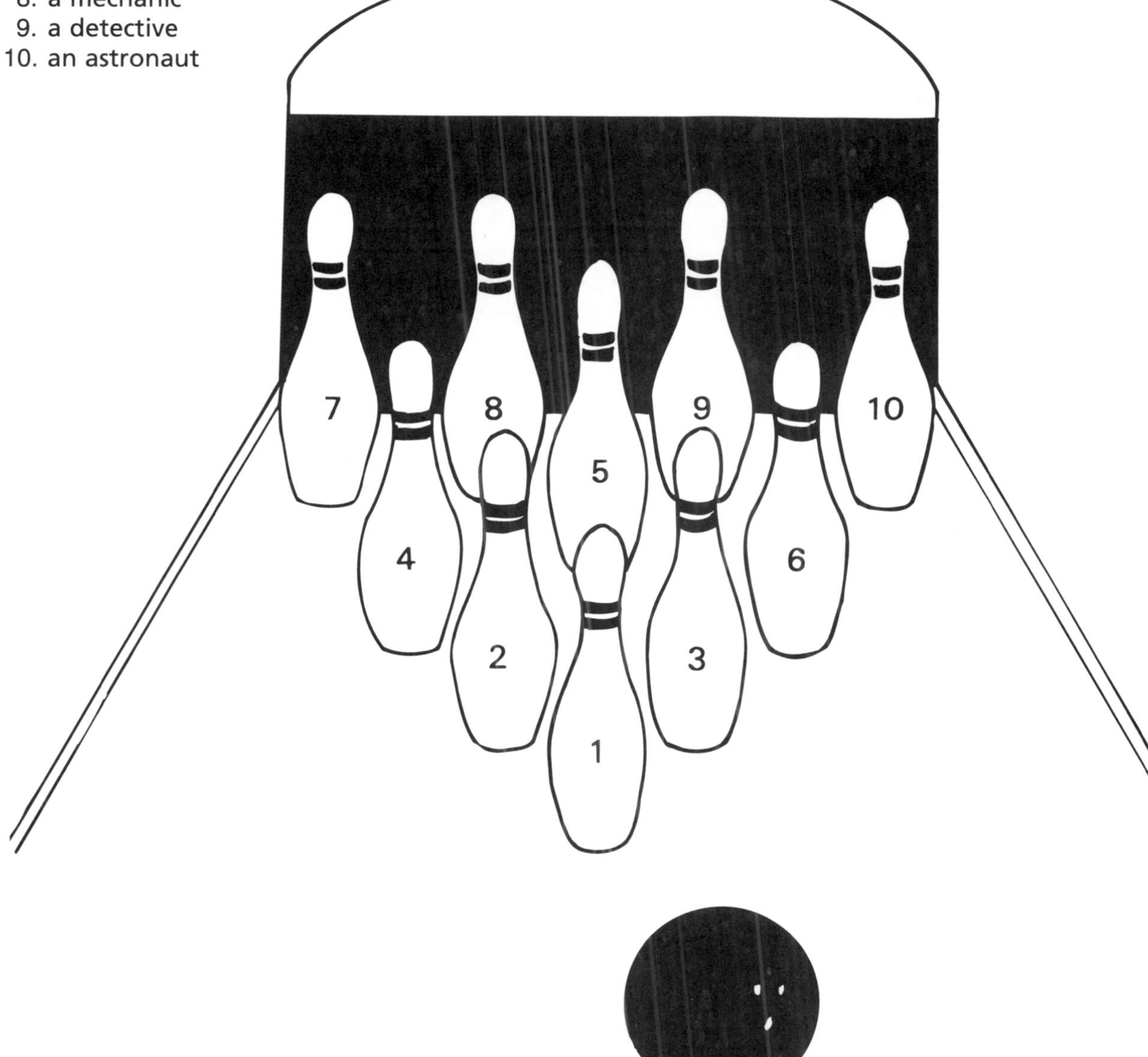

Good bowling!

Batter Up!

Name ______________________________

Trace a ball for the batter to hit each time you answer correctly. Hit a home run!

1. When do you take a bath?
2. When do you wake up?
3. When do you go to school?
4. When do you eat cereal?
5. When do you wear a coat?
6. When do you close your eyes?
7. When do you pack a suitcase?
8. When do you turn the lights out?
9. When do the leaves fall off the trees?
10. When does the sun go down?

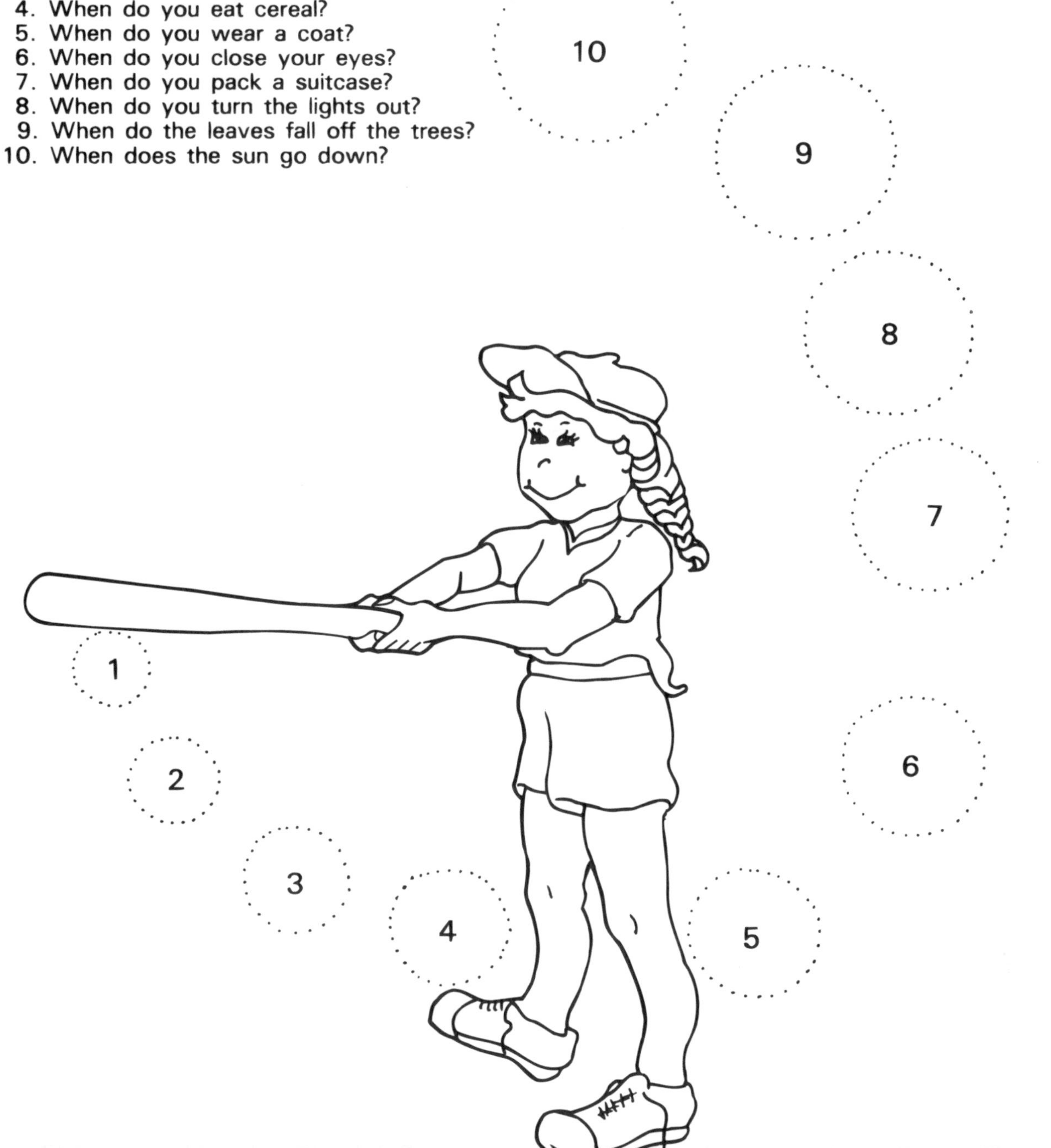

Congratulations, you're a hit!

Fetch, Fido!

Name ______________________________

Help Fido reach his bone by drawing an X on a line each time you answer correctly. Tell why these word pairs go together.

1. chalk · chalkboard
2. frame · picture
3. hand · glove
4. cone · ice cream
5. bed · pillow
6. finger · ring
7. piggy bank · money
8. key · lock
9. horse · saddle
10. bone · dog

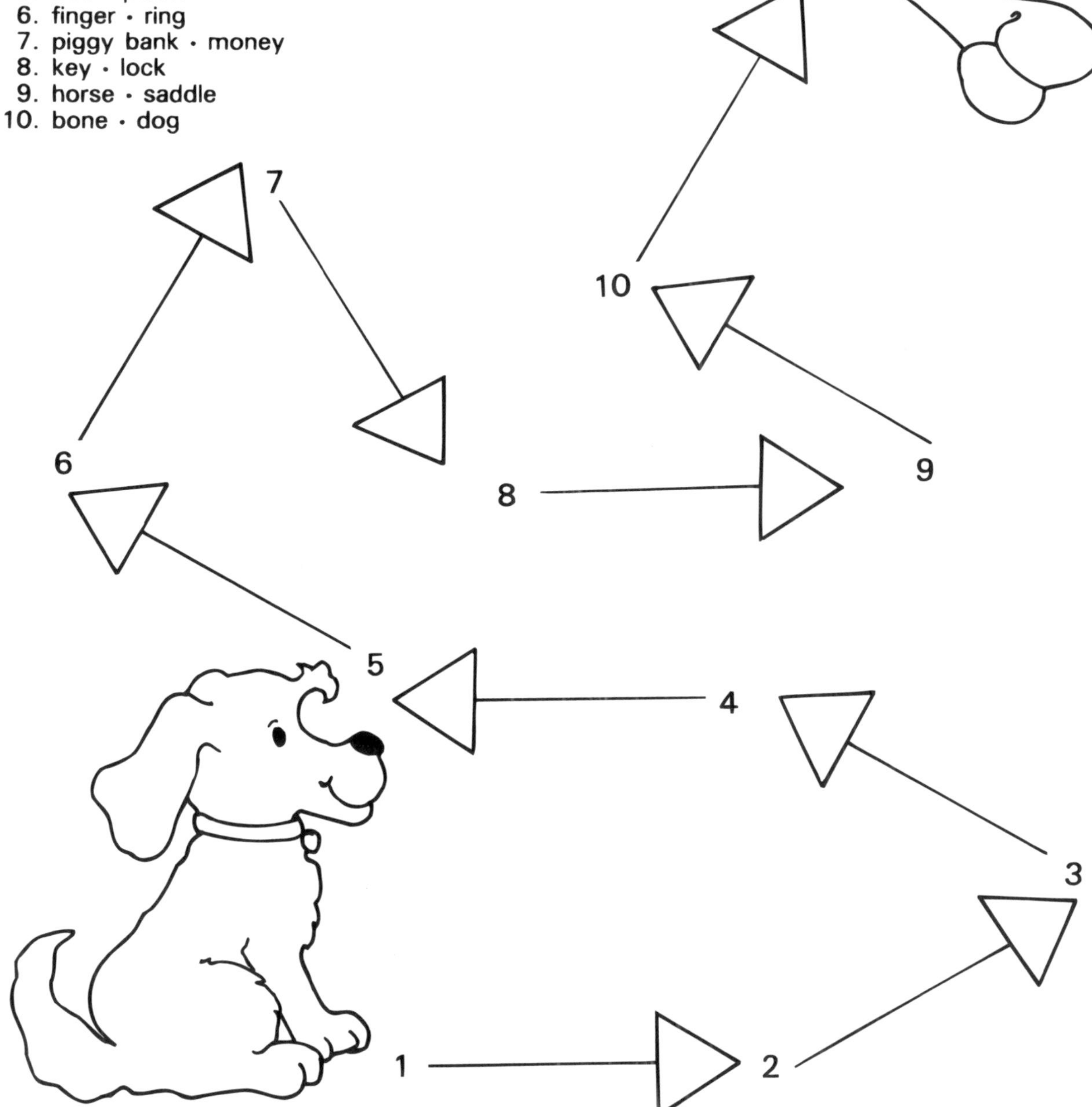

Woof woof! Fido says thanks!

Hip! Hip! Hooray!

Name ______________________

Trace a banner each time you answer correctly. Tell why the word pairs go together.

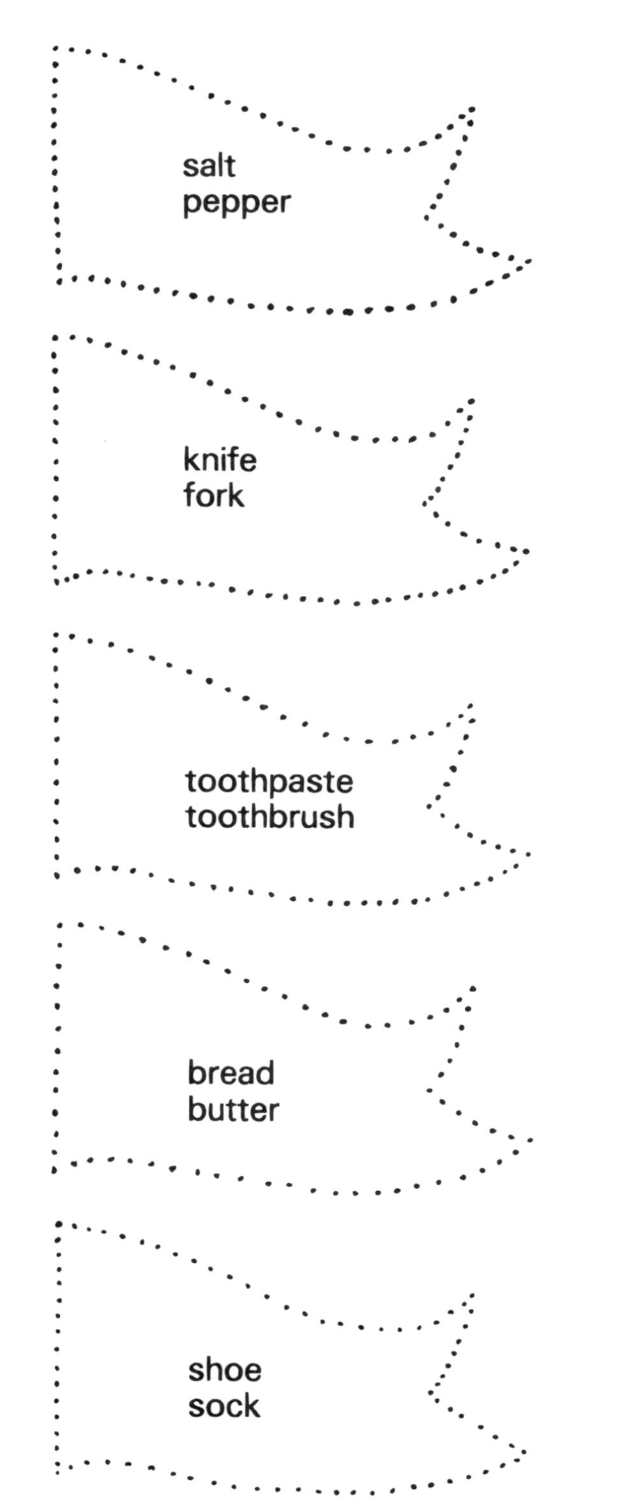

bat
ball

cereal
milk

soap
water

coat
hat

pencil
paper

Three cheers for a super job!

Yikes!

Name ______________________________

Color an eye on the monster each time you answer correctly. Don't let it catch you! Tell how these word pairs are alike.

1. bracelet • necklace
2. orange • banana
3. tape • glue
4. pin • needle
5. meow • bark
6. butterfly • bird
7. fingers • toes
8. rain • snow
9. penny • nickel
10. kitten • puppy

What an eyeful!

First Place

Name ______________________

Color a blue ribbon each time you answer correctly. Tell how these things are different.

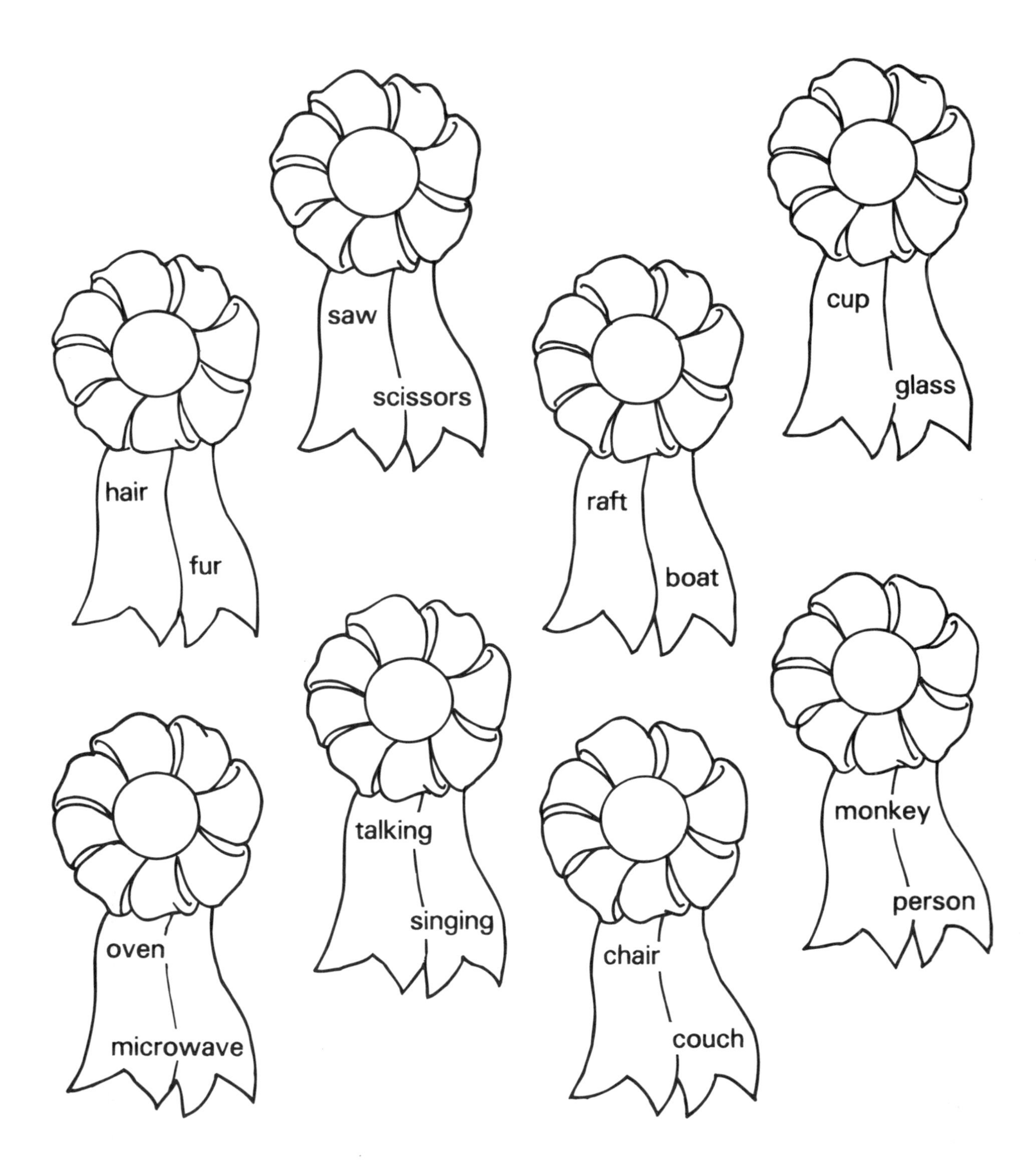

You're number one!

Pumpkin Patch

Name ______________________________

Draw a stem on a pumpkin each time you answer correctly. Tell whether or not the words are opposites by answering YES or NO.

1. over • under
2. dark • night
3. pull • push
4. short • little
5. old • young
6. slow • fast
7. hot • warm
8. day • noon
9. down • up
10. full • empty

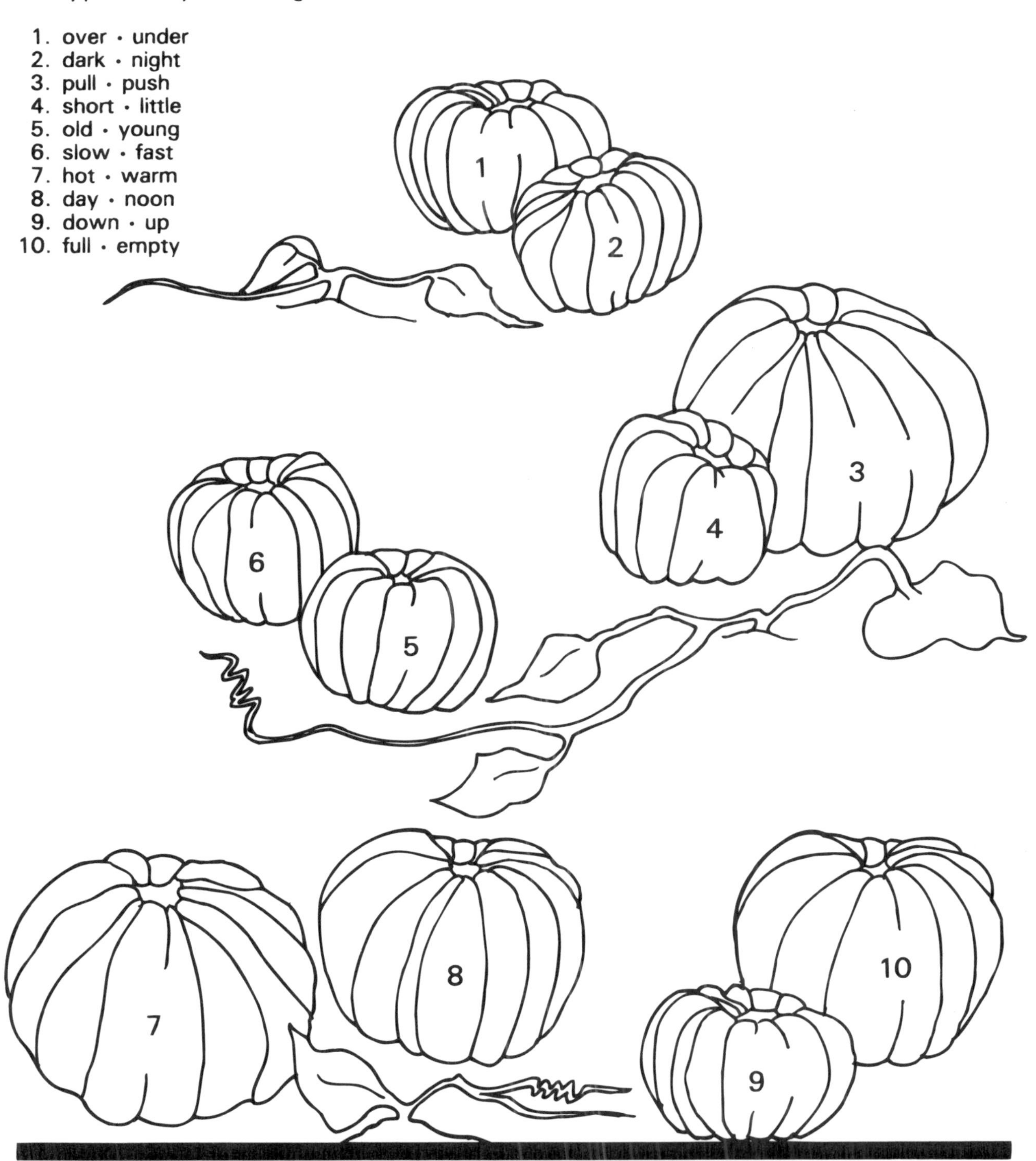

You worked hard! Now, make one of the pumpkins into a jack-o'-lantern just for fun!

Treat a Turtle

Name ______________________

Give Tommy Turtle a colorful home! Color a part of his shell each time you say the opposite of a word.

1. yes
2. woman
3. old
4. off
5. mother
6. good-bye
7. soft
8. black
9. come
10. dirty

Tommy is happy to have a pretty home. Draw a big smile on his face.

Window Words

Name ______________________________

Color a window frame each time you answer correctly. Tell the opposite for each word in a window.

What a lot of windows to wash!

Hearts to You!

Name ______________________

Be a sweetheart! Trace the unfinished half of a heart each time you answer correctly. Tell the opposite for each word in a heart.

Lovely work!

Cake Talk

Name ______________________

Decorate the frosting on a cupcake each time you answer correctly. Change the key (italicized) word to its opposite. I'll say the key word louder.

1. *All* of the boys are tall.
2. This end of the pool is *shallow*.
3. This food tastes too *sweet*.
4. Our class is often *quiet*.
5. That old tree is very *straight*.
6. What time did you *arrive*?
7. How many cookies will you *sell*?
8. This is a *difficult* test.
9. My knife is too *sharp*.
10. That's the *best* story I've ever heard.
11. My *aunt* is coming to visit.
12. I think Tony *forgets* the answer.

You take the cake!

Elf Errors

Name ______________________________

These elves lost their hats. Draw a hat for an elf each time you finish a sentence correctly.

1. Some people wake up early. Others wake up ___________.
2. A giant is big. A baby is ___________.
3. Summer is hot. Winter is ___________.
4. A rock is hard. A pillow is ___________.
5. A truck is heavy. A feather is ___________.
6. Sandpaper is rough. A mirror is ___________.
7. Lifting a book is easy. Lifting a desk is ___________.
8. Sugar is sweet. A lemon is ___________.
9. A princess is pretty. A monster is ___________.
10. A king is rich. A beggar is ___________.

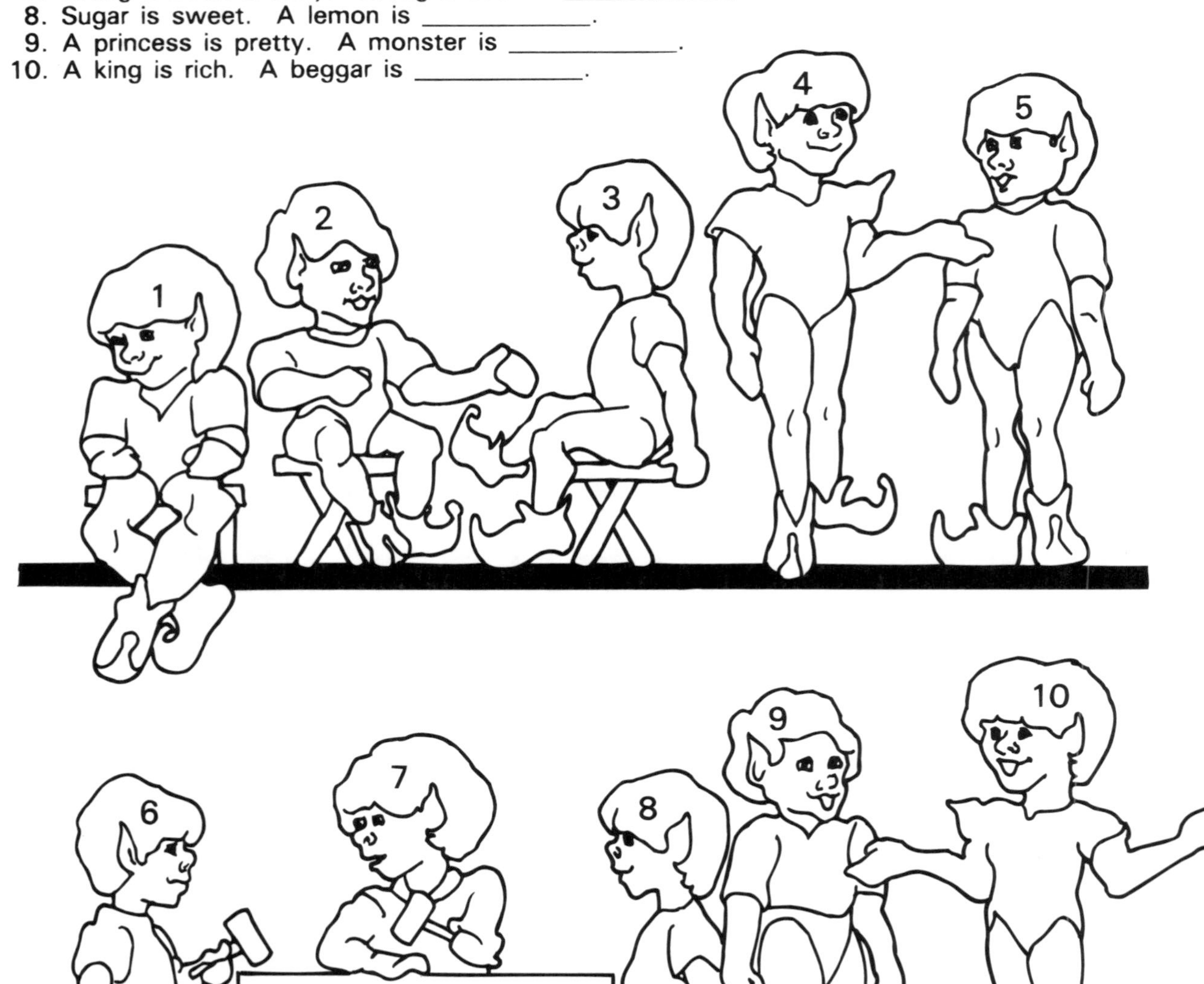

Thanks! Now, the elves can get back to making toys!

Climb on Up!

Name ______________________

Try to reach the top of the ladder. Circle a number each time you finish a sentence correctly.

1. A snake bites.
   A wasp ___________.
2. We sniff with our noses.
   We blink with our ___________.
3. Doctors have patients.
   Teachers have ___________.
4. A man has hands.
   A bear has ___________.
5. A firefighter uses a hose.
   A carpenter uses a ___________.
6. A guitar has strings.
   A piano has ___________.
7. A deer has antlers.
   An elephant has a ___________.
8. A person has a mouth.
   A bird has a ___________.
9. A bird lives in a nest.
   A bee lives in a ___________.
10. A bus travels on land.
    An airplane travels in the ___________.

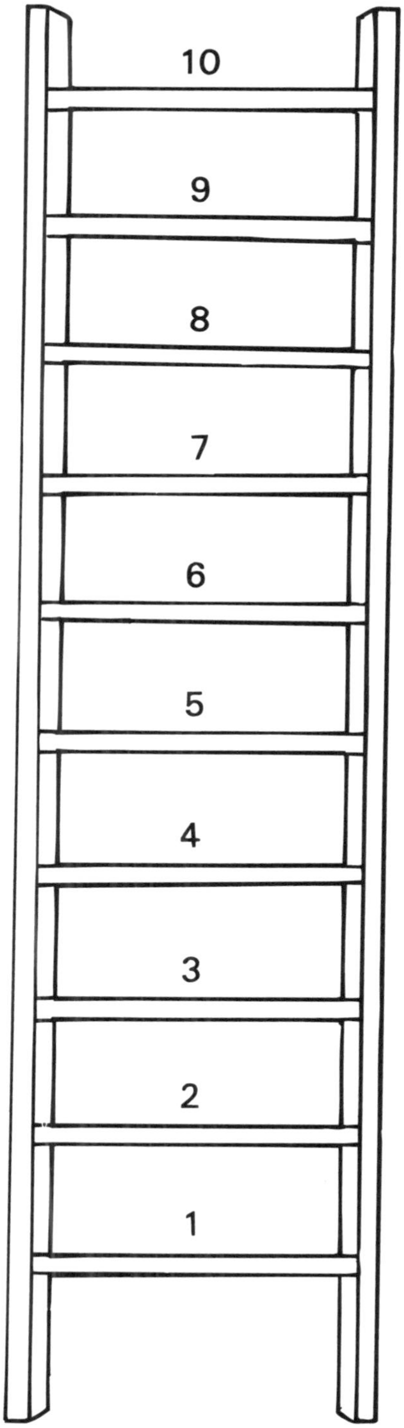

10

9

8

7

6

5

4

3

2

1

You made it!

Blow a Bubble

Name ______________________________

Color a piece of bubble gum each time you complete the sentence correctly.

1. I see with my eyes.
   I smell with my ____________.
2. Grass is green.
   The sky is ____________.
3. We listen to the radio.
   We watch ____________.
4. It is hot in the summer.
   It is cold in the ____________.
5. On my hands, I wear mittens.
   On my feet, I wear ____________.
6. A turtle is slow.
   A rabbit is ____________.
7. Jessica is a girl.
   Matthew is a ____________.
8. An ant is small.
   An elephant is ____________.
9. On my feet, I have toes.
   On my hands, I have ____________.
10. A cow says, "Moo."
    A cat says, "____________."

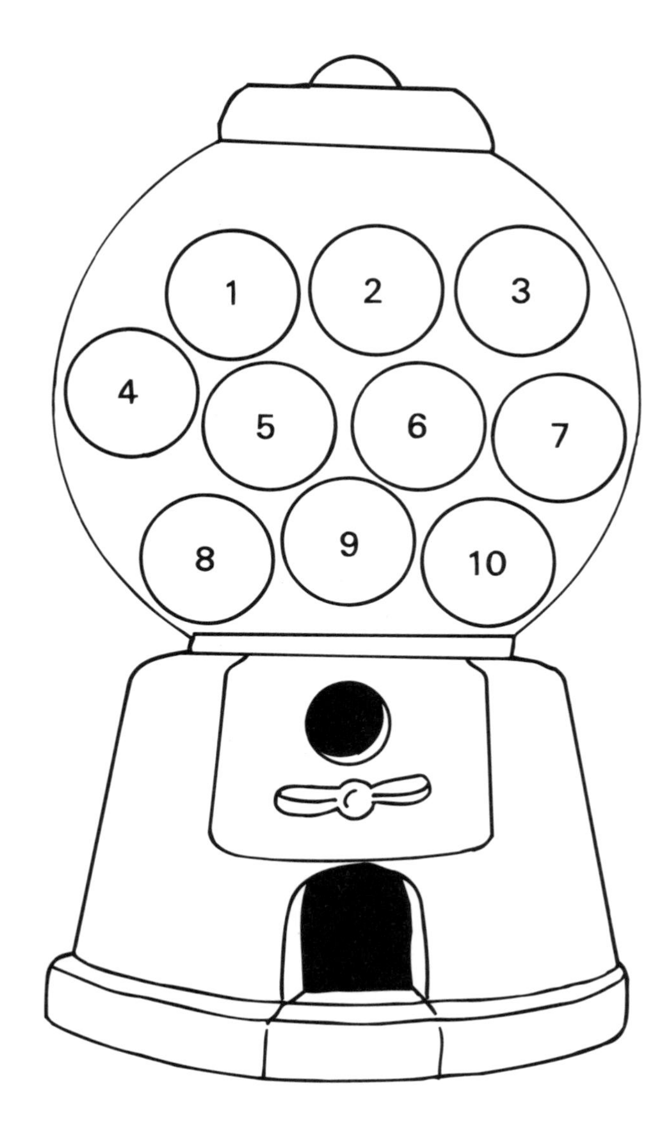

What's your favorite bubble gum flavor?

Wish Upon a Star

Name ______________________________

Reach for the stars! Color a star each time you guess the answer to a riddle.

1. I am an animal.
   I am black and white.
   I can make a bad smell.
   I am a ____________.
2. I taste sweet.
   Bees make me.
   I am sticky.
   I am ____________.
3. I have pages.
   I tell a story.
   I rhyme with *look*.
   I am a ____________.
4. I live on a farm.
   I eat hay.
   I give milk.
   I am a ____________.
5. I grow in a tree.
   I am red on the outside.
   I am white on the inside.
   I am an ____________.
6. I wear a hard hat.
   I ride on a big truck.
   I put out fires.
   I am a ____________.
7. I get very hot.
   I give off steam.
   I make clothes neat.
   I am an ____________.
8. You drink me.
   I have bubbles.
   I come in a can or a bottle.
   I am ____________.

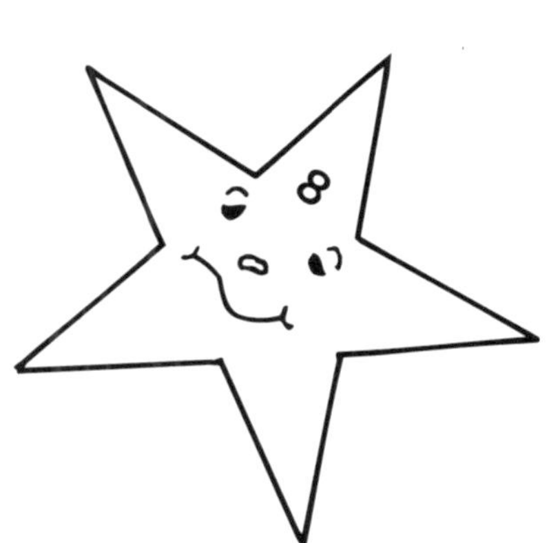

Congratulations, superstar!

What's Wrong?

Name ______________________________

Get ready to paint. Color a paint spot each time you tell what is wrong in a sentence.

1. The children listened to the radio with their eyes.
2. The ice cream froze in the hot snow.
3. My aunt shaved her beard.
4. Put on your socks after your shoes.
5. The dog's hands were on the couch.
6. The seeds in the lettuce were very large.
7. The baseball team scored a touchdown.
8. A brown cow makes chocolate milk.
9. Her hand hurt because her ankle was broken.
10. My pencil ran out of ink.

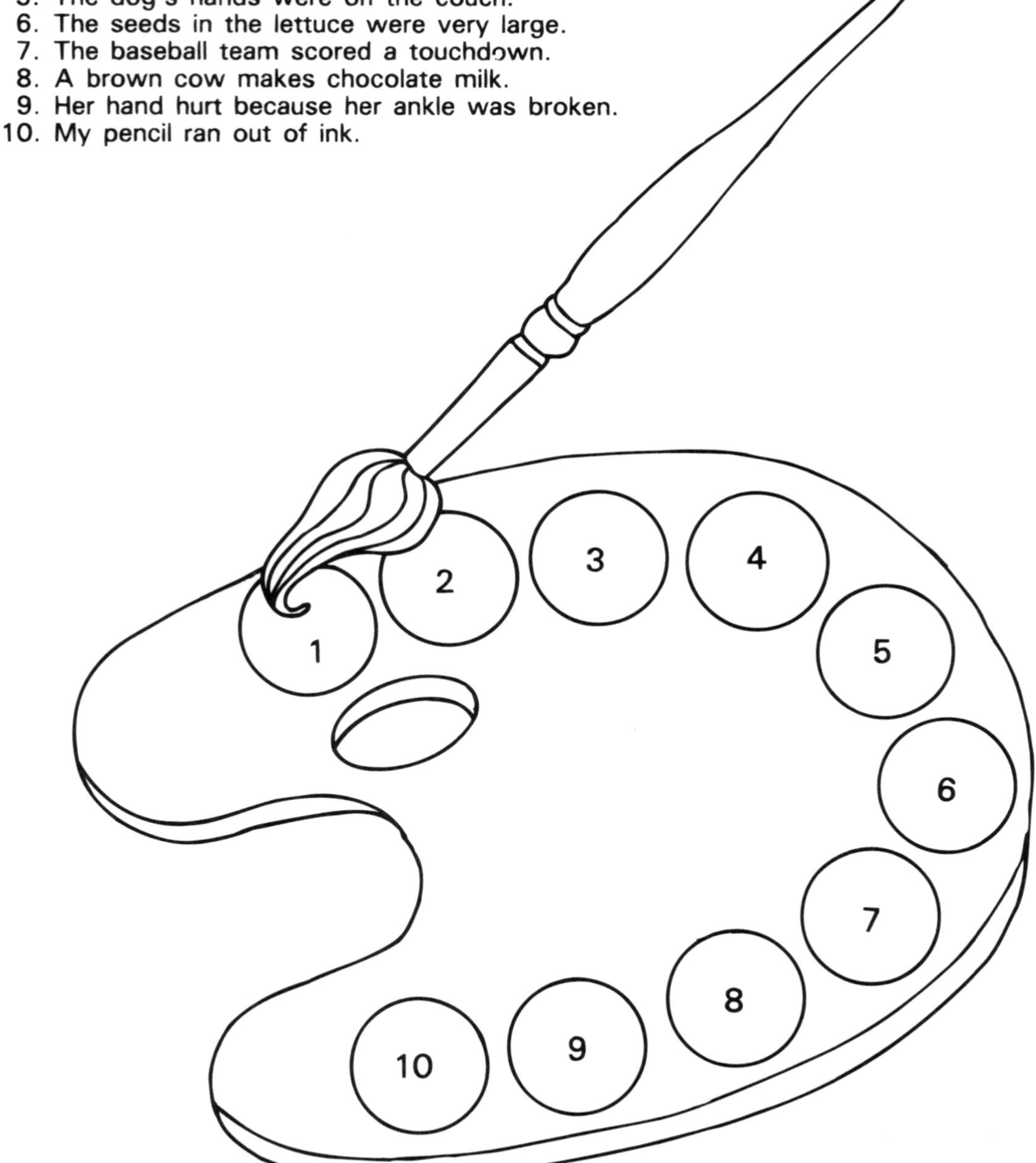

What's your favorite color?

Listening for Recall

Short-term auditory memory requires processing and retaining spoken information for a short time for the purpose of immediate recall. For example, we often remember a seven-digit telephone number long enough to call it, and then we allow the number to pass from our memory. This skill is helpful in forming new associations, in sequencing, and in adding new information to our long-term memory store.

Since a child learns most when learning is enjoyable, the listening activities in this section encourage the growth of short-term auditory memory skills in a fun way. These activities also help to improve the child's understanding and expression of language skills, and they may provide a basis for learning associated skills such as reading, math, and spelling.

These listening worksheets may be used with individuals or small groups in a therapy setting, within a classroom environment, or for homework assignments. The speech-language clinician, classroom teacher, or parent reads the statements and question, and the child answers aloud. For each correct answer, the child colors, traces, or draws a simple picture numbered to correspond with the question. To ensure that the activities are auditory tasks, the questions have been printed upside-down on each worksheet.

Trace a petal on a flower each time you repeat these words in the correct order.

1. fish • clam
2. chair • desk
3. fork • knife
4. clock • wall
5. doll • toy
6. horse • grass
7. wrist • hand
8. mom • boy
9. tie • shirt
10. foot • sock

Make It Beautiful!

Name ________________________________

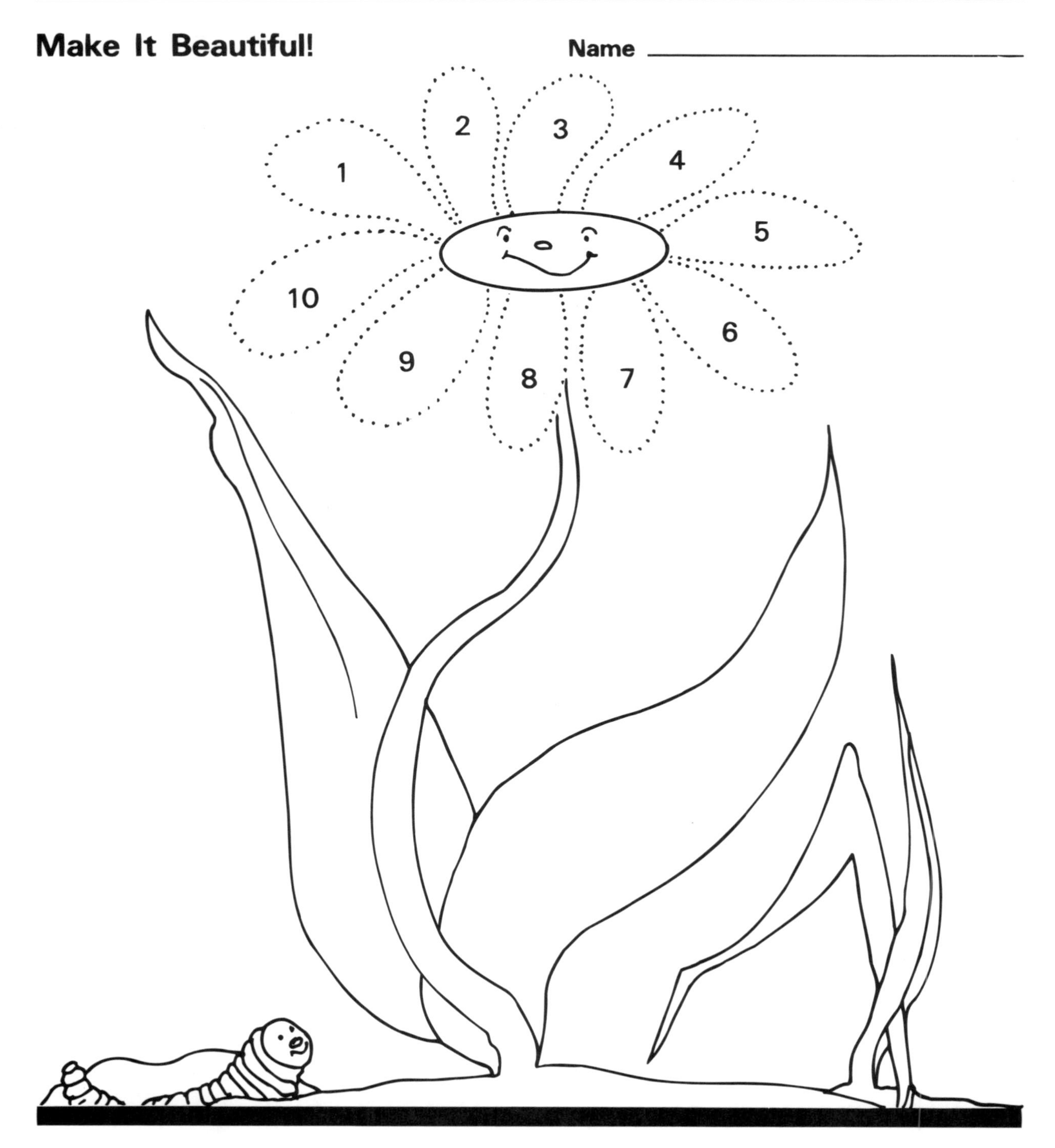

What a pretty flower!

Draw a circle around a number each time you repeat these words in the correct order.

1. ball · watch
2. tree · fork
3. nose · wall
4. thumb · ring
5. bird · line
6. sing · square
7. wing · check
8. talk · ear
9. toy · clock
10. spoon · bush

Make Each Answer Count!

Name ______________________

1 2 3 4

5 6 7

8 9 10

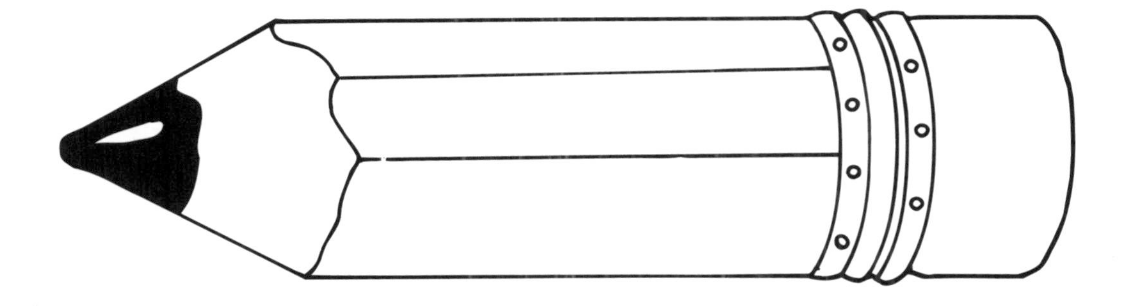

How far did you count?

Help Laura catch fish. Color a fish each time you repeat these words in the correct order.

1. chair • bed • desk
2. horn • drum • bell
3. pail • mop • broom
4. bag • box • jar
5. tooth • nose • arm
6. bus • boat • plane
7. slip • skirt • dress
8. bush • leaf • grass
9. pen • chalk • ink
10. orange • green • blue

Go Fish!

Name ______________________

How many fish did you and Laura catch?

Connect two dots each time you repeat these words in the correct order.

1. up • down • in
2. good • ugly • nice
3. run • hop • jump
4. roll • slide • fall
5. sing • talk • hum
6. cut • build • make
7. eat • swallow • drink
8. start • stop • go
9. cloud • moon • star
10. rope • chain • string

Spout Off!

Name ______________________

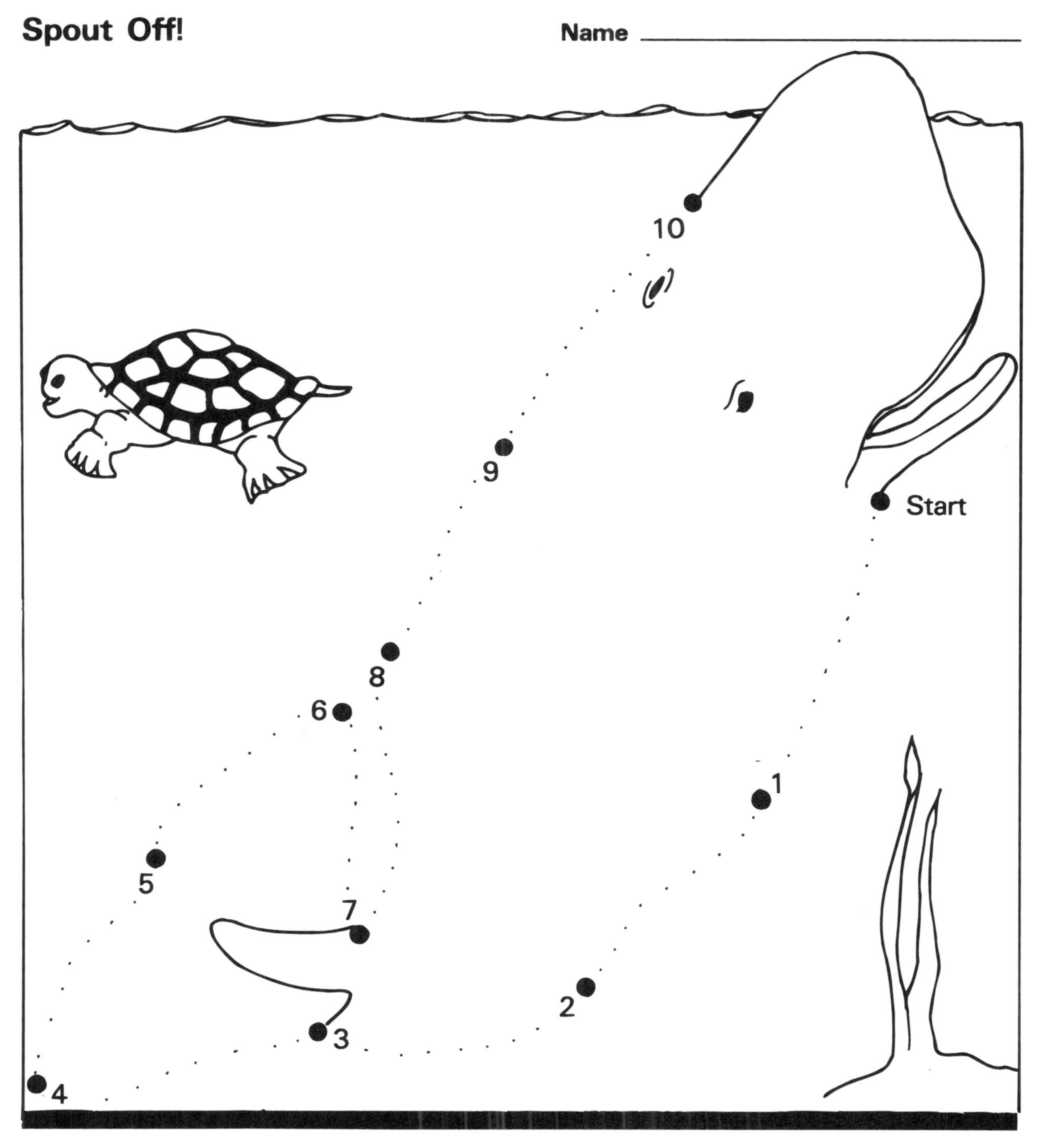

Those are whalin' good answers!

Color a heart each time you repeat these words in the correct order.

1. book • chart • magazine
2. salt • sugar • flour
3. across • down • through
4. throw • toss • catch
5. ask • say • tell
6. heart • lace • arrow
7. hot • cold • warm
8. fish • eel • shark
9. wrap • bow • ribbon
10. cherry • grape • orange

Have a Heart!

Name ______________________

1 2 3 4 5 6 7 8 9 10

Heart-felt congratulations!

Color a bird each time you repeat these words in the correct order.

1. cat • bird • dog
2. chair • box • book
3. cup • shoe • pen
4. toy • clock • ring
5. hat • boy • horse
6. grass • light • hand
7. light • boy • eye
8. shirt • rug • sink
9. ball • watch • tree
10. fork • nose • wall

Tweet! Tweet!

Name ______________________

Circle your favorite bird.

Color a coin each time you repeat these words in the correct order.

1. watch • coin • goat
2. heat • bean • fat
3. pick • light • win
4. wheel • tape • nail
5. soap • vest • ring
6. spoon • jail • grass
7. cake • kiss • bear
8. dark • lunch • red
9. knife • fall • can
10. long • fire • egg

Colorful Coins

Name ______________________________

Can you count the money?

Treat yourself to candy. Color a piece of candy each time you repeat these words in the correct order.

1. white · pen · wood
2. mouse · block · clown
3. crown · clean · pole
4. rain · nut · boat
5. seal · ten · bug
6. win · fruit · gum
7. game · men · west
8. bag · step · ride
9. luck · sun · jam
10. frown · horse · dirt

Dandy Candy

Name ______________________________

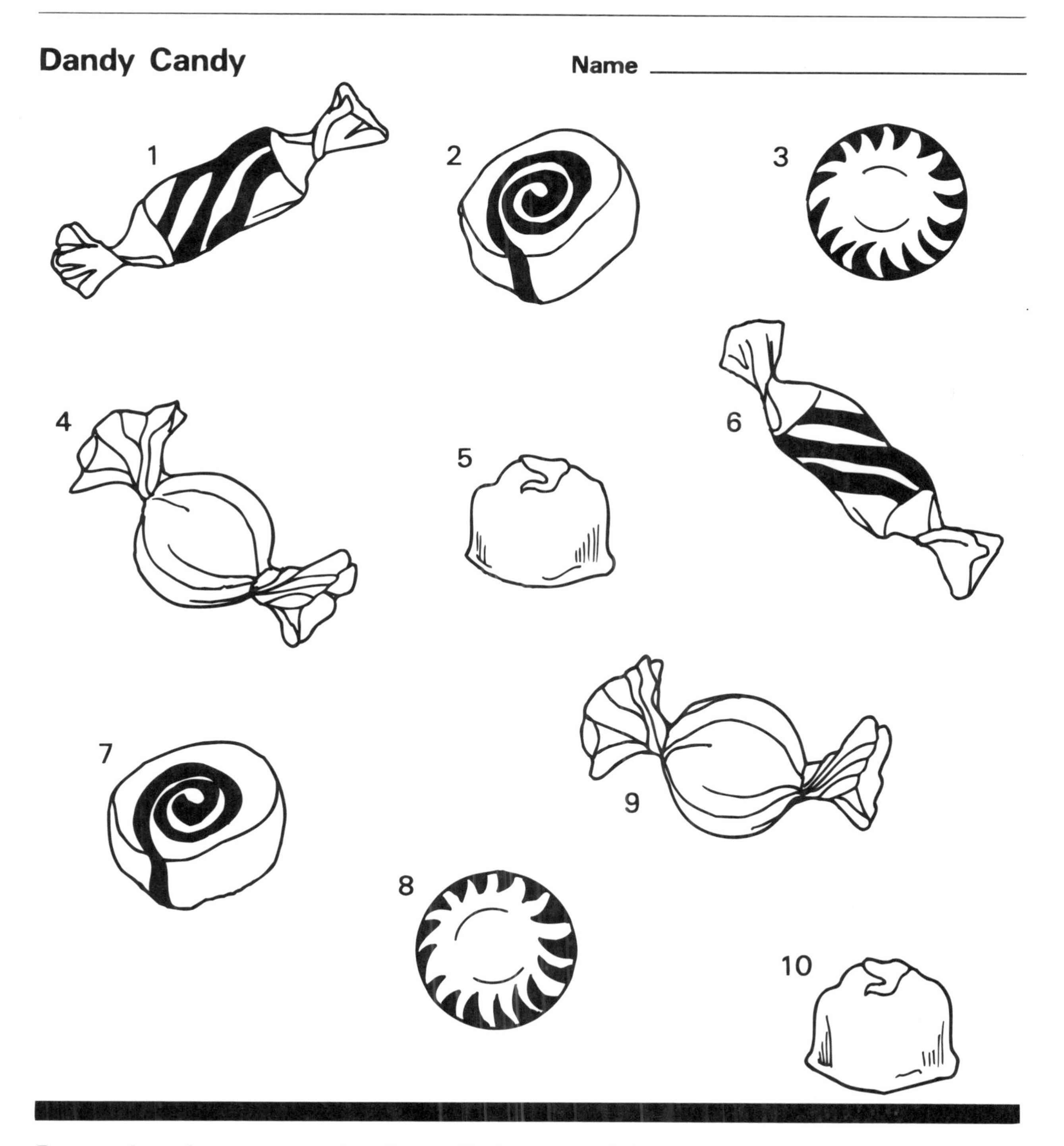

Better brush your teeth after all that candy!

Draw a face on a monster each time you repeat these words in the correct order.

1. sheep · cow · pig · horse
2. towel · wash · bath · bubble
3. toast · juice · cereal · milk
4. cup · knife · plate · fork
5. through · out · off · around
6. peas · beans · corn · broccoli
7. school · store · library · garage
8. smile · laugh · cry · frown
9. queen · prince · duke · king
10. dot · check · spot · mark

Monster Madness

Name ______________________________

Oooh! What great monsters you made!

Color a section of the thermometer each time you repeat these words in the correct order.

1. ball • game • jacks • dice
2. stripe • check • dot • line
3. rug • curtain • rag • towel
4. night • noon • day • morning
5. pie • cake • brownie • cookie
6. hat • cap • scarf • hood
7. zoo • farm • cage • tank
8. lamb • calf • puppy • kitten
9. pound • hit • smash • crush
10. price • cost • change • money

Hot Stuff

Name ______________________

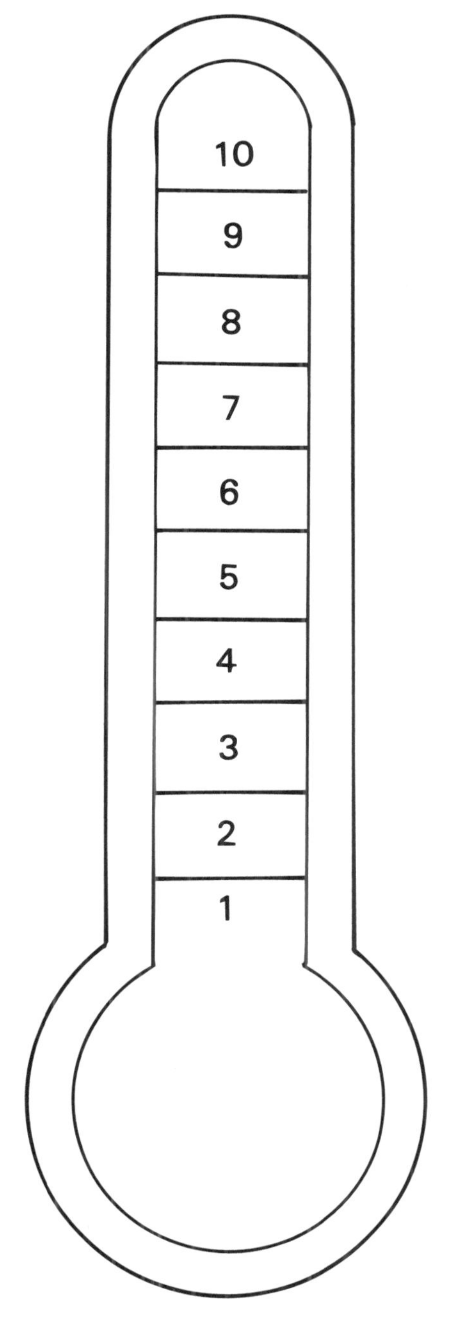

Boy, it's hot in here!

Keep the balloons in the air! Color a stripe on a balloon each time you repeat these words in the correct order.

1. tea • milk • pop • water
2. comb • wash • brush • hair
3. axe • saw • log • chop
4. clock • minute • hour • time
5. ice • slip • snow • skate
6. floor • wall • door • ceiling
7. hot • burn • steam • fire
8. music • note • song • play
9. beef • pork • ham • veal
10. lake • pond • ocean • river

Balloon Stripes

Name ______________________________

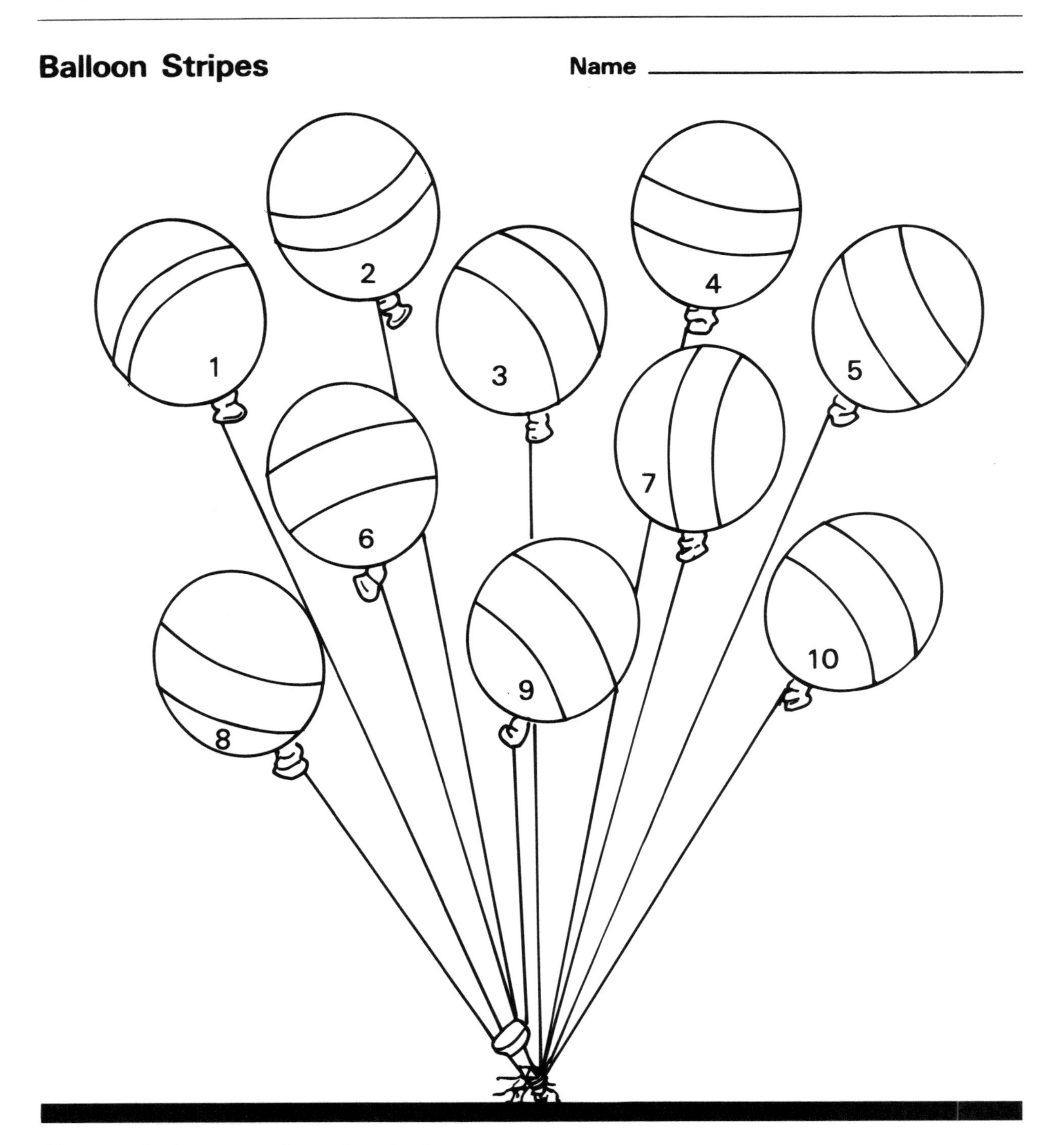

Now, circle your favorite balloon.

Color a section of the robot each time you repeat these words in the correct order.

1. sand • over • queen • toss
2. pink • ball • lip • coat
3. glove • rug • hot • fast
4. shoot • like • rock • swing
5. heel • flat • salt • say
6. nice • red • jump • cold
7. ask • line • keep • read
8. cool • top • did • couch
9. oil • bowl • paint • cup
10. fail • bat • cheese • beak

Robot Wonder

Name ______________________________

What a remarkable robot!

Color a section of the umbrella each time you repeat these words in the correct order.

1. flag • song • bow • rat
2. toe • bee • cough • sheet
3. farm • leg • mom • blue
4. spot • ice • night • crumb
5. bake • hole • fix • ear
6. look • cap • friend • hour
7. down • ride • nest • ham
8. safe • oil • brush • inch
9. paw • shelf • key • seed
10. good • high • loud • rain

April Showers

Name ______________________

What a colorful umbrella!

Match a pair of socks each time you repeat these words in the correct order.

1. pay • wide • feel • get
2. soap • line • more • road
3. dream • with • tag • four
4. store • hold • dear • come
5. right • all • now • close
6. will • out • my • song
7. love • egg • next • free
8. gift • eye • yours • week
9. touch • buy • foot • play
10. point • tongue • work • twelve

Sock It To 'Em!

Name ______________________

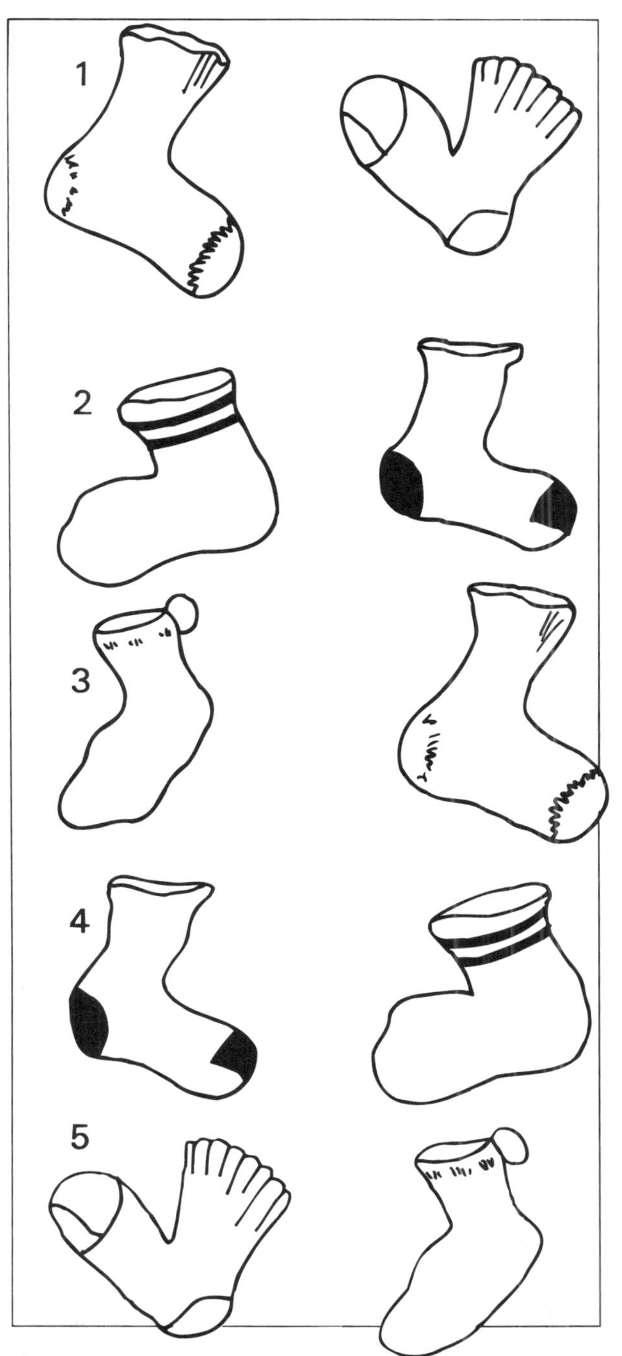

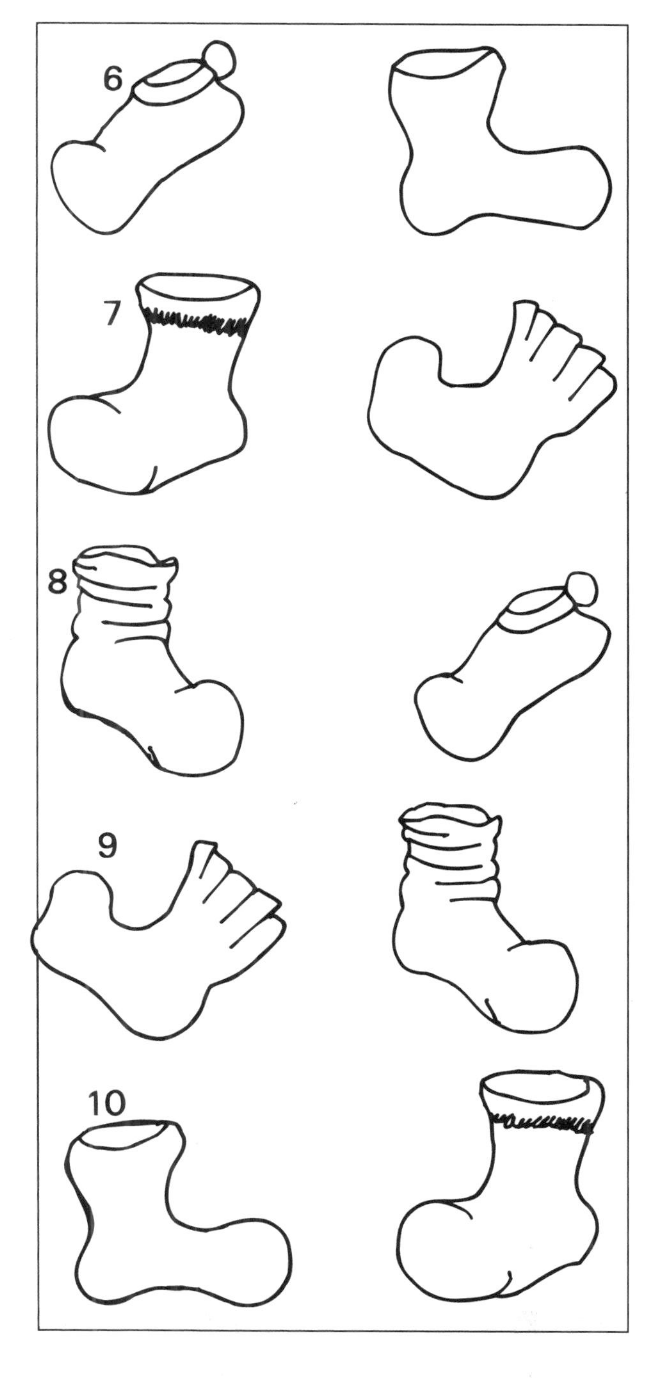

Great matching!

Color a banana each time you repeat these numbers in the correct order.

1. 6 · 9
2. 2 · 8
3. 1 · 7
4. 5 · 10
5. 3 · 4
6. 7 · 2
7. 9 · 6
8. 4 · 1
9. 5 · 3
10. 10 · 8

Murphy the Monkey

Name ______________________

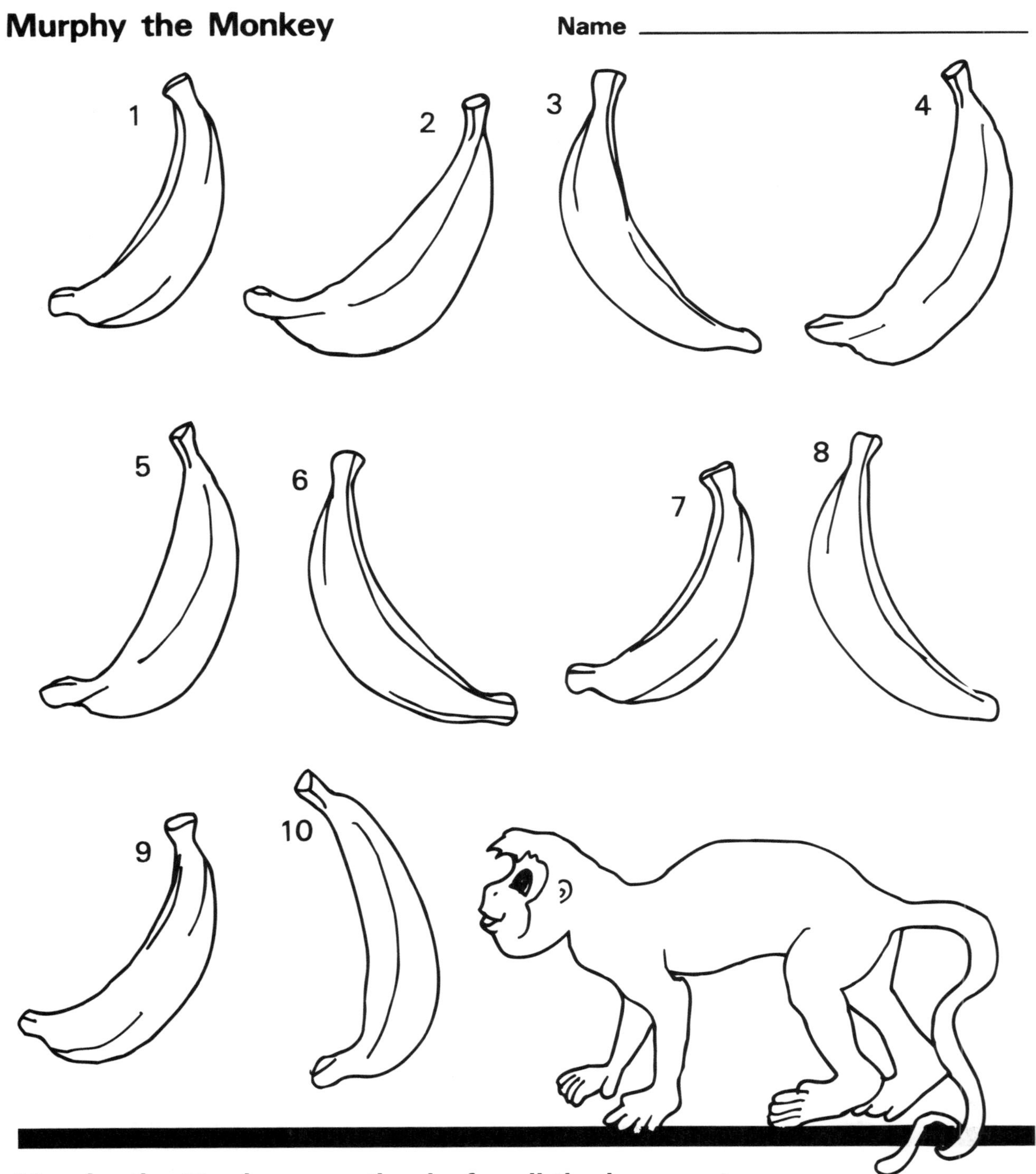

Murphy the Monkey says thanks for all the bananas!

Trace Kippy Kangaroo's path each time you repeat these numbers in the correct order.

1. 4 · 7 · 3
2. 5 · 10 · 2
3. 8 · 12 · 6
4. 11 · 1 · 9
5. 6 · 2 · 9
6. 1 · 0 · 6
7. 4 · 10 · 12
8. 3 · 2 · 5
9. 7 · 9 · 8
10. 11 · 6 · 4

Kippy Kangaroo

Name ______________________________

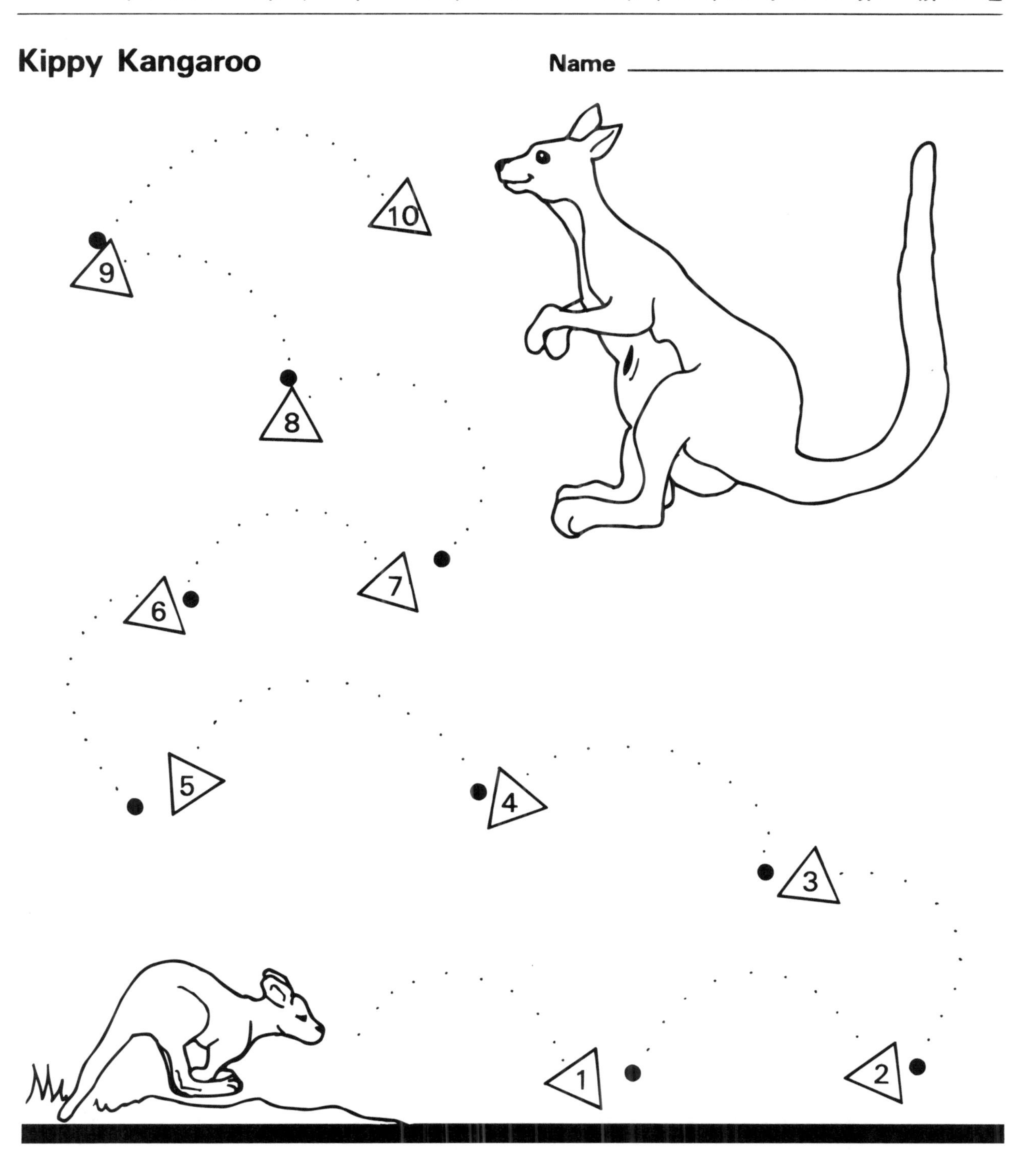

Nice hopping!

Color a marble each time you repeat these numbers in the correct order.

1. 9 · 10 · 5 · 8
2. 6 · 3 · 7 · 2
3. 1 · 2 · 4 · 6
4. 12 · 6 · 5 · 9
5. 4 · 0 · 6 · 7
6. 10 · 2 · 3 · 7 · 9
7. 1 · 0 · 4 · 11 · 2
8. 5 · 6 · 8 · 12 · 1
9. 4 · 1 · 11 · 8 · 4
10. 2 · 4 · 6 · 7 · 10

Marbles a Rollin'! **Name** ______________________

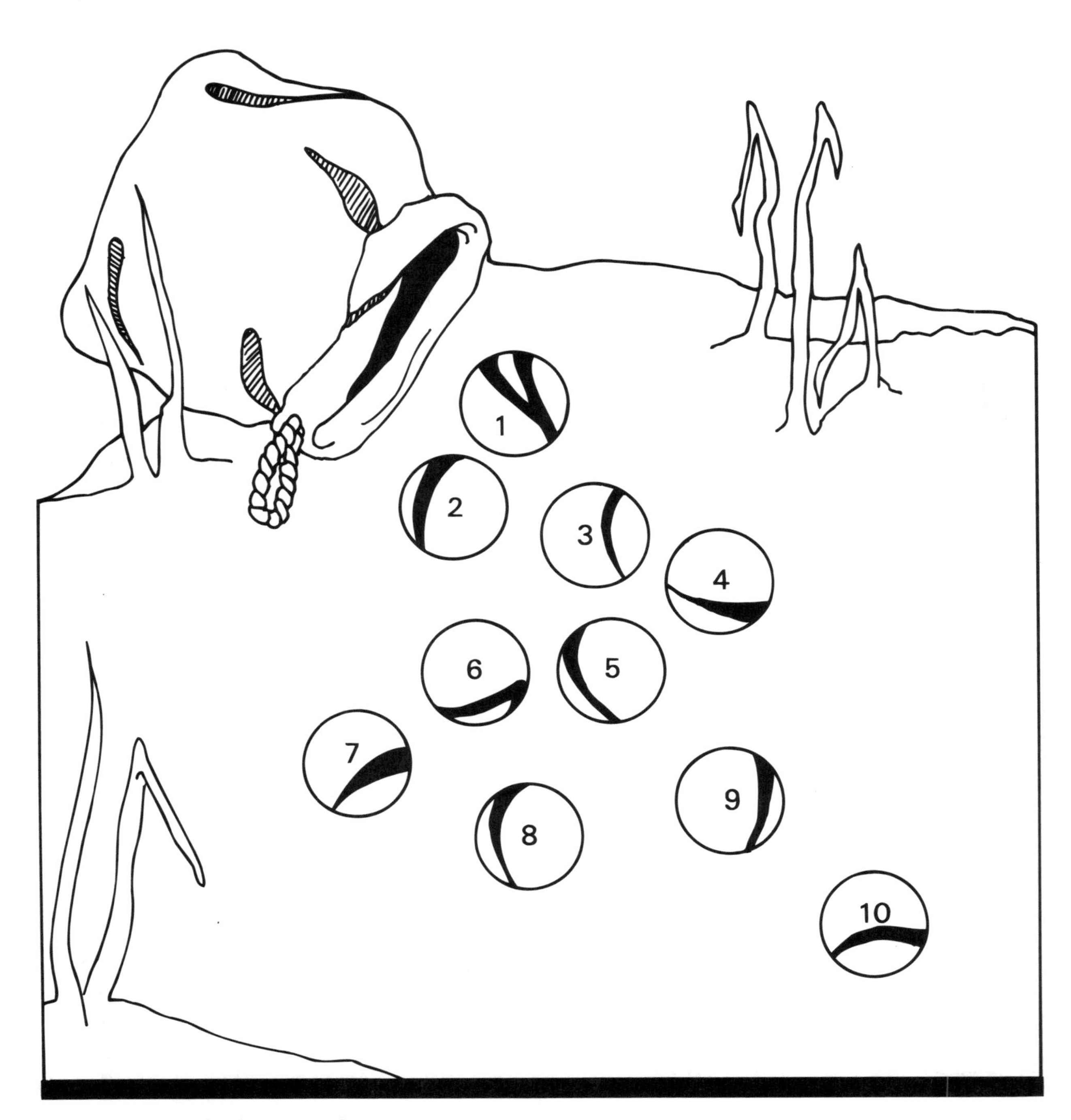

What a "marbelous" job!

Don't let Simon fool you! Color a rattle for the baby each time you follow these directions correctly.

1. Simon says, "Spell your name."
2. Simon says, "Tell me the alphabet."
3. Turn around three times.
4. Simon says, "Hop two times."
5. Simon says, "Count to twenty."
6. Fold your hands.
7. Stand up quickly.
8. Simon says, "Say the days of the week."
9. Simon says, "Name four vegetables."
10. Close your eyes.

"Simon Says"

Name ____________________

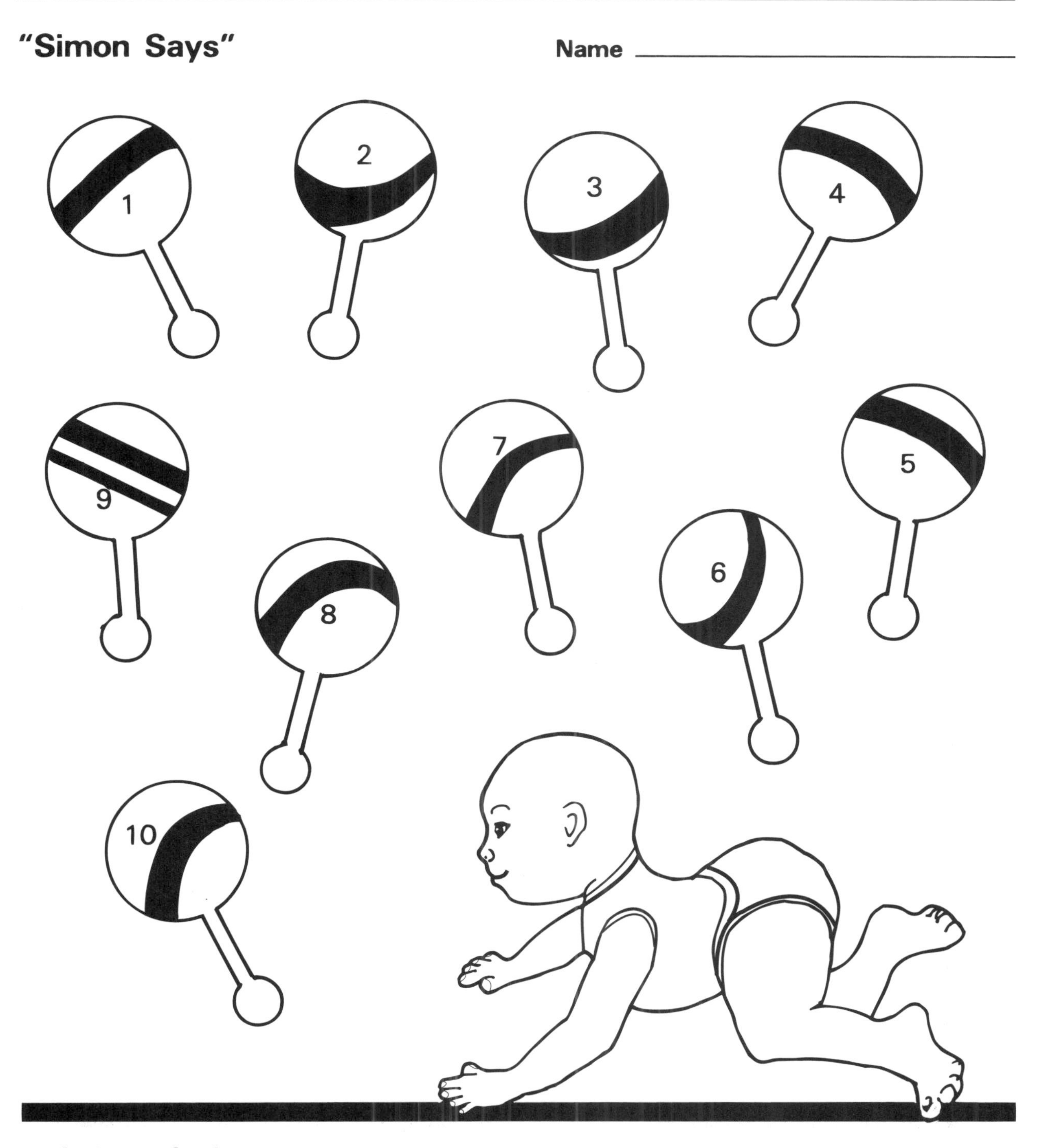

Did Simon fool you?

Use your crayon and follow these directions. Circle the number if you are correct.

1. Draw a line through the circle.
2. Complete the flower.
3. Trace the triangle.
4. Cross out the heart.
5. Put an X in the big square.
6. Draw a line from the house to the car.
7. Write a number 3 over the bee.
8. Underline the flag.
9. Circle both worms.
10. Color two of the crayons.

Super Listening

Name ______________________________

1

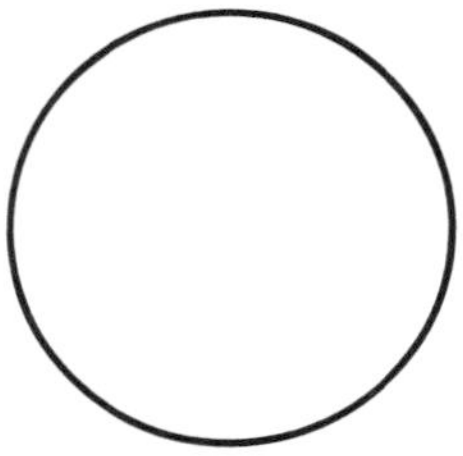

2

3

4

5

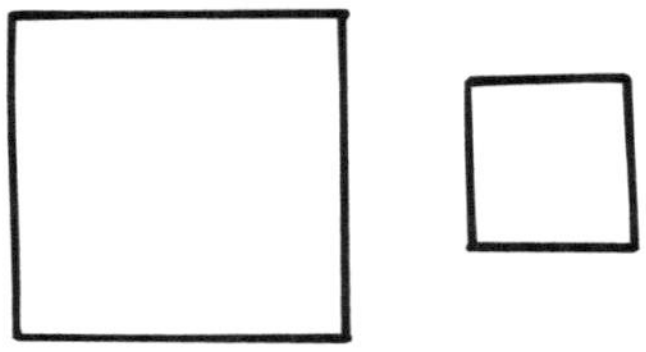

6

7

8

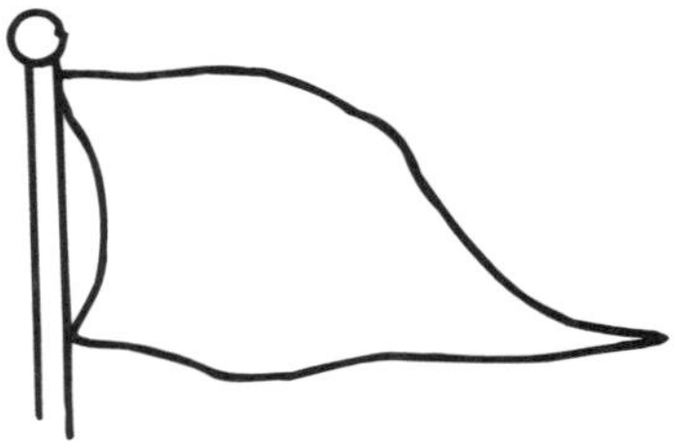

9

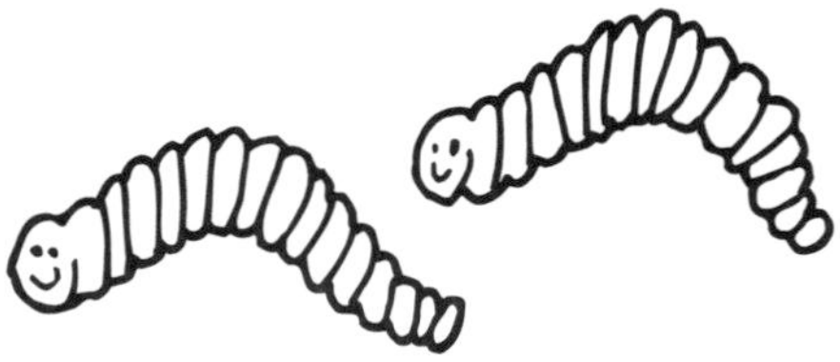

10

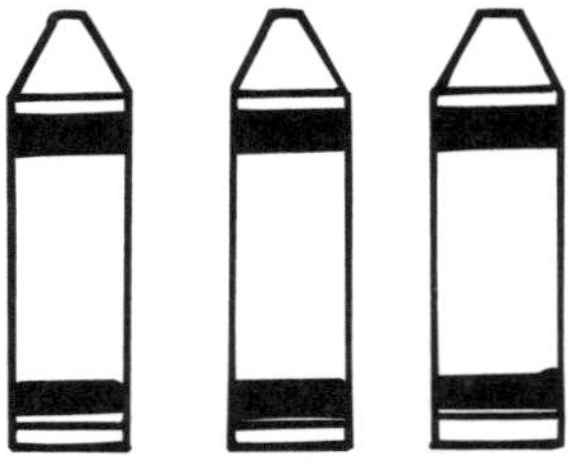

How many numbers did you circle?

Color a leaf each time you follow these directions in the correct order.

1. Snap your fingers.
   Clap your hands.
2. Jump once.
   Kneel down.
3. Hop on one foot.
   Touch your head.
4. Stick out your tongue.
   Close your eyes.
5. Kick out one foot.
   Say your name.
6. Laugh.
   Touch your ear.
7. Put your hand over your mouth.
   Touch your elbow.
8. Lick your lips.
   Sniff.
9. Smile.
   Blink your eyes.
10. Point to your stomach.
    Make a fist.

Colorful Leaves

Name ______________________

Did you "leave" out any actions?

How well can you follow these directions? Trace the number if you are correct.

1. Make an X on the balloon.
   Draw a scoop of ice cream for the cone.
2. Circle the shape.
   Draw a line above the sock.
3. Trace the big X.
   Circle the small X.
4. Draw a line from the banana to the kite.
   Underline the thing that you eat.
5. Draw a line from the bottom of the smallest snowman to the head of the medium-sized snowman.
   Color the largest snowman.
6. Write a number on the thing that you wear.
   Cross out the fruit.
7. Make a circle below the table.
   Write a number 5 above the table.
8. Cross out the smallest ball.
   Color the largest ball.
9. Draw two circles on the flowerpot.
   Make an X next to the pot.
10. Draw a line from the number to the letter.
    Trace the square.

Listen 'n' Follow

Name ______________________________

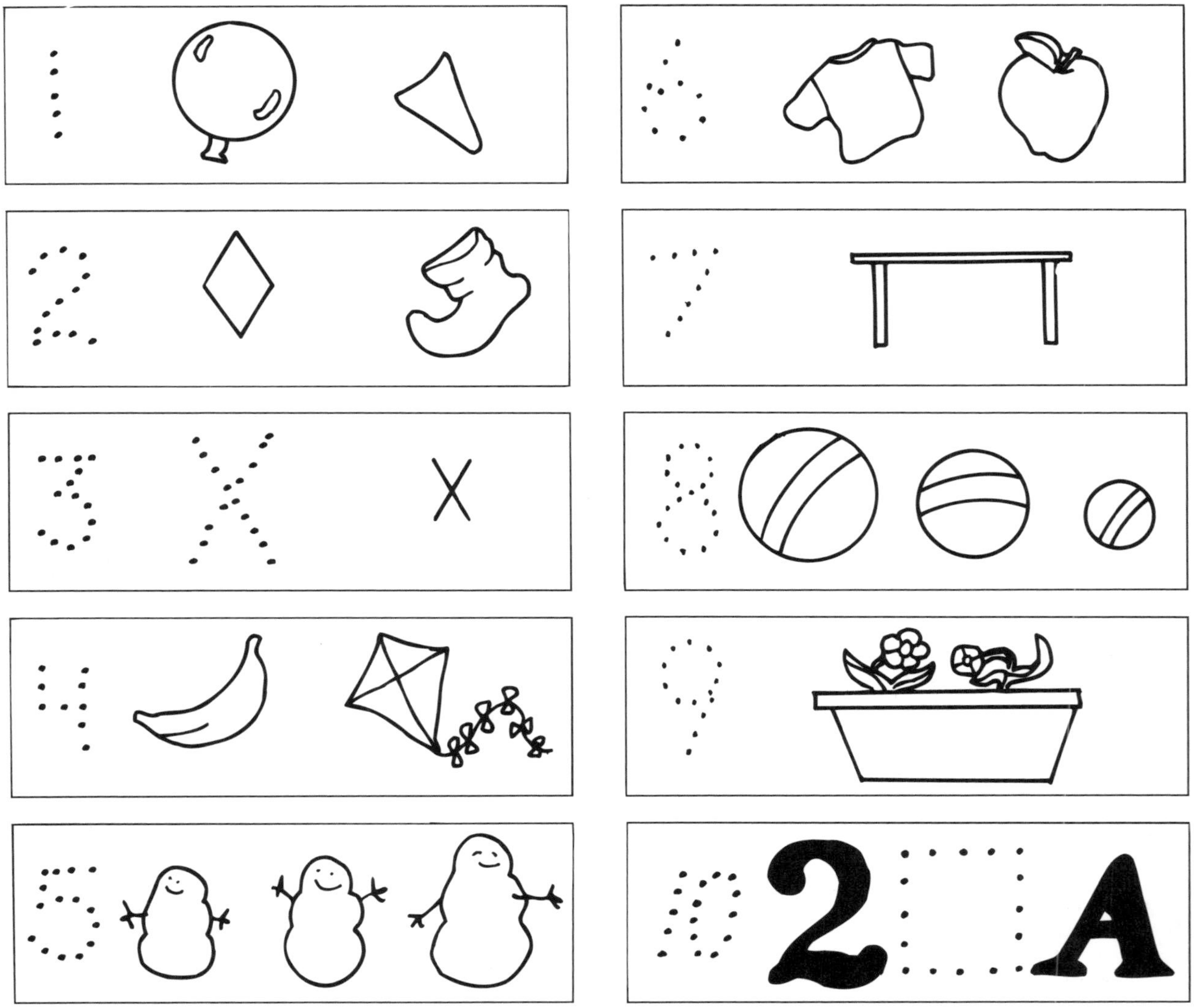

How many numbers did you trace?

It's fun to follow directions. Draw a smiley face in each box if you follow these directions correctly.

1. Draw two candles on the cake.
   Color the plate.
2. Make a smile for the sun.
   Color the eyes.
3. Write your name above the line.
   Write your age below the line.
4. Circle the high cloud.
   Put an X on the low cloud.
5. Color two circles.
   Cross out three squares.
6. Circle the middle flower.
   Underline the flower at the end of the row.
7. Color the bee's wings.
   Draw a square around the bee.
8. Underline the second shape.
   Write an L in the third shape.
9. Cross out the numbers.
   Draw a line above each letter.
10. Draw a line to connect the first cup to the first spoon.
    Draw a line to connect the last cup to the last spoon.

Smile! **Name** ______________________

How many smiley faces did you draw?

Gobble, gobble!

Name ____________________________

Make the turkey colorful! Color a tail feather each time you follow these directions in the correct order.

1. Cough once.
   Count to three.
   Tell how old you are.
2. Touch the floor.
   Pound on the table.
   Say the alphabet.
3. Touch your shoulder.
   Stamp your feet.
   Tell your favorite color.
4. Raise your arms.
   Point to your nose.
   Blink your eyes.
5. Wave your hand.
   Pull your hair.
   Point your finger up.
6. Touch your chin.
   Point to the door.
   Touch your chair.
7. Look at the ceiling.
   Hum a tune.
   Shake your head.
8. Open your mouth.
   Wiggle your tongue.
   Jump two times.
9. Slap your knee.
   Stand on one foot.
   Touch your toes.
10. Touch one hip.
    Turn your head.
    Touch your elbows together.

What a proud turkey!

Listen carefully! Use your crayon and follow the directions. Trace a check each time you are correct.

1. Circle the cold food.
   Cross out the fruit.
   Underline the candy cane.
2. Color the sun.
   Draw a line over the pipe.
   Write an X on the clock.
3. Draw a line in the square.
   Circle the *b*.
   Cross out the rainbow.
4. Trace the circle.
   Complete the table.
   Draw a line over the number 3.
5. Color the second umbrella.
   Cross out the first umbrella.
   Underline the third umbrella.
6. Write an X on the tie.
   Color the tooth.
   Draw a line to connect the balls.
7. Draw strings on the violin.
   Draw a fish in the fishbowl.
   Circle the higher number.
8. Complete the flower.
   Color the bee's wings.
   Write an X on the second door.

Listen 'n' Draw

Name ______________________

1

2

3

b

4

3

5

6

7

7 10

8

Look at all those checks you drew!

Trace the arms and legs of a stick person each time you repeat a sentence correctly.

1. Open the door.
2. Please don't go there.
3. I like raisins.
4. Call me tonight.
5. I want some milk.
6. Please answer the phone.
7. Emma walked up the steps.
8. I asked Carlos to go.
9. Chairs are for sitting.
10. I love cake and pie.

Stick People

Name ______________________

Isn't it fun to draw?

Fuzzy Wuzzy is too plain. Color a section of Fuzzy each time you repeat a sentence correctly.

1. I went to the drugstore.
2. My dog's name is Red.
3. My sister rode her bike.
4. The movie is on now.
5. What color do you like?
6. Write your name on the line.
7. You can play in the sand.
8. My friend is sick today.
9. Put the blocks together.
10. Sometimes I don't save my money.

Fuzzy Wuzzy

Name ______________________________

Fuzzy Wuzzy sure is fancy now!

Color a star on the hot air balloon each time you repeat a sentence correctly.

1. What time does the drugstore close?
2. The snowflakes melted quickly.
3. We went to the show last night.
4. My shirt has many colors.
5. Listen to the directions.
6. I'm building a big tower.
7. My bike needs a new pedal.
8. Her coat has fur on the hood.
9. These potato chips are fresh.
10. Are we going to eat lunch?

Stars

Name ______________________

You were a star listener!

Catch the dragons! Cross one out each time you repeat a sentence correctly.

1. I want to go to Noah's party.
2. My homework papers are all done.
3. I already saw this movie.
4. That phone is ringing too loudly.
5. They painted the wall of my school.
6. Somebody used my tube of glue.
7. We went to the circus last week.
8. The side door of the school is locked.
9. I learned to use a computer.
10. It's too late to buy a ticket.

Save the Princess!

Name ____________________

1 2 3 4 5 6 7 8 9 10

How many dragons did you catch?

Color a spot on a peacock feather each time you repeat a sentence correctly.

1. I had pancakes with syrup this morning.
2. The girl picked a couple of flowers.
3. The band stopped playing at ten o'clock.
4. The cold weather makes me shiver and shake.
5. Do you have any chocolate candy?
6. Emily is wearing a new red sweater.
7. I think that my homework is in my desk.
8. I can't play with you after school today.
9. Try to finish all of your work on time.
10. Our team won the basketball game yesterday.

Proud as a Peacock! **Name** ______________________

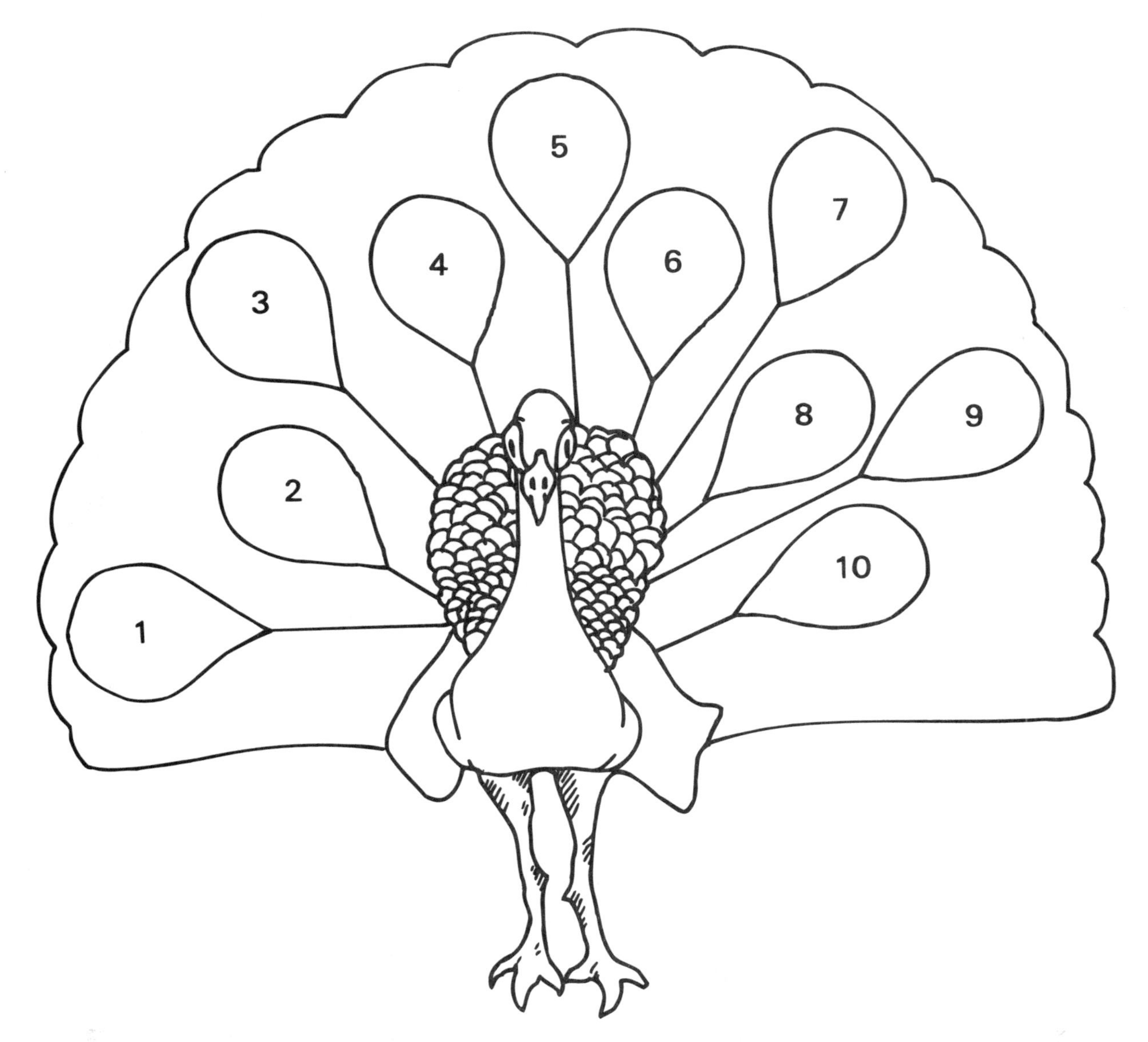

Be proud of yourself for a job well done!

Draw antennas for a bee each time you repeat a sentence correctly.

1. We learned how to make a graph on the computer.
2. I want you to make a copy for your parents.
3. My brother's red sports car won first place at the race.
4. I don't think I did this math problem correctly.
5. Sue and I don't think your plan is going to work.
6. How do you keep a cake from sticking to the pan?
7. My sister and I love to go see old movies.
8. Who is going to chaperone the high school prom?
9. Do these switches turn off the power in that room?
10. Dan lost his hall pass to get to computer class.

Busy Bees

Name ______________________

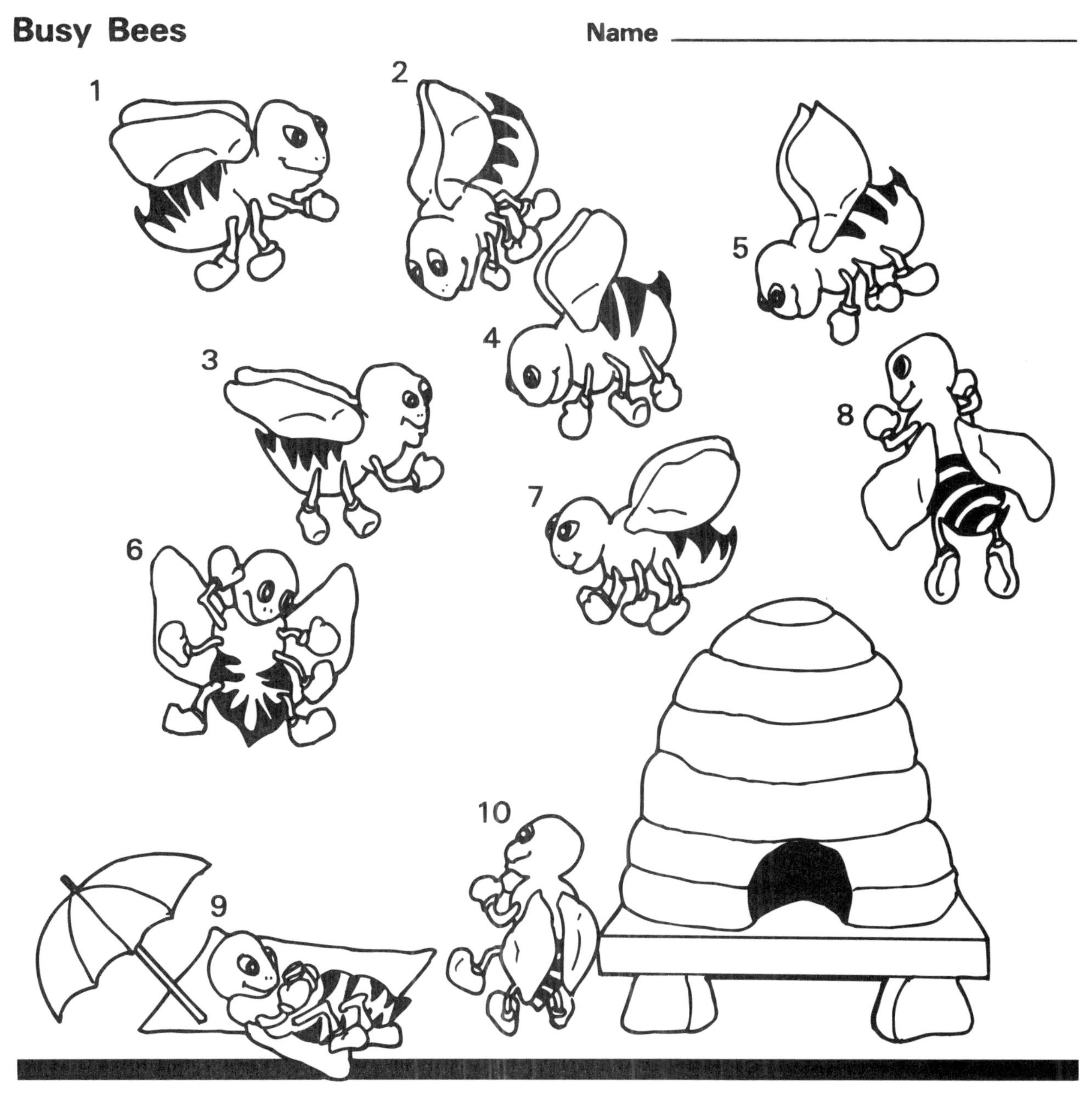

What a busy listener you are!

Draw an X on something that can be worn on your head each time you repeat a sentence correctly.

1. Dennis took his daughter, Leslie, to the baseball game.
2. Do you like pepperoni or mushrooms on your pizza?
3. My little brother thinks that ghosts are too scary.
4. I don't think my scissors are sharp enough to cut that paper.
5. I might need a new hat to wear on the beach in Florida.
6. One of the pieces of my puzzle is missing.
7. The batteries in my flashlight need to be recharged.
8. In class, we must follow the directions very carefully.
9. Helmets, hats, and caps are all things to wear on your head.
10. Our dog doesn't like to go for a walk in the winter.

Hats Galore!

Name ______________________

Hats off to good listening!

First, I will say a sentence. Then, I will ask you a question about it. Circle a number on the pyramid each time you answer a question correctly.

1. The dog ran home.
   Where did the dog run?
2. Jan likes to swim.
   Who likes to swim?
3. Matthew went to the store.
   Where did Matthew go?
4. The moon is in the sky.
   What is in the sky?
5. John ate a banana.
   What did he eat?
6. The cat runs quickly.
   What runs quickly?
7. The cup is on the table.
   Where is the cup?
8. The bird is in the cage.
   What is in the cage?
9. Kate is watching television.
   Who is watching television?
10. Jason went to Grandma's house.
    Where did Jason go?

Star Gazing

Name ______________________

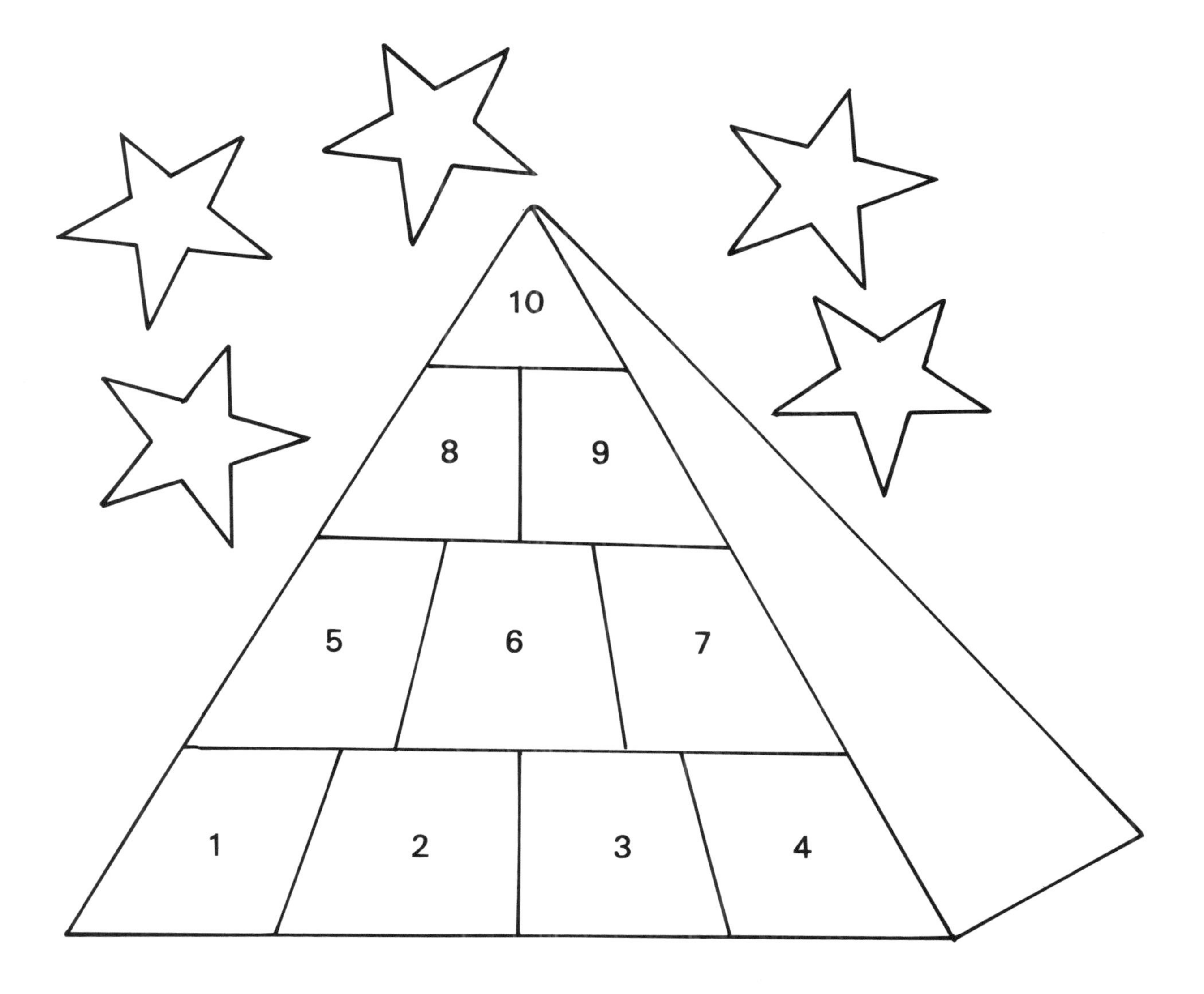

What a star listener you are!

First, I will say a sentence. Then, I will ask you questions about it. Draw a mouth on a ghost each time you answer the questions correctly.

1. Michael and Sarah will go out at 6:00.
   Who will go out?
   What time will they leave?
2. My five-year-old sister is dressing up like a princess.
   How old is my sister?
   What is her costume?
3. Last year I went to a party at Kathy Smith's house.
   When was the party?
   Who had the party?
4. My clown costume is in a big box in the attic.
   What is the costume?
   What is the costume in?
   Where is the box?
5. Maria had pizza and apple cider at her party.
   What did Maria serve?
   Where did Maria serve pizza and apple cider?
6. I carved my pumpkin with two triangle eyes and five teeth.
   What shape are the eyes?
   How many teeth does it have?
7. The man next door handed out stickers instead of candy.
   Who gave the treat?
   What did he hand out?
8. The skeleton has one hand on its hip and one on its shoulder.
   Where is one hand?
   Where is the other hand?

Boo Who?

Name ______________________

1 2 3 4

5 6 7 8

What a boo-tiful job!

First, I will say a sentence. Then, I will ask you questions about it. Draw a smile on a goofy face each time you answer the questions correctly.

1. For lunch, I ate a ham and cheese sandwich.
   What did I eat?
   When did I eat it?
2. My aunt gave me a pair of mittens.
   What did I get?
   Who gave them to me?
3. The tree fell over during the thunderstorm.
   What fell?
   When did it fall?
4. Melanie drank pop and ate potato chips.
   What did she eat?
   What was her name?
5. Yesterday, Dale fell off his bike and hurt his knee.
   What did he hurt?
   When did it happen?
6. John has a baseball in his closet.
   Where is the ball?
   What is the boy's name?
7. When I got home from school, I ate some crackers.
   What did I eat?
   When did I eat?
8. Tony got a puzzle for his birthday.
   What did he get?
   When did he get it?

No Time to Goof Off!

Name ______________________________

You're certainly no "goof-off"!

Help Pete Parakeet find his friends. Listen carefully! Draw a circle around a bird each time you answer a question correctly.

One Saturday afternoon, Pete Parakeet was feeling very lonely. He flew high above the clouds to find a friend. He flew under a rainbow, but he didn't see any other birds.

1. What day of the week was it?
2. What is the bird's name?
3. What did he fly above?
4. What did he fly under?
5. What was Pete looking for?

Suddenly, Pete Parakeet saw a large, gray bird coming toward him. It made a roaring noise. As it got closer, Pete saw that it wasn't a bird at all. It was an airplane! Pete swooped toward the ground, and there he found nine new friends.

6. What color was the thing Pete saw coming toward him?
7. What kind of noise did it make?
8. What was the thing that Pete saw?
9. What did Pete do when he knew that it was an airplane?
10. What did he find?

Pete the Parakeet

Name ______________________

Pete says thanks for helping!

Shamrocks and Leprechauns

Name ________________________

Follow the path of shamrocks to the pot of gold. Don't let a sneaky leprechaun fool you on the way. Draw an X on a shamrock each time you answer a question correctly.

Larry did not believe in fairies or leprechauns. One day, after a rainstorm, a beautiful rainbow appeared in the sky. Larry decided to follow the rainbow. During the trip, a leprechaun jumped out of the shamrock patch and told Larry, "Follow me!" The leprechaun led him to the end of the rainbow where Larry found a pot of gold. Now we call him "Lucky" Larry!

1. Who was the story about?
2. What didn't Larry believe in?
3. What appeared in the sky?
4. When did the rainbow appear?
5. What jumped out at Larry?
6. What did the leprechaun jump out of?
7. What did the leprechaun say to Larry?
8. Where did the leprechaun take Larry?
9. What did Larry find?
10. What is Larry's nickname now?

Lucky you!

Listening for Similarities

Comparing and categorizing involve the process of organizing words according to their similarities. For example, when we hear the words *bracelet*, *ring*, *necklace*, and *earrings*, we think of the word *jewelry*. By categorizing, we learn new concepts and vocabulary words, and we store them mentally for future retrieval.

Since a child learns most when learning is enjoyable, the listening activities in this section encourage the growth of comparing and categorization skills in a fun way. These activities also help to develop the child's word-finding ability and to improve his understanding and expression of language by providing a means of organizing thought.

These listening worksheets may be used with individuals or small groups in a therapy setting, within a classroom environment, or for homework assignments. The speech-language clinician, classroom teacher, or parent reads the statements and question, and the child answers aloud. For each correct answer, the child colors, traces, or draws a simple picture numbered to correspond with the question.

Whenever it is advisable to maintain a purely auditory task, have the child just listen to each item as you read it. After the child responds correctly, present the worksheet for the child to complete the appropriate reinforcing picture.

Pop, Pop, Pop!

Name ______________________________

Pop a soap bubble by coloring one each time you give a correct answer. Name as many things as you can that:

1. have motors
2. smell bad
3. are round
4. are loud
5. have wheels
6. have pockets
7. have zippers
8. you see in the forest
9. you find in an office
10. you find in a grocery store

You're a bubble expert!

B-r-r-r! It's Cold!

Name ______________________

Time for a cool treat! Color a Popsicle if you can name three:

1. kinds of candy
2. snacks
3. desserts
4. fruits
5. vegetables
6. kinds of meat
7. frozen foods
8. breakfast foods
9. dairy products
10. things to drink

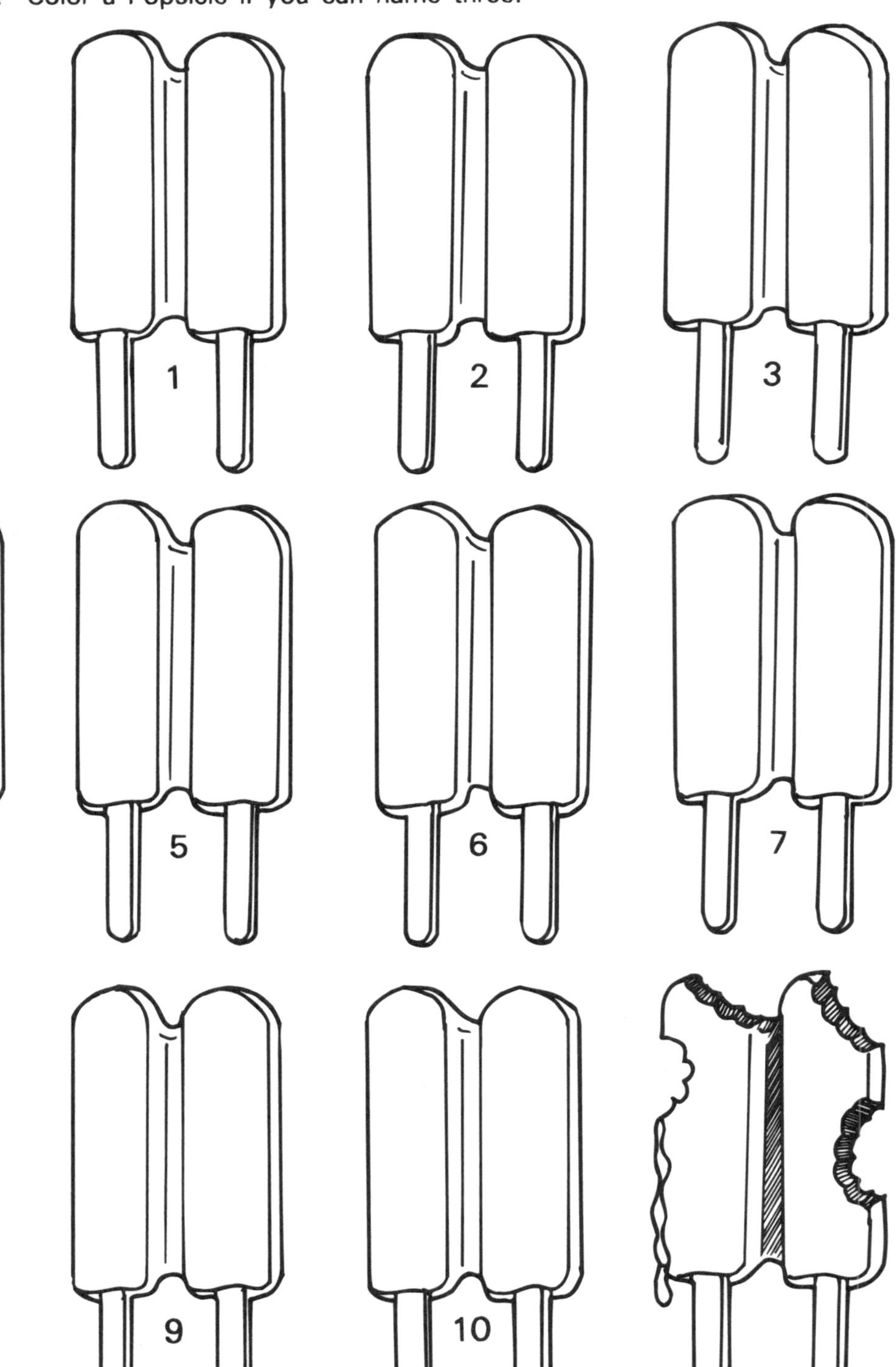

What's your favorite flavor?

Busy Bees

Name ______________________________

"Bee" a good thinker! Trace a bee's wings if you can name three:

1. liquids
2. birds
3. flowers
4. kinds of furniture
5. insects
6. kinds of jewelry
7. seasons
8. meals
9. coins
10. holidays

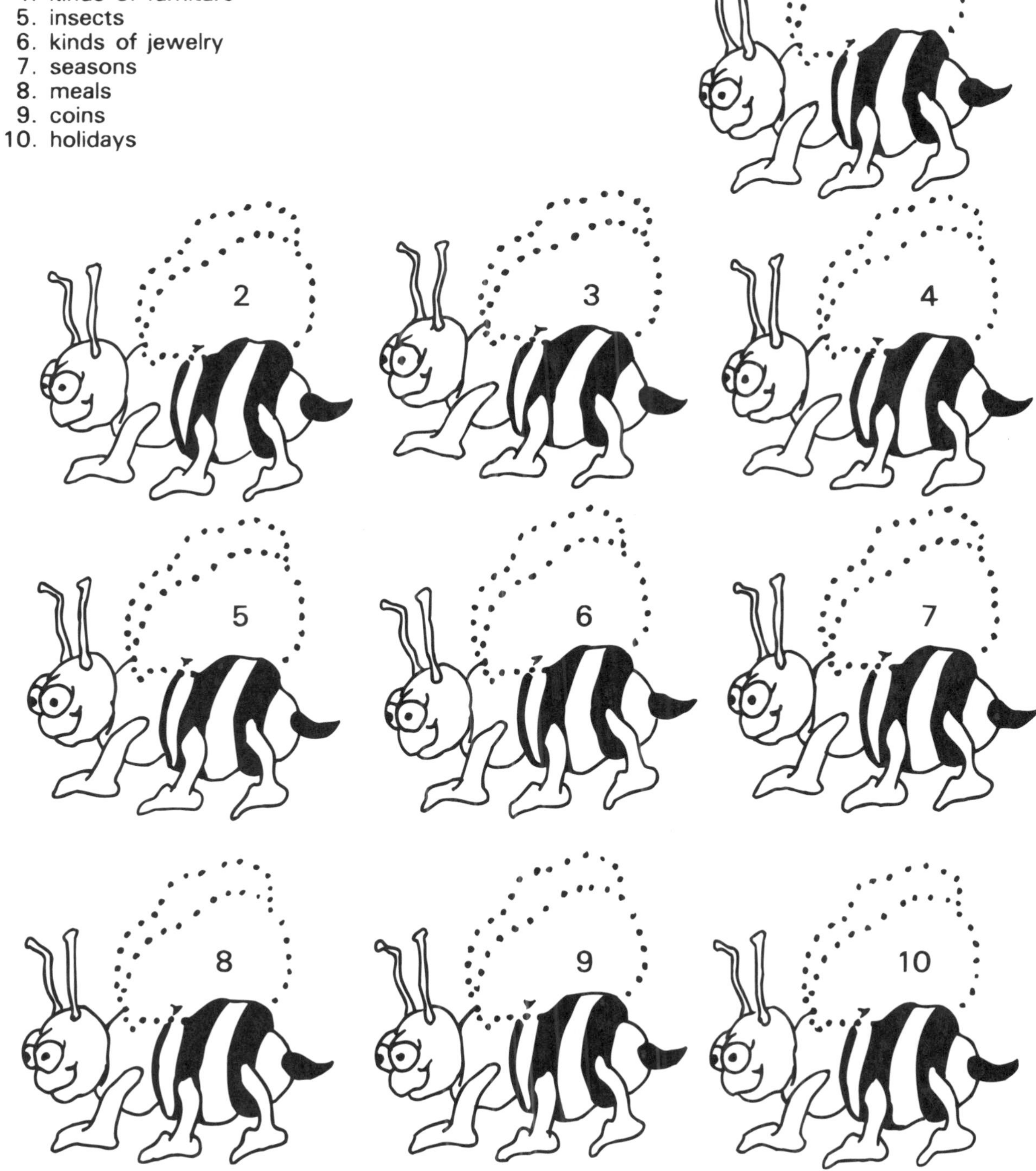

How many bees are buzzing?

Let's Go Fishing!

Name ______________________________

Fish for good answers! Trace the fins on a fish each time you answer correctly. Name three:

1. things you can sleep on
2. things you read
3. parts of the body
4. kinds of games
5. rooms in a house
6. boys' names
7. kinds of animals
8. colors
9. kinds of relatives
10. kinds of clothing

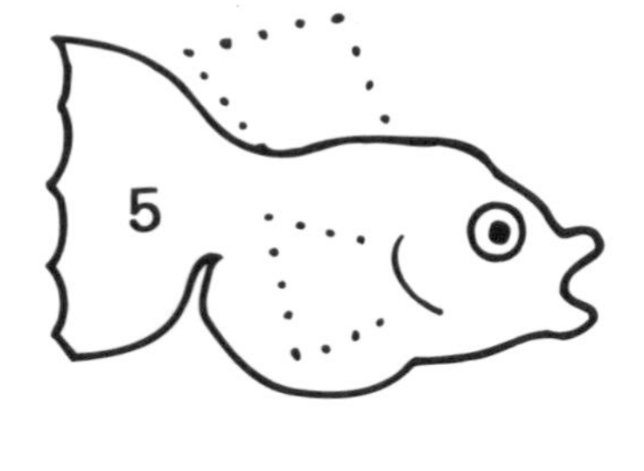

Good fishing!

It's Summertime!

Name ______________________

Get all of the watermelon seeds! Color a watermelon seed each time you give three correct answers. Name three things:

1. we drink
2. we draw with
3. that go on your feet
4. that shine in the sky
5. we can pet
6. we sit on
7. we drink out of
8. that are sticky
9. that come in pairs
10. we wear for jewelry

M-m-m-m!

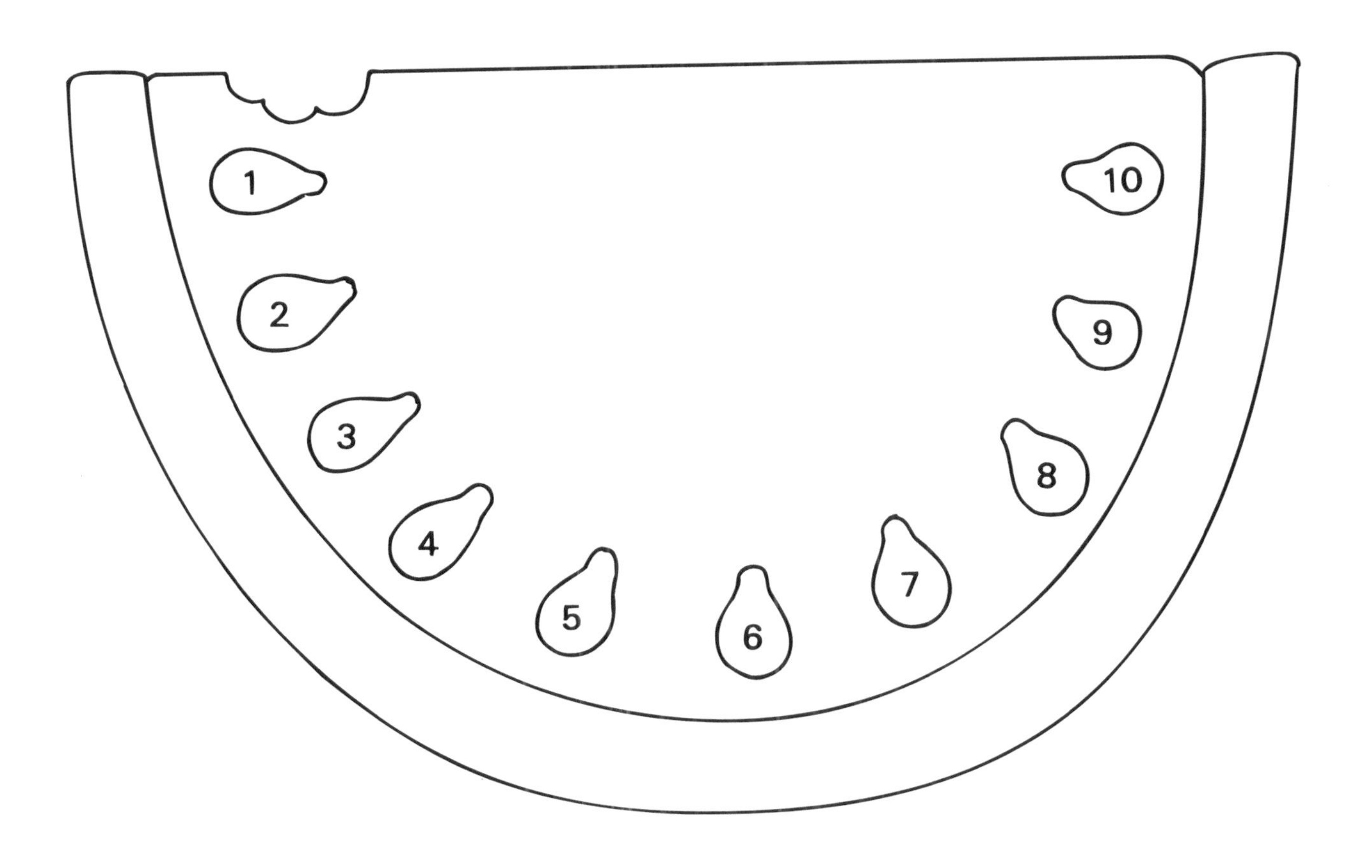

How many seeds are in the watermelon?

Game Time!

Name ______________________________

Make a touchdown! Color a football each time you give three correct answers. Name three things:

1. people use for cutting

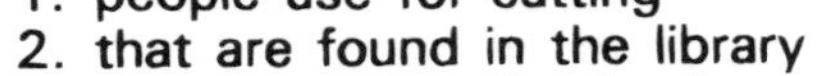
2. that are found in the library

3. that are parts of a book
4. that are found in the jungle
5. that are usually frozen

6. people use for transportation

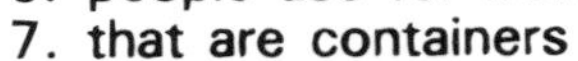
7. that are containers

8. people keep money in

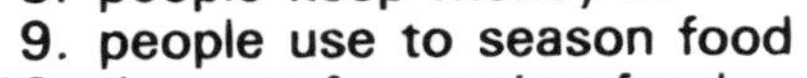
9. people use to season food

10. that are for storing food

10

9

8

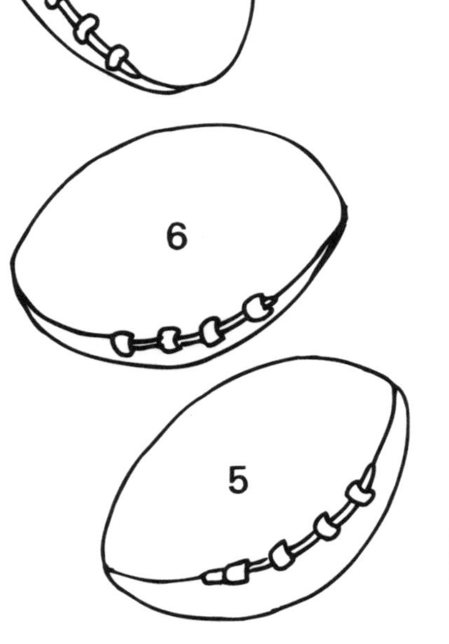

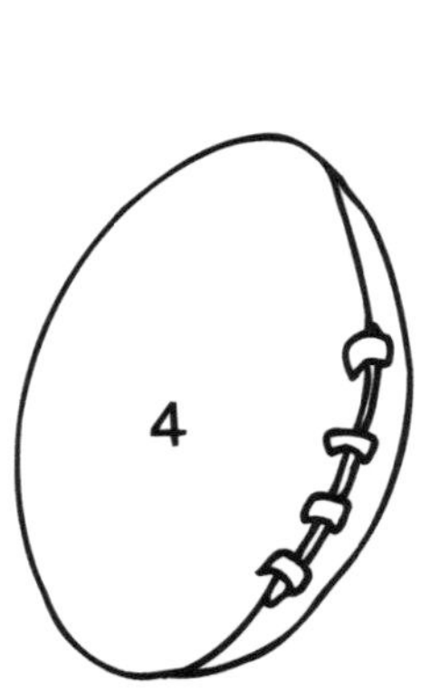

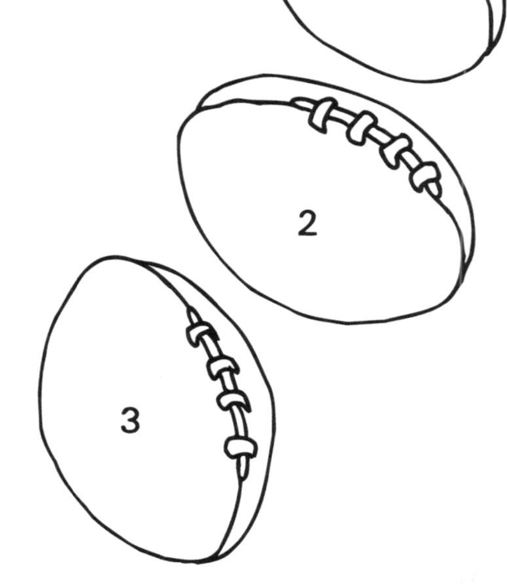

Touchdown!

Count Down

Name ______________________

Count down to blast off! Color a number each time you give three correct answers. Name the parts of your body that can do these things.

10. We can twist our ________________.
9. We can lift our ________________.
8. We can bend our ________________.
7. We can open our ________________.
6. We can tap with our ________________.
5. We can spread our ________________.
4. We can wiggle our ________________.
3. We can stretch our ________________.
2. We can shake our ________________.
1. We can kick with our ________________.

Blast off!

Change the Channel

Name ____________________

Draw a picture on a TV screen each time you answer correctly. Name three parts of a:

1. telephone
2. bicycle
3. pizza
4. flower
5. room
6. shoe
7. book
8. hand
9. television
10. house

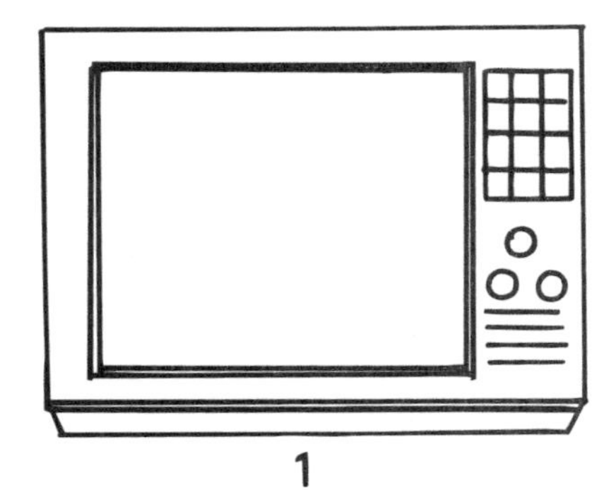

1

2 3

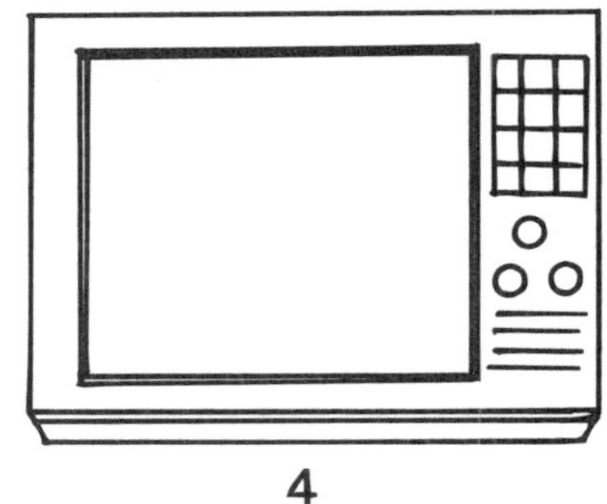

4

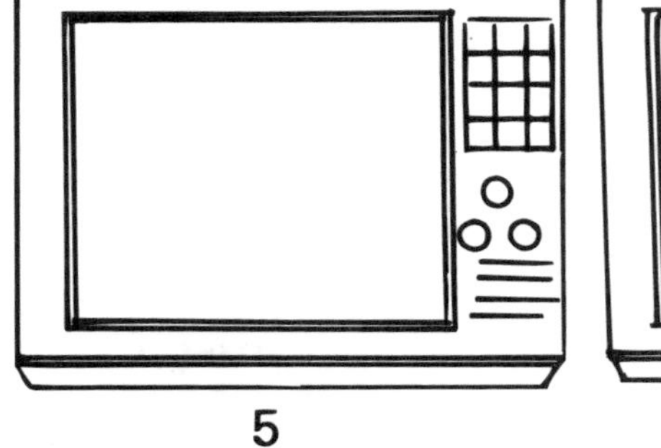

5

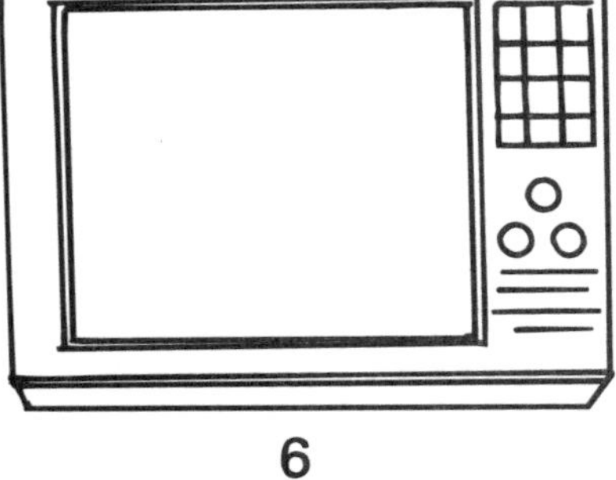

6

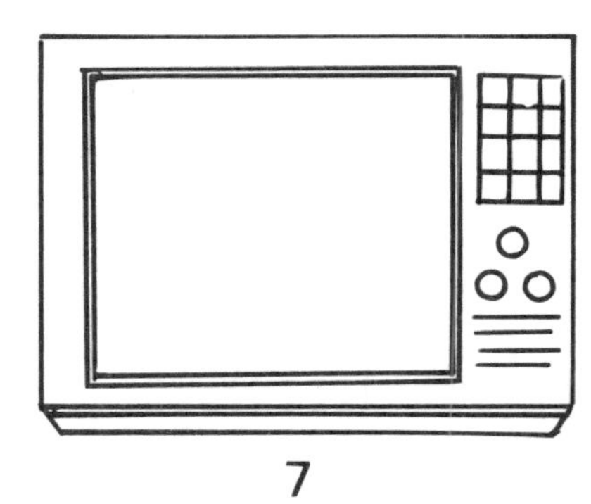

7

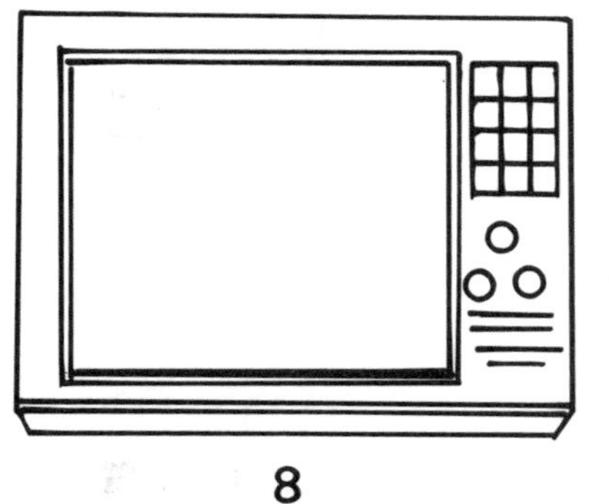

8

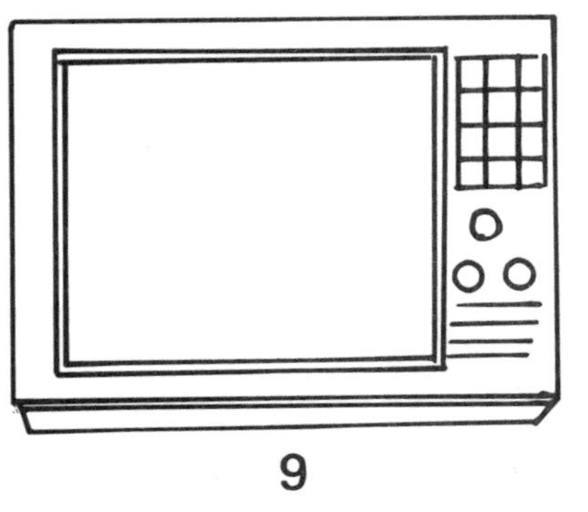

9

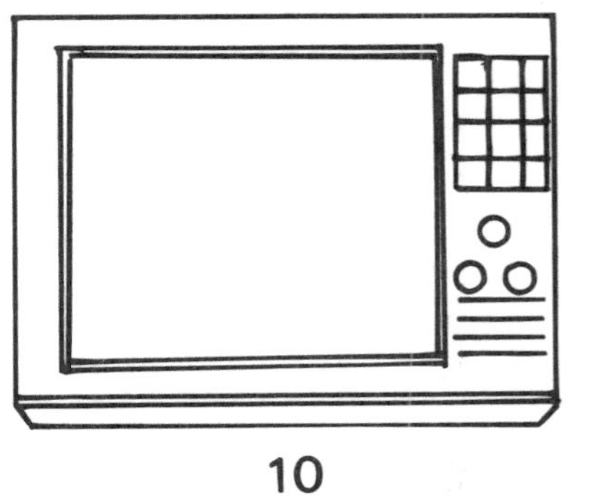

10

What is your favorite TV show?

Toot Toot!

Name ______________________________

Trace a car on the train each time you answer correctly. Name three parts of a(n):

1. apple
2. deer
3. watch
4. bathtub
5. piano
6. tree
7. bed
8. elephant
9. train
10. computer

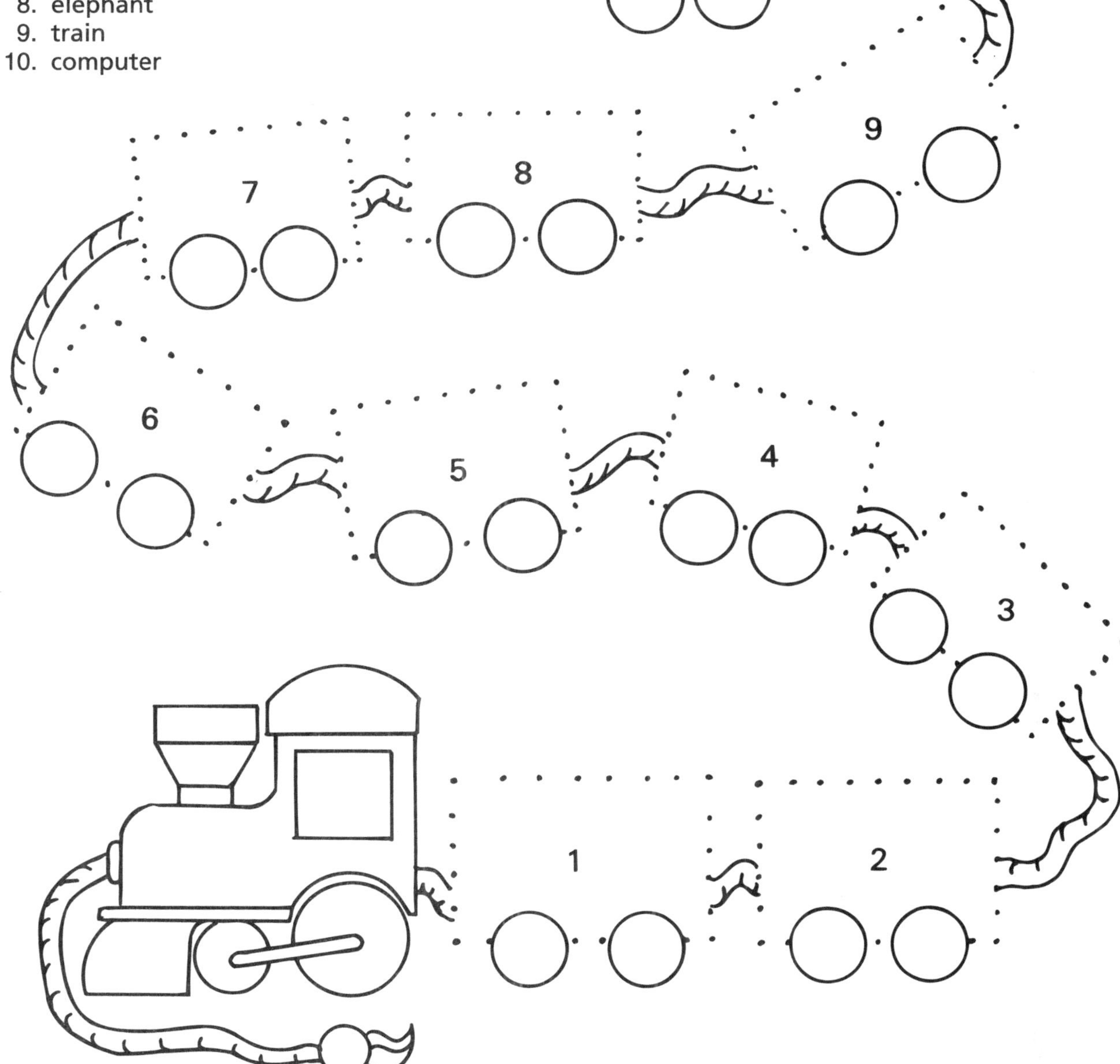

All aboard!

Poppin' Good Time!

Name ____________________

Color a piece of popcorn each time you answer correctly. Name three things you might need to:

1. build a house
2. wash windows
3. paint a house
4. wash dishes
5. wrap a present
6. take a bath
7. make a cake
8. set the table
9. make popcorn
10. make your bed

It's popcorn time!

Gifts Galore

Name ______________________________

Color a bow each time you give three correct answers. What three things do you need for __________?

1. planting a garden
2. playing baseball
3. having a party
4. brushing your teeth
5. making a cake
6. going swimming
7. going camping
8. having a picnic
9. growing flowers
10. taking a trip

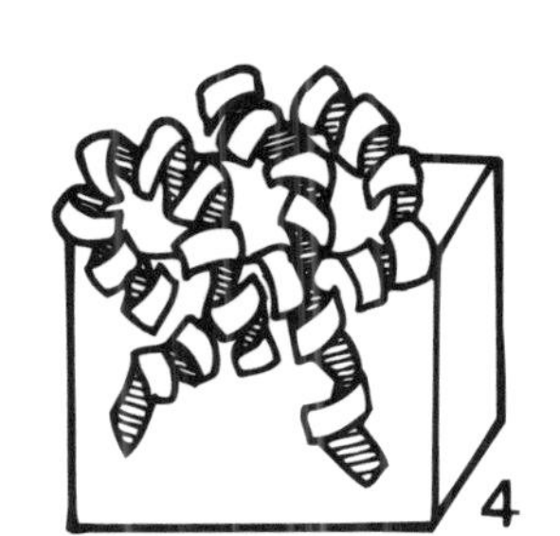

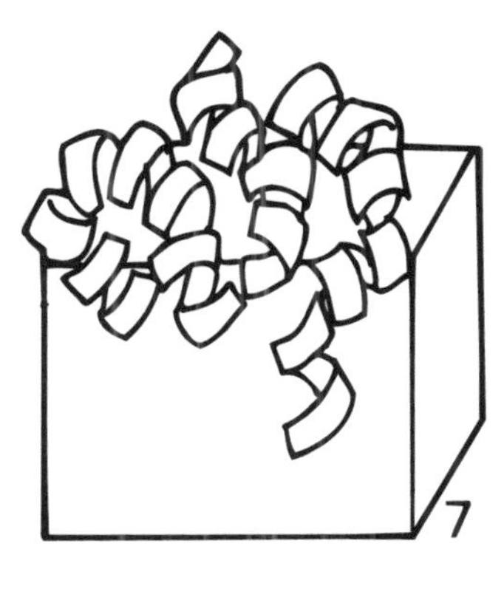

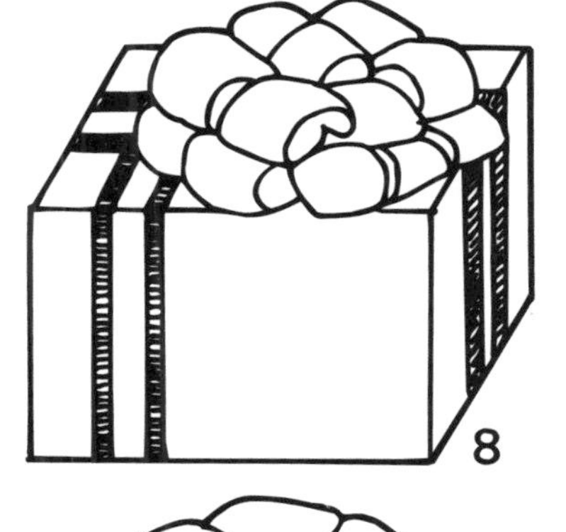

How many presents did you color?

Holiday Fun!

Name ______________________________

Name three things that go with each holiday. Color a jelly bean each time you answer correctly. What three things go with ____________?

1. Halloween
2. Thanksgiving
3. Christmas
4. Valentine's Day
5. St. Patrick's Day
6. Easter
7. Hanukkah
8. the Fourth of July
9. Memorial Day
10. New Year's Day

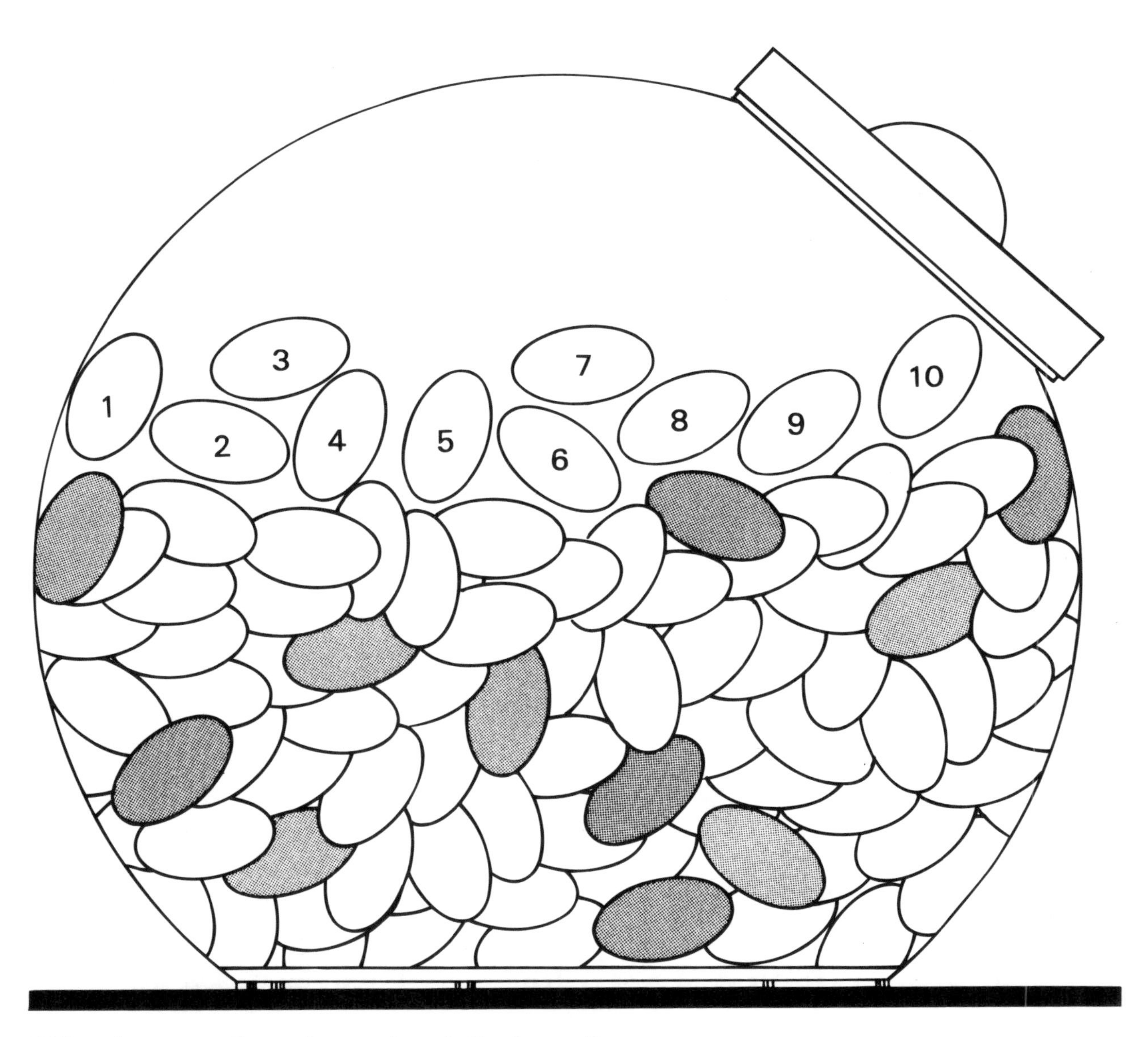

What's your favorite color jelly bean?

Onesies, Twosies, Threesies

Name ______________________

Circle a jack each time you answer correctly. Name three things that you can do:

1. in the bathroom
2. in the bedroom
3. in the water
4. in a haunted house
5. at an amusement park
6. on the playground
7. to your hair
8. with a pet
9. in gym class
10. with a door

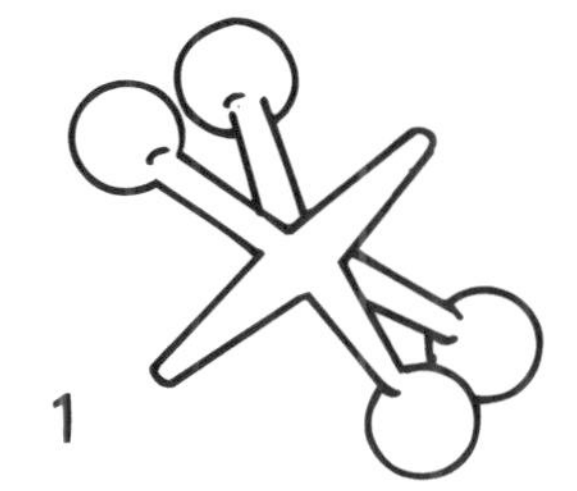
1

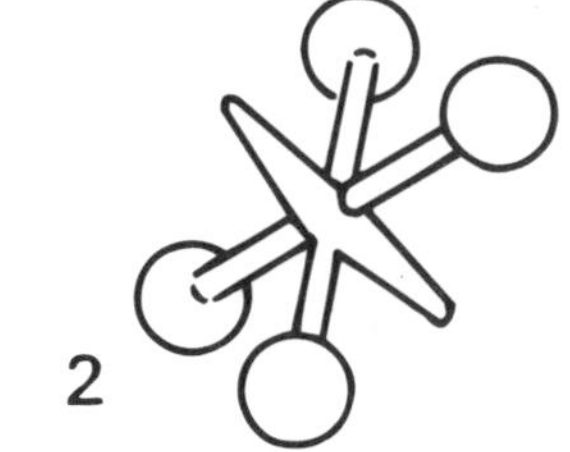
2

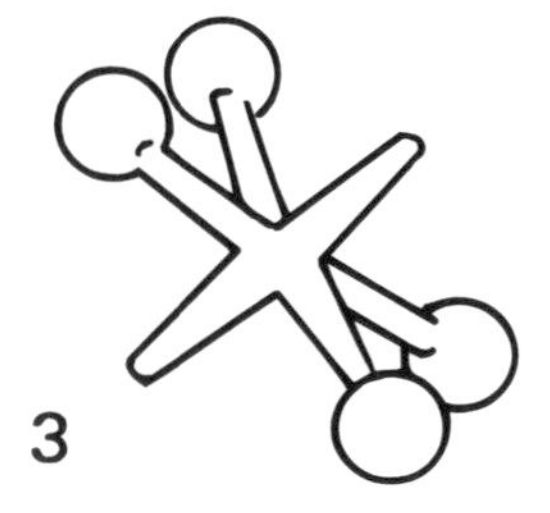
3

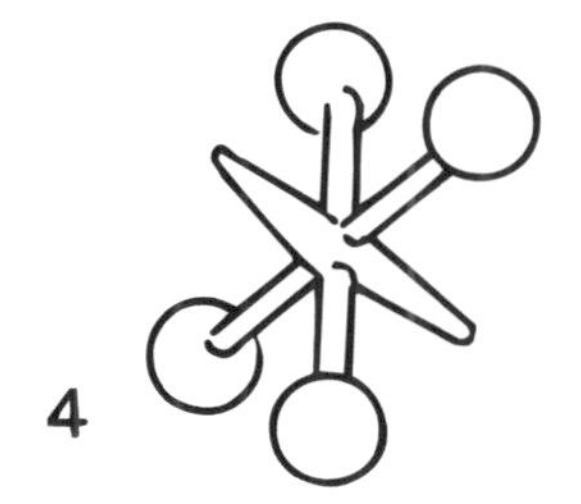
4

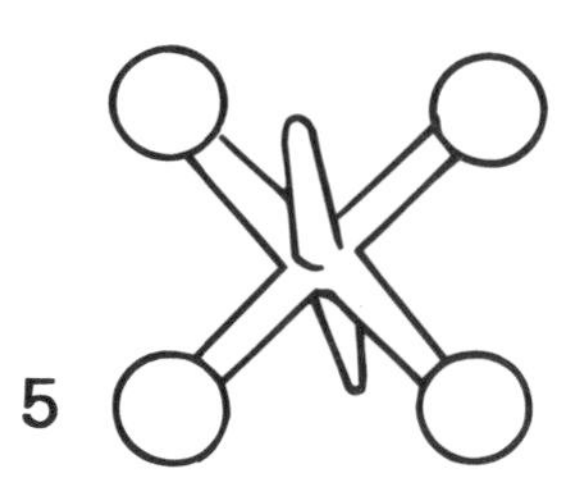
5

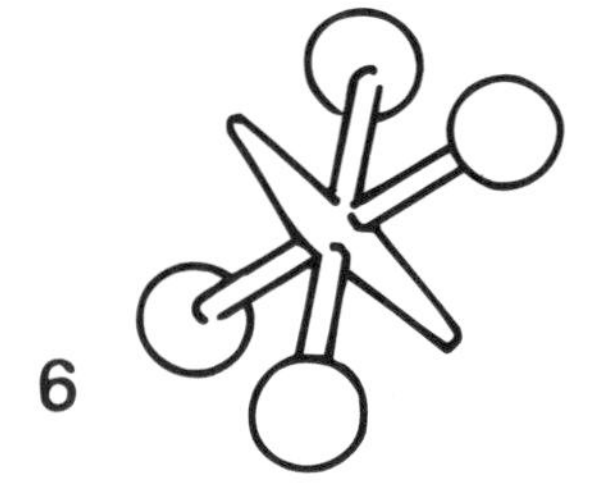
6

7

8

9

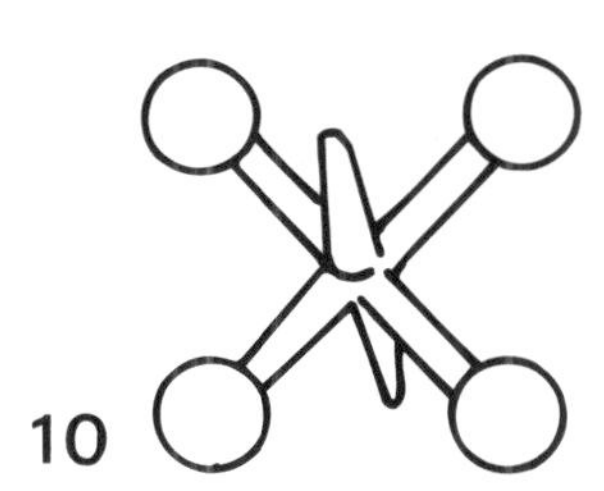
10

Did you get to "tensies?"

Rainbow Colors

Name ______________________

Color a rainbow stripe each time you answer correctly. Name three things that you can do:

1. at the beach
2. at Halloween
3. in your classroom
4. in the park
5. at a party
6. on a farm
7. in the snow
8. on the playground
9. with a ball
10. to get ready for bed

1 2 3 4 5 6 7 8 9 10

Decisions, Decisions!

Name ______________________________

Color a paint spot each time you name three things each person needs for his or her job.

1. baseball player
2. baker
3. gardener
4. pilot
5. artist
6. plumber
7. clown
8. teacher
9. secretary
10. sailor

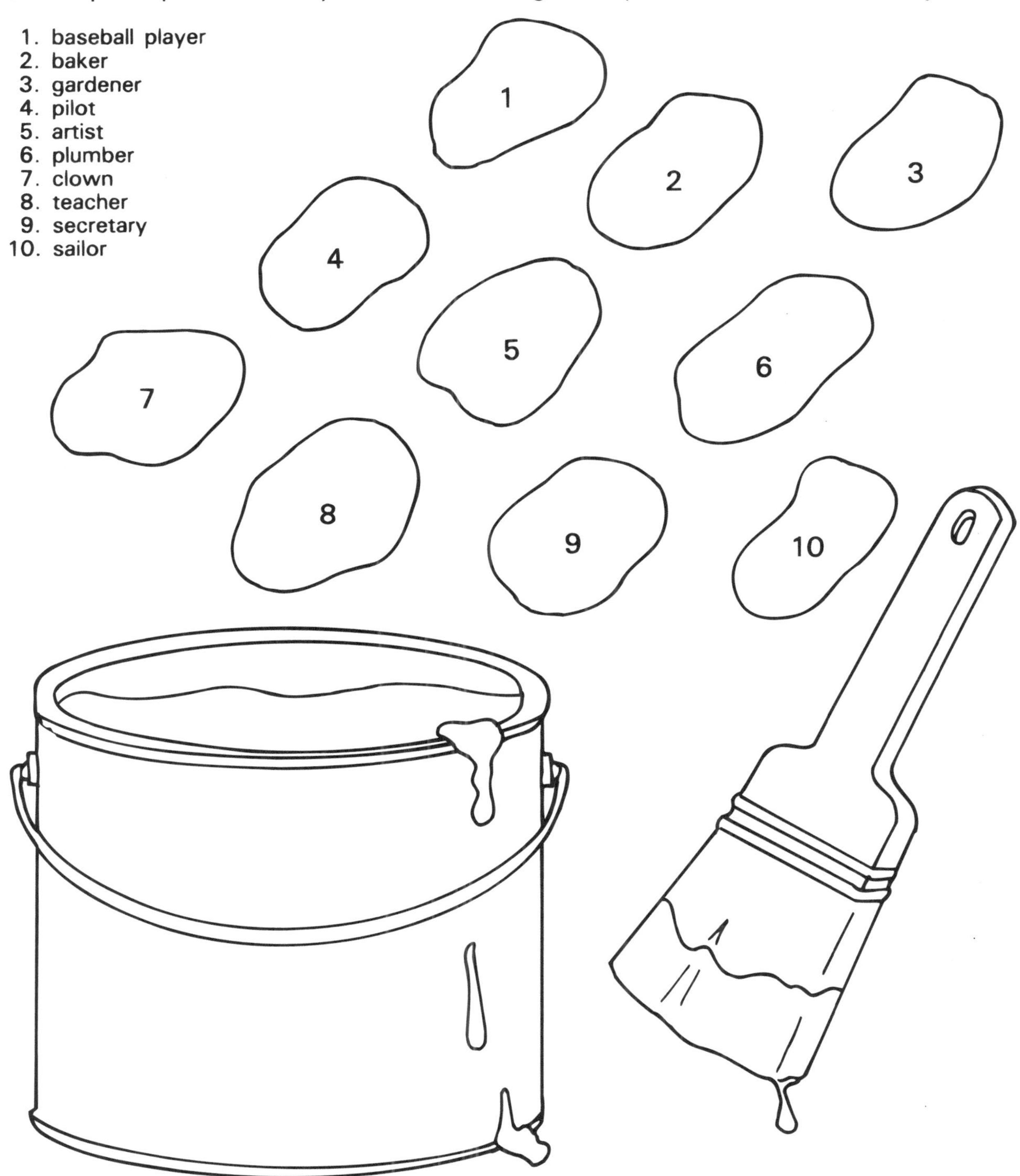

What color paint would you choose?

Circus Time!

Name ______________________________

Draw a hat for a clown each time you name three things each person needs for his or her job.

1. carpenter
2. photographer
3. maid
4. veterinarian
5. food server
6. musician
7. butcher
8. rock singer
9. hair stylist
10. mechanic

Good work! Now, circle your favorite clown.

Hee Haw!

Name ______________________________

Let's decorate the tail on the donkey. Color a bow for the donkey's tail if you can name three:

1. red fruits
2. cold drinks
3. loud noises
4. water sports
5. small insects
6. large animals
7. garden tools
8. girls' names
9. animal sounds
10. ice cream flavors

How long is the donkey's tail?

Cents Sense

Name ______________________________

Draw an X on a penny each time you answer correctly. Name three:

1. things that are noisy and heavy
2. things you wear that are soft
3. vehicles that fly
4. liquids that you don't drink
5. things you eat but don't cook
6. clothes that come in pairs
7. things that are round but don't bounce
8. things you don't eat that smell good
9. animals that are taller than a person
10. kitchen things that can break

1 

2 

3 

4 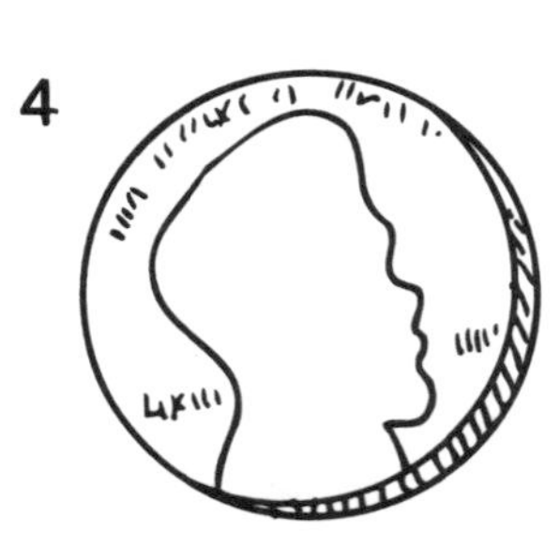

5 

6 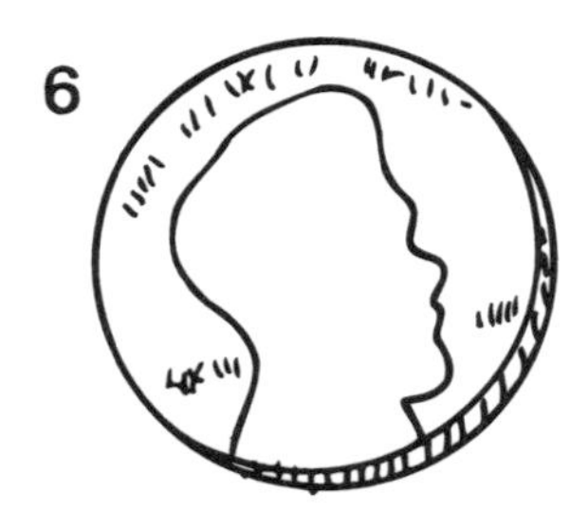

7 

8 

9 

10 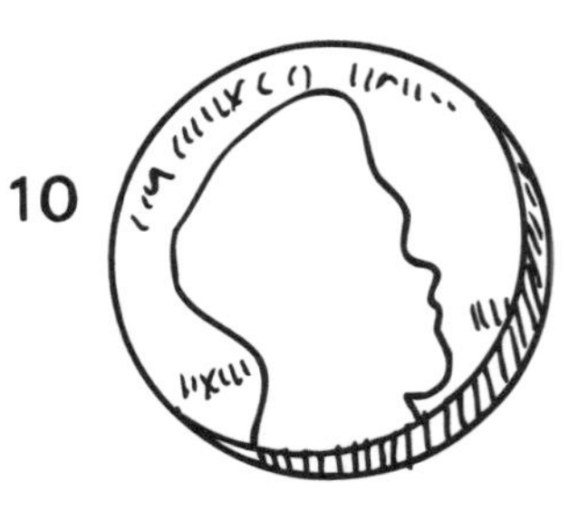

Will you save or spend your pennies?

Snowy Days!

Name ______________________________

Draw a face on a snowman if you can name three:

1. large appliances
2. round containers
3. baby animals
4. musical instruments
5. foreign countries
6. board games
7. circus performers
8. winter sports
9. flying insects
10. warm months

B-r-r-r, it's cold!

Outdoor Fun!

Name ______________________

Let's have a ball! Decorate a beach ball each time you answer correctly. Name something that goes with these things:

1. tent, lantern, camp fire
2. pop, tablecloth, picnic basket
3. water rides, merry-go-round, Ferris wheel
4. sand, waves, raft
5. hook, line, bait
6. goalposts, field, bleachers
7. mitt, diamond, bat
8. trapeze, clown, lion tamer
9. zookeeper, cages, monkeys
10. court, racket, net

1

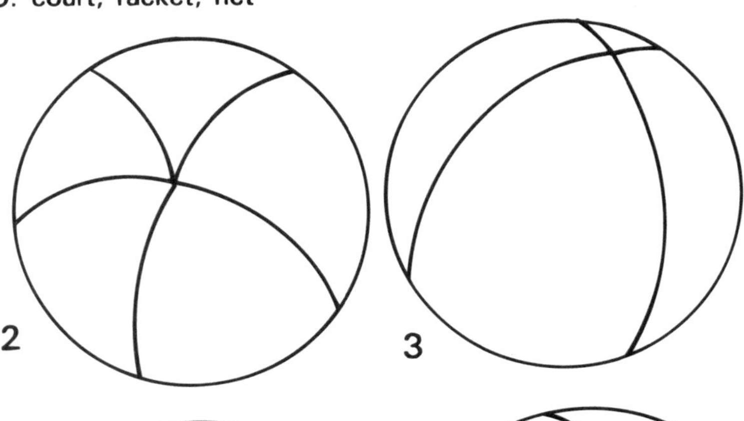

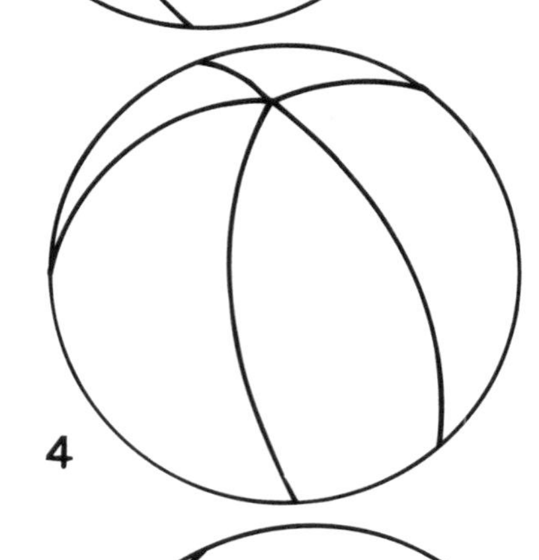

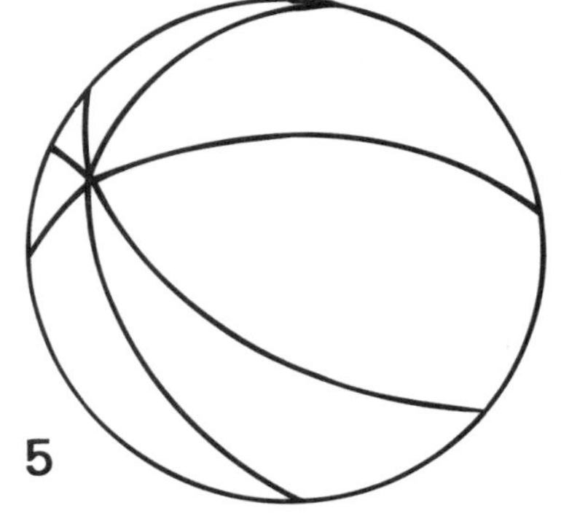

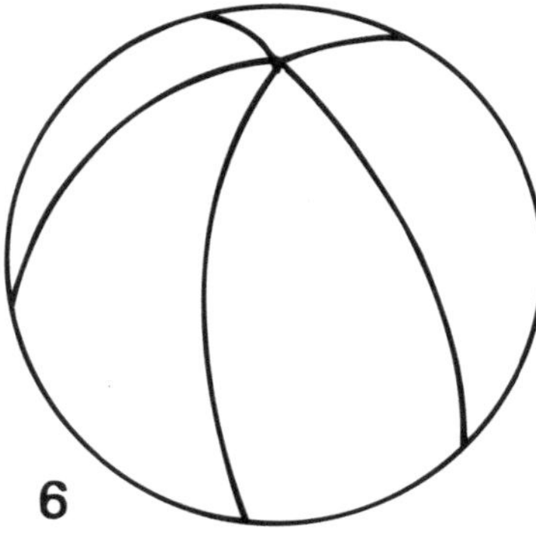

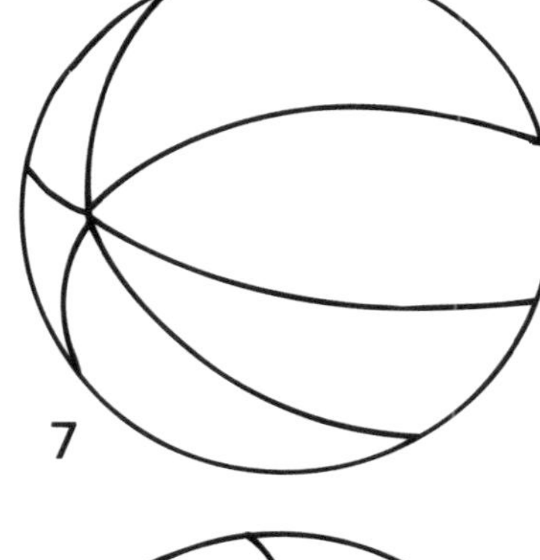

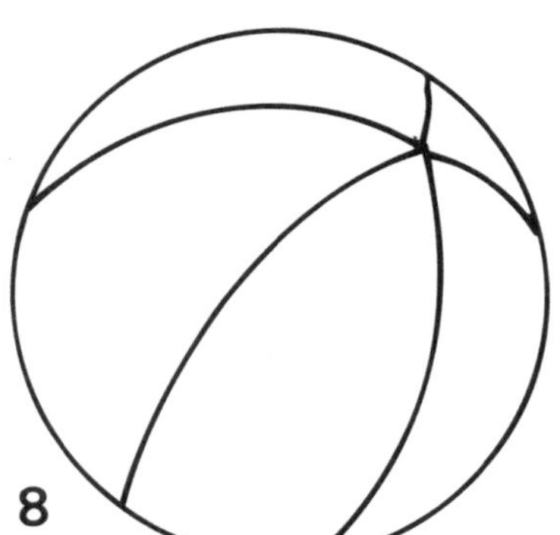

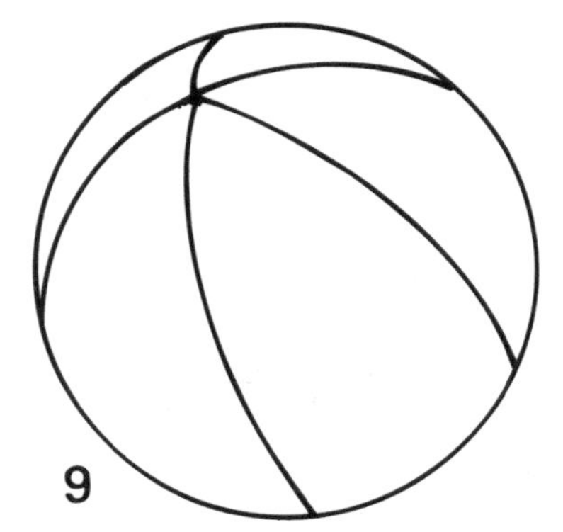

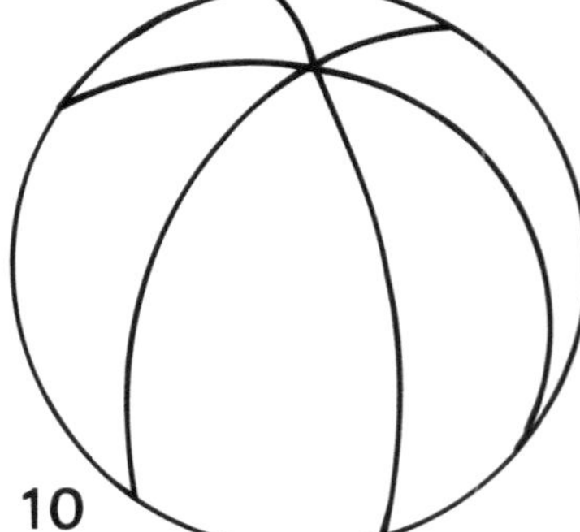

Nice decorating!

Bunny Hop

Name ____________________

Help the bunny reach the carrot by tracing a line each time you answer correctly. Name something that goes with these things:

1. ant, bug, wasp
2. jar, box, cage
3. newspaper, magazine, book
4. pretzel, crackers, popcorn
5. windbreaker, coat, sweater
6. address, stamp, letter
7. king, prince, queen
8. hook, clip, snap
9. knife, axe, saw
10. paper clip, pin, staple

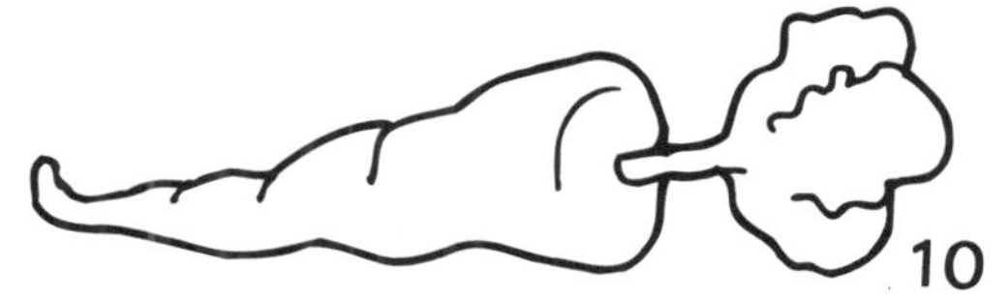

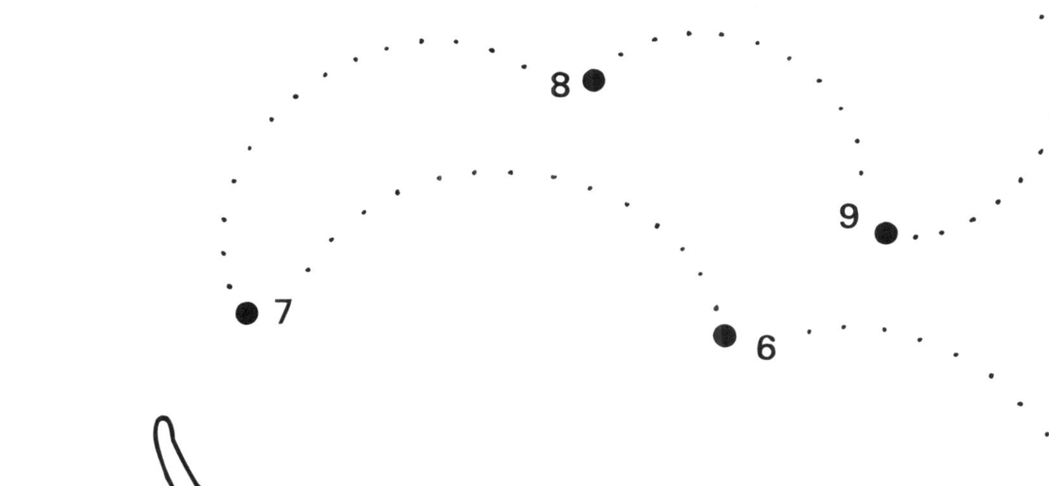

Hop, hop, c-r-r-runch!

Homer's Hungry

Name ______________________________

Feed Homer, the hungry elephant! Color a peanut each time you answer correctly. Name two more things that go with these:

1. pencil, marker
2. flowers, grass
3. boots, hat
4. nose, ear
5. brother, aunt
6. drum, flute
7. whale, shark
8. swings, sand
9. wrench, saw
10. napkin, cup

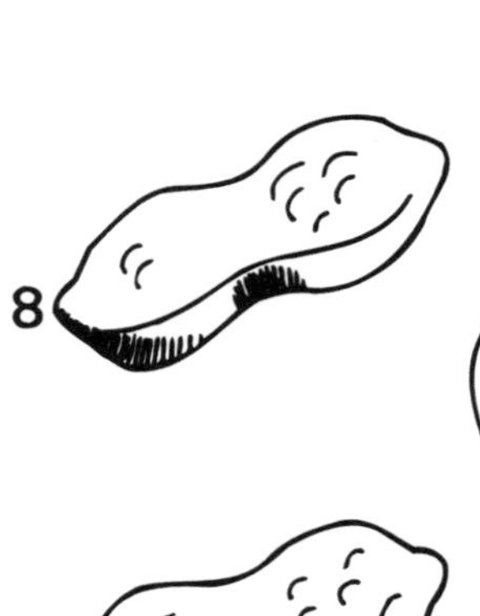

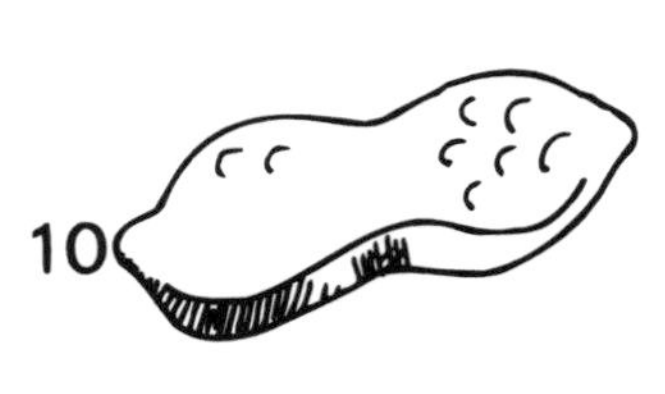

M-m-m, Homer the elephant says thanks!

Pizza Party Time!

Name ______________________

Color a piece of pepperoni each time you answer correctly. Name two more things that go with these:

1. brownie, cake
2. orange, apple
3. broccoli, peas
4. ham, roast beef
5. pop, water
6. rolls, buns
7. yogurt, cheese
8. mints, suckers
9. oatmeal, ice cream
10. sherbet, Fudgesicle

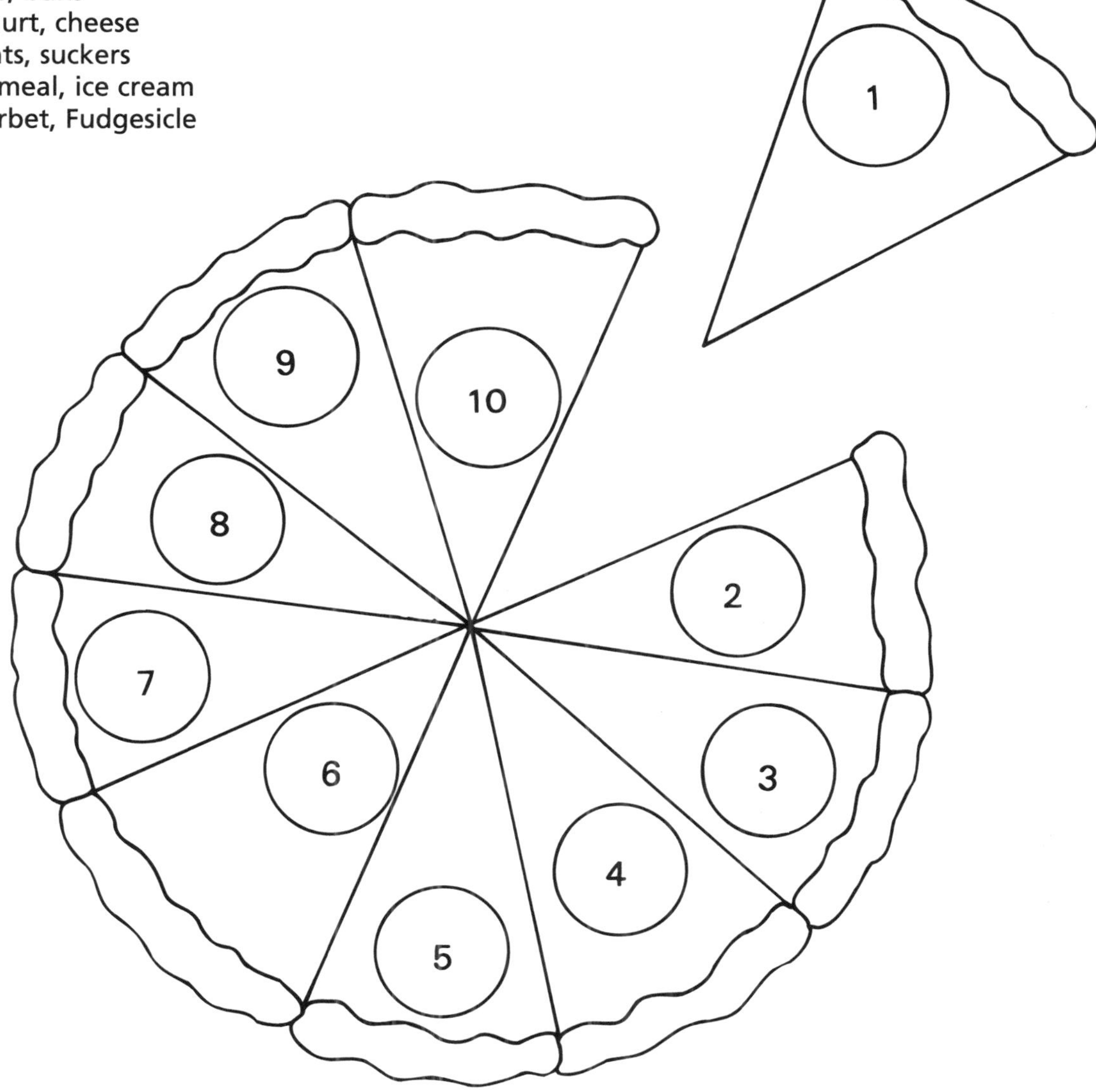

Time to eat!

Pretty Polly

Name ______________________

Make Polly Parrot beautiful! Color a section each time you give three correct answers for each question.

1. I'm going outside. It's raining. What should I take with me?
2. Mike wants to buy some pop. What kind of store could he go to?
3. Paul is going on a trip. What does he need to bring with him?
4. Uncle Rick's car broke down. What could be wrong with his car?
5. Sarah wants to buy a present for a friend. What could she choose?
6. Tina and Juan are trying to think of a name for their baby daughter. What could they name her?
7. Benito wants to buy a pet that will live in a cage. What pet could he choose?
8. Shavonne is making soup for lunch. What kind of soup could she make?

Polly want a cracker?

Surprise!

Name ______________________________

Color a party hat each time you answer a question correctly.

1. Nicole put eggs, bacon, and toast on a plate. What meal was she eating?
2. Ryan picked up an ace, a king, and a jack. What was he playing?
3. Brian put on his badge, his gun, and his uniform. What kind of job does he have?
4. Leroy took out a bat, a mitt, and a ball. What sport was he going to play?
5. Megan put on her hat, her scarf, and her mittens. What was the weather like outside?
6. Jason looked at the stove, the cupboard, and the refrigerator. Which room was he in?
7. Amanda took out the tent, a lantern, and some firewood. What kind of vacation was she taking?
8. The children saw candles, a cake, and presents. What kind of party was it?

Let's have a party!

Mind S-t-r-e-t-c-h **Name** ______________________

Color a spot on Jerry Giraffe each time you tell how these words go together.

1. chicken, horse, sheep
2. robin, blue jay, cardinal
3. leg, neck, face
4. spinach, corn, carrot
5. chair, desk, bed
6. house, school, hospital
7. coffee, pop, lemonade
8. shoes, skates, boots
9. Friday, Monday, Sunday
10. boy, baby, woman

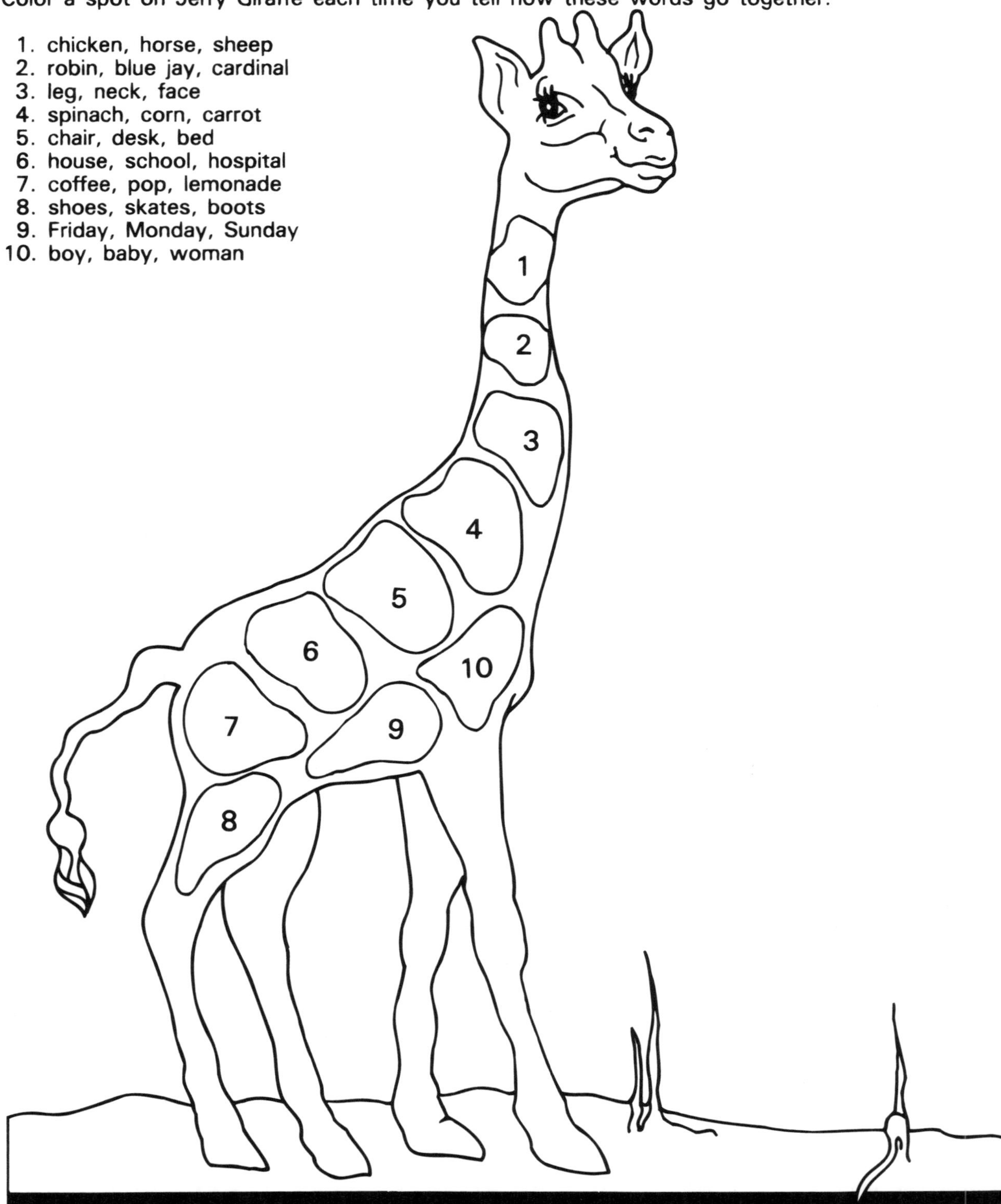

Jerry is very proud of his new spots. Thank you!

Word Web

Name ______________________________

Add legs to a spider in the web each time you tell how these words go together.

1. oak, maple, elm
2. ant, fly, mosquito
3. Popsicle, ice cream, Fudgesicle
4. necklace, bracelet, ring
5. shampoo, soap, detergent
6. Cleveland, Boston, Los Angeles
7. candy, cake, sugar
8. nurse, teacher, barber
9. pickup, Jeep, van
10. slippers, tennis shoes, boots

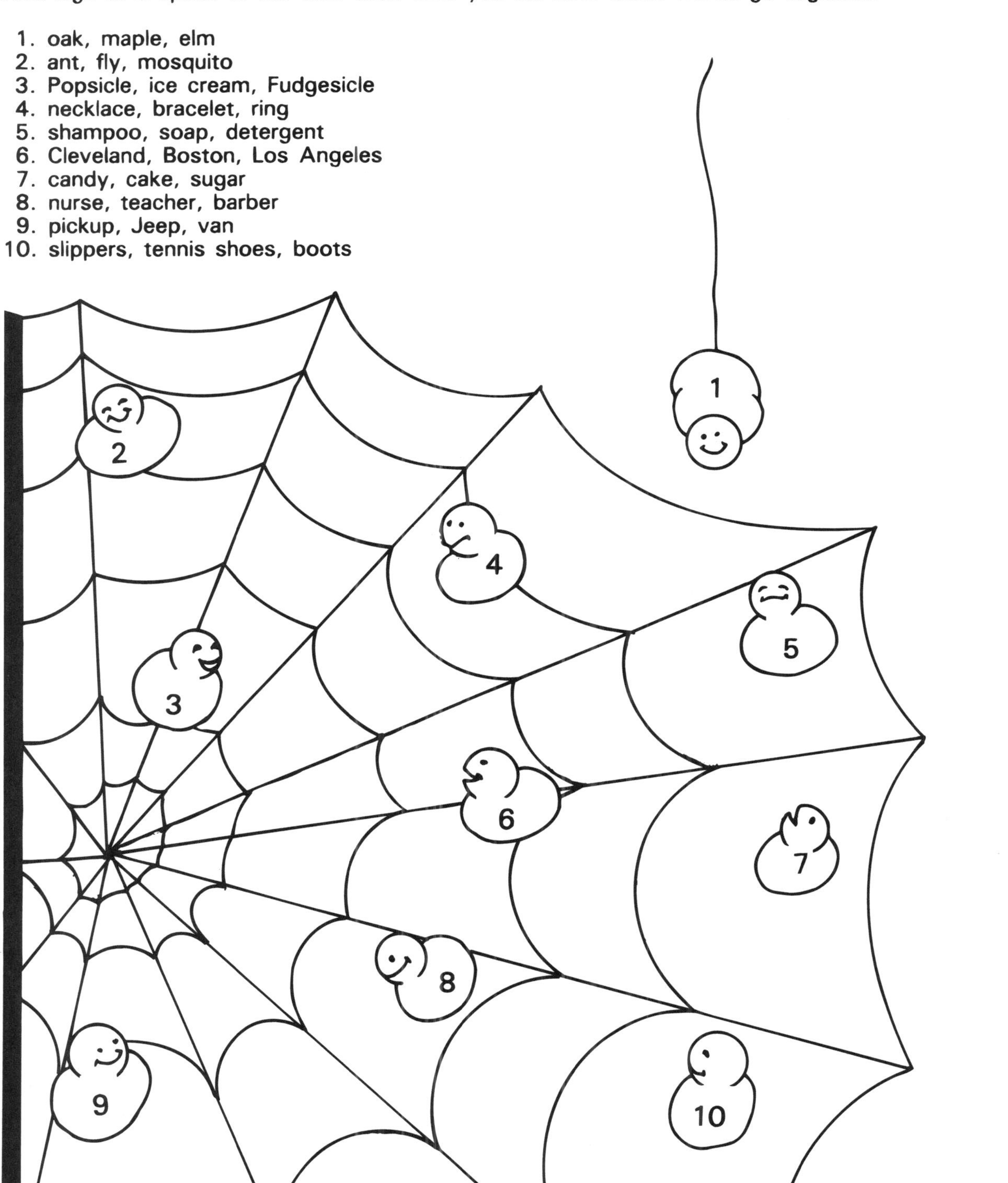

Look at all those spiders!

Super Treat!

Name ___________________________

Draw chocolate chips in a cookie each time you answer correctly. Tell where you can find these things.

1. books, shelves, card catalog, magazines
2. meat, dairy products, vegetables, fruit
3. gas pumps, air hose, cars, oil
4. safe, money, tellers, guard
5. food server, booths, tables, cashier
6. hoses, truck, alarms, ladders
7. badges, bars, prisoners, uniforms
8. computer, secretary, stapler, phone
9. cashier, aspirin, pills, cough medicine
10. stove, toaster, sink, cupboards

Now you're cookin'!

Crowning Glory

Name ____________________

Color a jewel on the crown each time you tell how these words go together.

1. sweet, sour, bitter
2. sad, angry, hurt
3. tall, pretty, fat
4. loud, noisy, quiet
5. wart, mole, birthmark
6. headache, sprained ankle, stomachache
7. chew, swallow, talk
8. roar, growl, quack
9. house, apartment, tent
10. radio, newspaper, television

What a beautiful crown!

Nuts!

Name ______________________________

Help Sammy Squirrel gather acorns! I am going to say some words. Color an acorn each time you answer a question correctly.

monkey, tiger, lion, horse

1. How do all of these things go together?
2. Where does a monkey live?
3. Where does a tiger live?
4. Where does a lion live?
5. Where does a horse live?
6. Which one doesn't belong?

dress, blouse, tie, bracelet

7. How do all of these things go together?
8. Who wears a dress?
9. Who wears a blouse?
10. Who wears a tie?
11. Who wears a bracelet?
12. Which one doesn't belong?

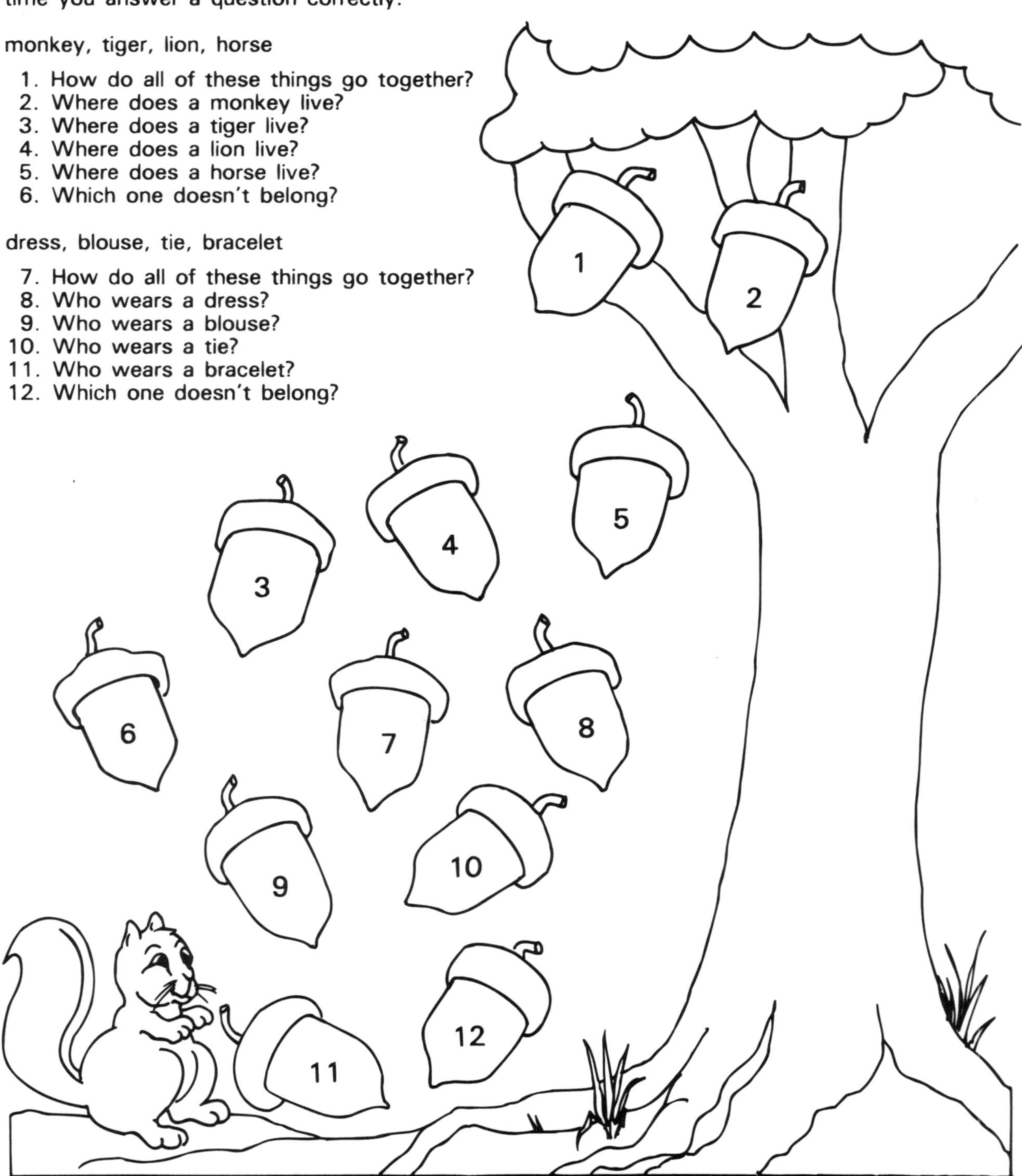

Sammy Squirrel says thanks for all the acorns!

Be a star! Trace a star each time you tell which word does not belong with the others.

1. peach, apple, *cup*, strawberry
2. *car*, dog, cat, hamster
3. truck, *pen*, car, bus
4. *bird*, shoe, shirt, dress
5. one, three, *can*, eleven
6. couch, chair, table, *tree*
7. *stove*, window, door, ceiling
8. brother, sister, father, *dog*
9. letter, *goat*, stamp, envelope
10. car, gas, *bed*, pedal

Stardom

Name ______________________________

You're a star!

These fish are really hungry! Draw some food for a fish each time you tell which word does not belong with the others.

1. cup, bowl, plate, *tree*
2. spoon, fork, *hat*, knife
4. *table*, book, magazine, newspaper
4. bird, kite, plane, *train*
5. *cat*, bee, mosquito, ant
6. red, *five*, green, blue
7. head, arm, *shirt*, leg
8. *bike*, earring, bracelet, necklace
9. corn, *milk*, peas, beans
10. crayon, marker, *paper*, pen

Food for Thought

Name ______________________________

Nice feeding!

Color a coin each time you tell which word does not belong with the others.

1. pen, pencil, *school*, chalk
2. rabbit, frog, grasshopper, *fly*
3. *goat*, whale, shark, eel
4. sun, star, *tree*, moon
5. woodpecker, blue jay, owl, *bee*
6. run, jump, *car*, hop
7. happy, *boy*, bored, angry
8. sunny, windy, cloudy, *far*
9. *three*, Monday, Thursday, Saturday
10. *Andrew*, Jennifer, Marissa, Ashley

A Penny Saved, A Penny Earned

Name ______________________________

You're rich!

I'm going to say four words. Then, I will ask you some questions. Color a sun each time you answer a question correctly.

red, *ten*, green, yellow

1. Which word doesn't belong?
2. What are *red, green*, and *yellow*?
3. Why doesn't *ten* belong?

potato chips, pretzels, *carrot*, popcorn

4. Which word doesn't belong?
5. What are *potato chips, pretzels*, and *popcorn*?
6. Why doesn't *carrot* belong?

doctor, nurse, teacher, *goat*

7. Which word doesn't belong?
8. What are *doctor, nurse*, and *teacher*?
9. Why doesn't *goat* belong?

fork, knife, *pen*, spoon

10. Which word doesn't belong?
11. What are *fork, knife*, and *spoon*?
12. Why doesn't *pen* belong?

Ray Out!

Name ______________________

Look at all those suns. Better wear your sunglasses!

Trace a shape each time you tell which word doesn't belong and why.

1. cherries, *sun*, strawberries, apples
2. tasting, hearing, seeing, *digging*
3. *John*, Ohio, New York, Oregon
4. suitcase, *book*, bag, purse
5. Mars, Jupiter, *December*, Saturn
6. *lettuce*, petals, stem, leaves
7. bang, boom, click, *hit*
8. waffles, pancakes, *spaghetti*, French toast
9. zebra, *bear*, candy cane, flag
10. *toaster*, glass, pitcher, vase

Shape Up!

Name ____________________

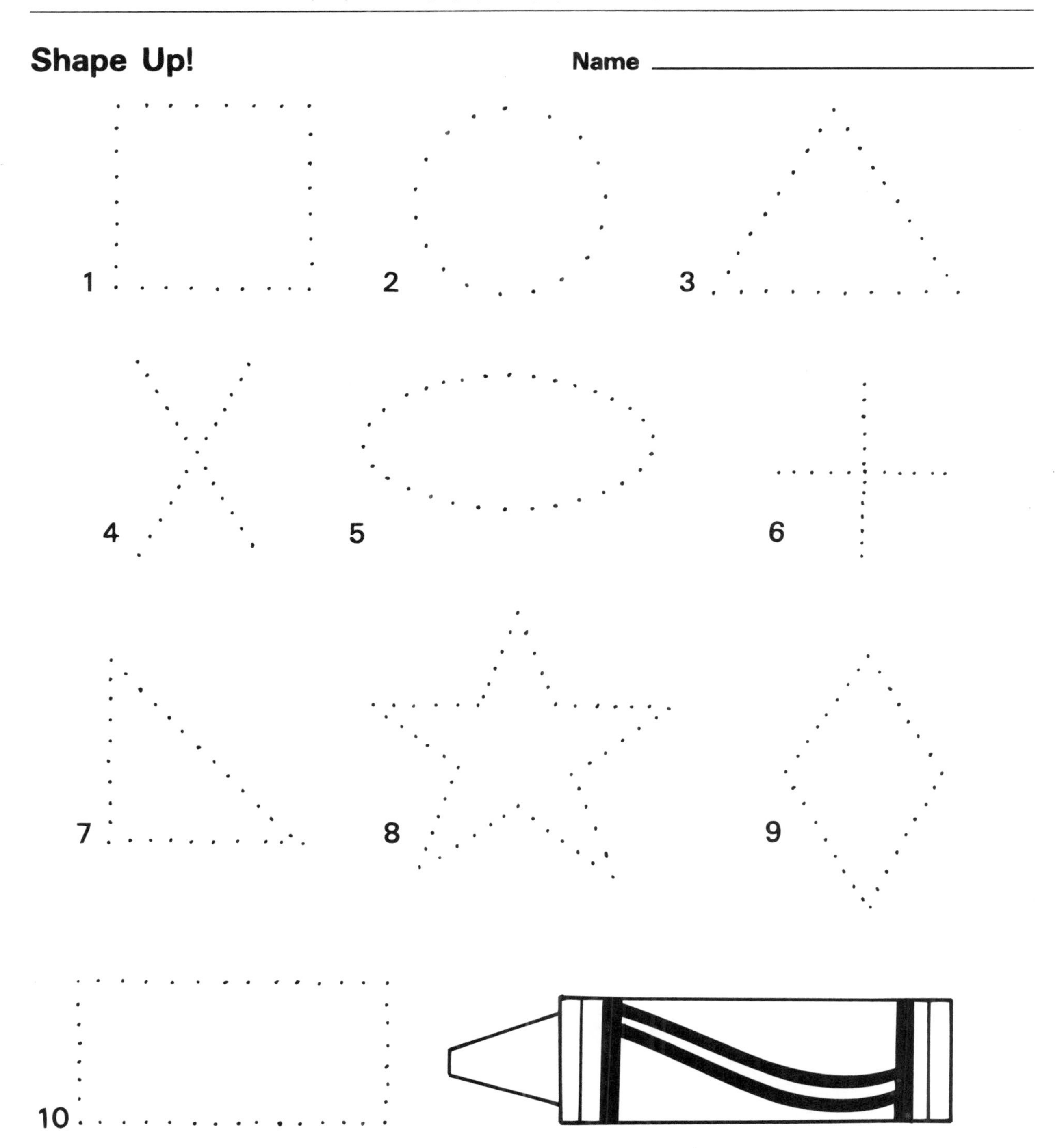

You're in good shape!

Don't let the ants get in the picnic basket! Color an ant each time you tell which word doesn't belong and why.

1. Bonnie, Melanie, *Joseph*, Nicole
2. second, year, day, *mile*
3. moon, *kite*, sun, star
4. whale, octopus, *boat*, porpoise
5. *spoon*, hammer, wrench, screwdriver
6. calf, *pig*, lamb, chick
7. rainy, foggy, cloudy, *lazy*
8. *late*, angry, happy, disappointed
9. large, tall, *good*, tiny
10. *purse*, dime, penny, nickel

Picnic Pests

Name ______________________

Whoa! You stopped the ants just in time!

19-04-98765432